D0998407

MANAGERIAL ETHICS

*Moral Management
of People and Processes*

MANAGERIAL ETHICS

*Moral Management
of People and Processes*

Edited by

Marshall Schminke
Creighton University

LEA LAWRENCE ERLBAUM ASSOCIATES, PUBLISHERS
1998   Mahwah, New Jersey   London

Copyright © 1998 by Lawrence Erlbaum Associates, Inc.
All rights reserved. No part of the book may be reproduced in any form, by photostat, microform, retrieval system, or any other means, without the prior written permission of the publisher.

Lawrence Erlbaum Associates, Inc., Publishers
10 Industrial Avenue
Mahwah, New Jersey 07430

Cover design by Kathryn Houghtaling Lacey

Library of Congress Cataloging-in-Publication Data

Managerial ethics : moral management of people and processes / edited by Marshall Schminke.
    p. cm.
    Includes bibliographical references and index.
    ISBN 0-8058-2492-8 (pbk. : alk. paper)
    1. Management--Moral and ethical aspects. 2. Business ethics.
I. Schminke, Marshall.
HF5387.M3345 1998
174' .4--dc21   98-26312
                                                            CIP

Books published by Lawrence Erlbaum Associates are printed on acid-free paper, and their bindings are chosen for strength and durability.

Printed in the United States of America
10 9 8 7 6 5 4 3 2 1

Contents

174.4
S348

Preface   vii

Foreword   ix
André L. Delbecq

1 Management and Ethics: Distant Neighbors
    in Theory and Research   1
    Marshall Schminke

2 Fairness as Moral Virtue   13
    Robert Folger

3 A Multiple Stakeholder Model of Privacy in Organizations   35
    Dianna L. Stone and Eugene F. Stone-Romero

4 Electronic Performance Monitoring: A Consideration of   61
    Rights
    Maureen L. Ambrose, G. Stoney Alder, and Terry W. Noel

5 Employee Selection and the Ethic of Care   81
    Beverly Kracher and Deborah L. Wells

6 Punishment in Organizations: Descriptive and Normative   99
    Perspectives
    Linda Klebe Treviño and Gary R. Weaver

7   Building Organizational Integrity and Quality
    With the Four Ps: Perspectives, Paradigms, Processes,
    and Principles   115
    Joseph A. Petrick

8   If Politics Is a Game, Then What Are the Rules?:
    Three Suggestions for Ethical Management   133
    Russell Cropanzano and Alicia A. Grandey

9   Interpersonal Manipulation: Its Nature and Moral Limits   153
    Mark A. Seabright and Dennis J. Moberg

10 Software and Hard Choices: Ethical Considerations
    in the Facilitation of a Sociotechnical System   177
    Terri L. Griffith, Gregory B. Northcraft, and Mark A. Fuller

11 The Magic Punchbowl: A Nonrational Model
    of Ethical Management   197
    Marshall Schminke

Contributors   215

Author Index   221

Subject Index   231

Preface

Ethics and ethical issues surround our lives, and libraries abound with great thinkers' attempts to understand them. Business ethics is no exception. In recent years, some of the finest minds from philosophy, business, and management have converged to explore the forces at work in the ethics of business. These scholars presently provide more useful and interesting approaches to business ethics than at any point in our history.

This book attempts to add to and (I hope) to improve on that pool of knowledge. It is a book for organizational and management scholars, philosophers, students, and, yes, even managers, interested in thinking about—and thinking differently about—business ethics.

As with many new projects, this book arose from a small and personal frustration. As I have become more involved in research on business ethics during the past several years, like others, I have been troubled by what seems to be a two camp approach to thinking about and researching ethical issues. On the one hand, management scholars—armed with impressive empirical skills and a penchant for addressing concrete real-world problems—explore the practical ethical concerns of today's managers. On the other hand, moral philosophers—equipped with sophisticated theories of human nature and a broad worldview—develop and refine theoretical models of ethical development and decision making. Business ethics represents the interface of these two camps and teems with current and potential insightful, intriguing research. However, most of what we do falls into one camp or the other, rather than both. That is, we often produce sound business or management theory and research and equally often produce sound ethics theory and research. However, we seldom produce work that integrates fully—at both empirical and theoretical levels—what we know about business, management, and ethics.

Clearly, this critique of our field is neither original nor unique to this book. Calls for theory integration have been common, but like the weather, we have talked about it at length but have not been very successful at doing much about it. The point of this volume is to take an important step in that direction, to initiate conversations, and to provide some models for thinking about how to integrate more fully our thinking about business ethics.

As a result, this volume may raise more questions than it answers. I hope that is true. Furthermore, it remains to be seen how effective this volume will be in its mission of cultivating new conversations about business ethics. The simple act of creating this work has already led to nearly a dozen new proposals with and between the contributing authors of this volume! However, the real test lies not with these writers—they already shared my view that integration is necessary and useful—but with the readers. Will these chapters foster more integrative, more creative ways of linking management and ethics research among management and ethics researchers? I hope so.

ACKNOWLEDGMENTS

No project like this can be successfully concluded without an abundance of work, advice, and support from a number of fronts. First, I thank the editorial team and staff at Lawrence Erlbaum Associates. Before meeting these good people, the ideas in this book were just that: ideas. They have provided unbounded professionalism and invaluable guidance at every step of the process. Second, I thank Creighton University and its College of Business Administration for supporting this project and I thank my Creighton colleagues for supporting me through this project (especially during those times when my preoccupation with it pulled me away from my local duties!). Finally, my deepest thanks and gratitude to those who labored so hard to contribute the chapters that follow. To a person, they were insightful, creative, responsive, and just generally good souls. I could not have hoped for a more pleasurable editing experience than I had with this stellar group. I learned much from working with each one of them and even more from each final contribution. I hope the reader does as well.

—*Marshall Schminke*

Foreword

André L. Delbecq
Santa Clara University

As we approach the turn of the century the contemporary business organization is the institution that shapes much of our destiny. In modern societies it is the primary creator of wealth, provider of goods and services, and source of employment. The majority of people spend their day within its confines. It is here that community is or is not experienced and individual talents are engaged to benefit society.

There was a period in history when time spent within the business organization was "just a job" taking a portion of the day but from which we returned to other more primary groups such as neighborhood, village, and church. At the beginning of the century it was in these nonbusiness settings that our self-expression and self-realization occurred, and in which our moral character was forged. Now, as the information age matures, the employing organization takes up the greater psychological space, capturing our energies, creating networks (real and virtual) that inform and shape both behavior and character, and displacing the preeminence of other settings.

As business educators we spend much of our time portraying the positive side of modern business. We praise its potential for enhancing both the economic and social well being of its members and the society it serves. We talk about loosely coupled empowering organizations unleashing individual creativity. We laud the movement away from hierarchy toward transformative leadership. We speak of diversity within high-performance teams allowing for both individual expression and group creativity. In short, we portray modern business organizations as positive institutional forms creating not only economic surplus but also individual and social surplus. In focusing on examples of high-performance organizations populated by satisfied workers we suggest a world of bright fulfillment.

But there is another side of organizational life we tend to understate—the dark side of exploitative and destructive behavior, which is also encountered. Modern organizations, with their ability to create wealth and exercise power, can also be places where narcissism abounds, greed pervades, political ruthlessness emerges, and injustices are perpetrated on employees, communities, and nations by very capable individuals engaged in unethical practices. Because of our neglect of the dark side, our critics justifiably accuse us of failing to prepare our students for the encounter with evil. It is as if a parent never prepared their child to recognize the less laudable forms of human behavior, with the consequence that the child easily becomes the victim of the malevolent.

Consequently, part of our responsibility as business educators is to help our students understand the need for countervailing forces against organizational darkness. The historical evidence shows that laws, regulations, employee unions, consumer advocacy organizations, and other external controls have played an important role in making capitalism successful. Our students must not have a romantic and historically inaccurate view that businesses are always benign and inexorable forces for good, and that good practices will always be in place. But in the end, our most important task in dealing with organizational darkness as management educators is to shape the individual character of our students, who are destined to become future participants within the contemporary organization. An understanding of ethical principles is one of the foundations of character that they must possess.

The melding of an understanding of ethical principles with the complex milieu of the modern organization is no small challenge. Simplistic ethical cases do not capture the nature of contemporary dilemmas. There is a need to locate ethical challenges in realistic contexts that our students will encounter complete with their varied and subtle forms of seduction. Those students who are able to recognize challenges to business ethics and have formulated correct habits of mind and heart (at times requiring not simply choice but also courage) will be important influences impacting the destiny of many within and outside the powerful institutions of business.

Therefore, this effort by Marshall Schminke and his colleagues seeking to integrate ethics and management is not at the margin of business education, but central to its soul. We are in their debt for their assistance with this important task.

CHAPTER ONE

Management and Ethics: Distant Neighbors in Theory and Research

Marshall Schminke
Creighton University

Strike up a conversation about business and before long the talk will turn to ethics. Business and ethics are wedded in our social consciousness like Gilbert and Sullivan, Laurel and Hardy, or Fred and Ginger (albeit not always as positively!). This chapter explores the often stormy relationship between business and ethics theory and research and seeks to understand and to strengthen the ties between the two.

The chapter begins with a brief review of recent work addressing the state of business ethics research. Next, it proposes an agenda for overcoming some of the well-noted problems in integrating business and ethics. Finally, it outlines the remaining chapters in the volume, thus providing a template for expanding our thinking about business ethics research.

RESEARCH IN BUSINESS ETHICS

Popper (1972) distinguished between social systems that are like clocks and those that are like clouds (Cropanzano & Schminke, in press; Guzzo & Shea, 1990). Clocks are rational, orderly machines. Their parts move in predictable ways and in predictable relationships to other parts. Alternatively, clouds are neither predictable nor orderly. To the extent that they have parts, they do not move in clearly defined or predictable ways in relation to their other parts. From a distance, they appear to be substantial objects with clear boundaries. However, up close, they are fuzzy, flexible, organic creations.

This metaphor for social systems also describes research systems. Here, I distinguish between research systems that are like clocks and those that are like clouds. Business ethics research is more cloud-like than clock-like. From a distance, it appears to be a singular, solid, substantial thing. But, up close, it is fuzzy, flexible, and organic.

One of the greatest strengths of business ethics research lies in the diversity of those interested in knowing more about it. Where else could we find moral philosophers, industrial psychologists, political scientists, management scholars, and organizational sociologists all exploring the same issue? Scholars from these and other disciplines bring to the table an intriguing mix of skills and perspectives. In doing so, they reflect a common interest in questions regarding business, ethics, and the relationship between the two. However, with this strength also comes a weakness. Researchers from such diverse backgrounds often find it difficult to communicate with one another in meaningful ways. Nowhere has this been more true than with business ethics.

Several recent essays address the natural conflicts that arise between those with different perspectives on the field. Most of this work echoes two central themes, and those themes compose the agenda for this volume. First, how might we best integrate the two very different areas—philosophy and social science—that provide the foundation for the field? Second, how might we create closer ties between business ethics research and real business settings?

THE FIRST CHALLENGE: INTEGRATING PHILOSOPHY AND SOCIAL SCIENCE

Business ethics research consists of two distinct subdisciplines. One, primarily descriptive and based in the social sciences, addresses the question of "what is." The other, primarily normative (or prescriptive) and based in moral philosophy, addresses the question of "what ought to be." Historically, these two approaches represented distinct areas of inquiry, and recent works point to a number of issues that inhibit efforts to integrate them: fear, purpose, and background.

For example, Victor and Stephens (1994) pointed out that historically, philosophy and social science have exhibited a sort of division of labor with respect to business ethics. Philosophers address normative issues; social scientists, descriptive ones. However, forces in each area impede attempts to integrate the two. For example, philosophers fear a creeping "naturalistic fallacy" in the face of advancing empiricism. That is, they fear that discoveries of what is may come to define our thinking of what ought to be. Similarly, social scientists express concern over breaking ranks with a positivist tradition, which asserts that facts are distinct from values. If truth cannot carry with it any value judgments, how can empiricists consider addressing questions regarding what ought to be?

Others note ways in which the two areas differ in basic purpose. For example, Fleming (1987) noted "an almost complete lack of integration between normative and descriptive research efforts" (p. 21) in business ethics. He predicted the two may eventually converge by developing distinctive contributions to practicing managers. That is, the normative approach would evolve into an instructive tool, identifying what constitutes moral behavior, how it is learned, and how it may be converted into business practices. The descriptive approach would develop predictive competence, to be implemented into practical business decision making.

Treviño and Weaver (1994) distinguished between business schools' concentration on the business perspective of business ethics, and liberal arts philosophy and theology departments' focus on the ethics perspective. They pointed out that researchers from each area differ in a number of important ways, including academic background, language, and underlying assumptions, as well as how they use, apply, and evaluate theory. Although they reiterate recent calls for unity, they note that these calls for integration have, for the most part, failed to provide clear guidance as to what an integrated field would look like or how it might be accomplished.

Background

Kahn's (1990) essay on creating an agenda for business ethics research may play a role in addressing that question. Like others, he distinguished between normative (prescriptive) and contextural (descriptive) traditions in the field. He argued that, at present, the two areas resemble distinct circles in a Venn diagram that overlap little, if at all. Because the two areas rise from relatively distinct underlying disciplines, little shared ground exists. Further, individuals possess strong theoretical and methodological ties to their primary disciplines. As scholars attempt to reinforce their own areas, those areas may become even more impenetrable to others. Researchers continue to be grounded inadequately in at least one of the two disciplines, and often differ significantly in how they identify ethical issues in business. Therefore, shared ground is not likely to grow and may even shrink! He related one author's comments regarding the dilemma facing business ethics researchers: "[Researchers] in applied ethics are in the inherently comic position of carrying water from wells they haven't dug to fight fires they can't quite find" (Kahn, 1990, p. 313).

Kahn (1990) sketched four images—conversation, history, vision, and community—that he believes outline an ideal ethical system. Members of such a system would talk to each other. They would respect and understand each other's historical roots. They would provide clear and imaginative ideas.

Finally, they would work within the larger community toward shared goals. These images provide a sound basis for integrating business ethics researchers, as well. That is, they would be an interactive community of scholars with diverse historical backgrounds and imaginative ideas, working toward a shared goal of understanding and creating more ethical organizations and business systems.

A common theme emerges from each of these essays. Most business ethics scholars agree that the question is not whether the two traditions should interact. They should. The more important question is what that integration should look like. When the circles in the Venn diagram overlap, what should be going on in that shared territory?

Parallel, Symbiotic, and Integrative Approaches

Weaver and Treviño (1994) proposed three categories for thinking about the relationship between normative and empirical approaches in business ethics research: parallel, symbiotic, and integrative views. The three views represent a continuum of how tightly integrated normative and empirical approaches can be (or, to take a more normative perspective, should be).

Parallelism suggests that normative and empirical approaches are, and should remain, distinctly separate paths to understanding business ethics issues. Both practical and conceptual conflicts drive this view (e.g., differences in training and methodology, and differences in whether "is" or "ought" represents the correct question to be asked, respectively). *Symbiosis* reflects a cooperative, collaborative relationship between normative and empirical approaches. Shared research agendas and theoretical foundations may guide and inform the progress for each path of inquiry. Finally, *integration* represents an even stronger melding of normative and empirical approaches. Moving beyond simply sharing theoretical or methodological models, the integrative view seeks to create a unified hybrid theory of business ethics by melding the theoretical foundations of each area.

In the end, Weaver and Treviño (1994) viewed symbiotic inquiry as the most promising, a position Donaldson (1994) echoed. He rejects parallelism, acknowledging that research in business ethics should include both normative and empirical insights. However, he also strongly rejects integration, stating that "the temptation to [fully] integrate must be boldly resisted" (p. 157). He asserted that such a move to combine the fundamentally different normative and empirical approaches is akin to "combining triangularity and circularity" (p. 157). Further, he believes that such a combination would lead to confusion within and without the field and, eventually, irrelevance for the entire discipline. In the end, he supports a balanced, symbiotic approach.

These papers identify a rift in business ethics research that distinguishes between philisophical (normative) and social science (empirical) roots. Consensus within the field suggests that a symbiotic relationship between norma-tive and empirical approaches is not only possible, but also desirable. How-ever, the real issue is broader than a simple debate between normative and empirical issues. Not all of philosophy is normative. Not all of social science is empirical. Therefore, integrating the two is more complicated than simply applying sound empirical research methods to test ethical theory. For a true symbiosis to emerge—and to work—business ethics researchers need to think beyond how one perspective's research methodology or intellectual processes can inform the other's thinking. They need to rethink the rela-tionships between their basic theoretical models.

A Meta Business Ethics View

Meta ethics addresses the development of ethical theories and the relation-ships between different theoretical systems and disciplines (Fleming, 1987). Therefore, first we should step back and take a "meta business ethics" view of the field. That is, a theoretical symbiosis must precede meaningful and enduring methodological symbiosis. Thus, business ethics researchers must first consider and map the relationship between ethical and social science theories in order to discover and capitalize on synergies between the two.

A striking example of the efficacy of such an approach already exists in the literature: Kohlberg's (1984) work on moral development. Kohlberg wed-ded an array of ethical theoretic bases (egoism, utilitarianism, deontology) with Piaget's emerging social science theories of cognition and developmen-tal psychology. This, and related work (e.g., Rest, 1986), probably exerts a more profound impact on current business ethics theory, research, and prac-tice than any other. That is no accident. It demonstrates that well-crafted theory that first integrates ethics and social science at the theoretical level provides a foundation on which additional significant work may build. For example, Rest's Defining Issues Test, which draws heavily on Kohlberg's work, has itself spawned over 500 studies (Rest, 1994). Kohlberg's work has exhibited "legs," not in spite of its theoretical duality, but because of it.

This joint theoretical approach holds the greatest promise for researchers to make lasting, meaningful contributions. The most significant research, that which gets noticed and has a lasting impact, is, at its core, interesting (Davis, 1971). It is interesting because it violates some key assumptions of its audience. Research that denies no assumptions may be disregarded as ho-hum, whereas, if it denies all assumptions, it risks being dismissed as irrelevant (Campbell, Daft, & Hulin, 1982). Joint theoretical approaches to business ethics research are likely to reach that middle ground. On the one hand, research conceived, conducted, and distributed within either philoso-phy or social science is obviously more likely to conform to the theoretical and methodological assumptions of that field. Thus, it is less likely to break with the core assumptions of the field. On the other hand, research conceived and conducted within one field, but then distributed across the other, will likely violate so many basic assumptions of the target audience as to be dismissed out of hand. However, crafting symbiotic theoretical approaches may strike closer to Davis' (1971) notion of moderate assumption violation. Thus, each area maximizes its opportunities to create not only new, but also meaningful, research contributions.

Promising joint theoretical approaches have begun to surface in the literature. For example, Donaldson and Dunfee (1994) united the organization studies constructs of bounded rationality and satisficing with the philosophical concepts of social contracts in creating their theory of integrative social contracts. Greenberg and Bies (1992) considered utilitarian, egoism, and Kantian approaches to ethics and their relationship to how we theorize about issues surrounding organizational fairness, rewards, and punishment. Ciulla (1995) melded normative theories of ethics with traditional models of leadership to shift the question from "What is leadership?" to "What is good leadership?" Others have sought to combine ethical theory with the economic concept of agency theory (Bowie & Freeman, 1992; Noe & Rebello, 1994), decision and attribution theory (Decker, 1994), and social psychology theories, such as impression management and cognitive distortions (Payne & Giacalone, 1990). These approaches provide the greatest chance of creating truly symbiotic partnerships between philosophers' and social scientists' quests to understand business ethics.

THE SECOND CHALLENGE: BUSINESS ETHICS IN REAL BUSINESS SETTINGS

The second theme that emerges from researchers' recent self-examination of the field reflects an interest in forging closer ties with real business settings and issues. In an essay entitled "What's the matter with business ethics?" Stark (1993) wondered why professions like law, medicine, and government have had much greater success than business in integrating ethical philosophy with practitioners' daily concerns. More than three fourths of major U.S. corporations are active in building ethics into their organizations. However, many still lament what seems to be a misfit between the type of expertise and advice business ethics scholars bring to their organizations and the organizations' needs.

Stark (1993) suggested that business ethicists must shoulder much of the blame. Historically, business ethics has tended to be too general, too theoretical, and too impractical to be of much use to practicing managers. It is perceived as too general, often attempting to address meta issues like the moral justification for capitalism or broad corporate social responsibility issues, rather than the workaday concerns of organization members. It is thought to be too theoretical in that it often couches ethical issues in lofty terms like formalism, utilitarianism, teleology, and deontology. Managers wonder how these relate to everyday work experiences. Finally, it is seen as too impractical in that it does not give very clear guidance to managers trying to behave morally in a complex world with often-conficting business, personal, family, and moral pressures.

In response, Stark proposes a new business ethics. This approach may be more business-friendly in that it allows for conflict to exist between individuals' ethics and their pursuit of organizational and self-interests. It seeks to guide managers as they try to behave ethically and socially responsibly, without jeopordizing their careers or companies. It calls "the creation of actionable strategies for the pragmatists" (Stark, 1993, p. 48) the most critical task in business ethics.

Others echo this view, questioning how researchers might contribute more to understanding what Treviño and Weaver (1994) referred to as morally significant business practices, with particular empasis on practices. For example, Kahn (1990) proposed a multidimensional research agenda for business ethics. He suggested that researchers should pursue research questions that reflect philosophical ethical principles, organizational context, and a balance between philosophic ideals and pragmatic work demands. He not only tolerated but also embraced the potential conflict between ideal ethical settings and pragmatic workplace pressures. He noted that ethical principles and organizational contexts carry equal relevance to those struggling to live morally, and that meaningful ethical systems will be created where those forces intersect.

Robertson (1993) also called for a more applied approach to business ethics research, and provided three suggestions that relate directly to this issue. First, provide an increased normative focus for ethics research. She noted investigators' common reluctance to address the what-ought-to-be issue because of questions about what exactly constitutes ethical behavior. Yet, she correctly noted that normative decisions have always played a role in descriptive research; experimental treatments often reflect implicit normative ethical positions. (For example, studies may assume that kickbacks, padding expense accounts, churning clients' investment portfolios, and so on, are unethical.) Even such basic decisions as what issues are worth studying carry normative overtones (Forsyth, 1980).

Second, emphasize behavior as the key dependent variable. Robertson (1993) believed that because the purpose of business ethics research is to discover the meaning and causes of ethical behavior, then behavior should be the focus. Moral attitudes and moral reasoning may represent important determinants, but behavior is key. Because managers commonly seek assistance in understanding what to do, this suggestion addresses those concerns.

Third, build links to managerial and public policy applications. Robertson contended that the ultimate purpose of business ethics research is to guide higher-quality ethical decision making. Therefore, researchers must focus on how to make research results useful to those in positions to influence policy, such as by providing assistance in creating corporate codes of ethics.

This issue of increased applicability of research goes beyond business ethics; it emerges in organizational studies in general. For example, Daft and Lewin (1990) stated that "organization studies have been a recurrent souce of disappointment for practitioners" and that "the body of knowledge published in academic journals has practically no audience in business or government" (p. 1). Campbell, Daft, and Hulin (1982) identified several characteristics of significant research in organizational studies. In particular, three of these suggest that significant business ethics research must address real business issues:

1. *Significant research is an outcome of investigator involvement in the physical and social world of organizations.* Investigators should go into organizations, talk to managers and practitioners, and use these contacts to inform their thinking about worthwhile research subjects.
2. *Significant research focuses on real problems.* Abstract academic notions are useful. They provide theoretic guidance and understanding. But, research that addresses real problems of real people in real organizations carries the greatest chance of enduring.
3. *Significant research reaches into the uncertain world of organizations and returns with something clear, tangible, and well understood.* Investigators might view organizational actors and actions through lenses thick with theory and jargon. However, the final product should be precise and ordered and, most important, usable.

In all, these broad and recurring calls make a clear statement: For business ethics research to be useful, it must eventually touch business.

OUTLINE OF THE BOOK

The purpose of this book is twofold. First, it attempts to initiate conversations between researchers with similar interests but different perspectives. By doing so, it seeks to create a symbiotic mix of ethical and managerial theory, one that might allow us to take our research to a higher level of sophistication and rigor from both perspectives. Second, it attempts to focus those conversations on topics of interest to today's managers. The chapters cut across theoretical and practical arenas, and address individual as well as systemic issues. I am confident that some will be controversial. However, all address current, relevant issues that affect the people and processes that make up organizational life.

The remainder of the book opens with a chapter by Folger that provides the backdrop for the other chapters (chap. 2). At the heart of much of our thinking about ethics lies fairness. Folger suggests that fairness is, and should be, a morally laden construct. However, he suggests that organizational researchers have not treated it this way; current approaches all eventually focus on self- or group-interested definitions of what it means to be fair. His call is to take justice to a higher level of analysis, from an issue of self-interest to one of more general social and moral interest.

Next, Stone and Stone-Romero explore privacy issues from a multiple stakeholders perspective (chap. 3). They consider the natural tensions that exist between individuals' desire for and right to privacy and other organizational stakeholders' (e.g., management, owners, customers) desire and need for reasonable monitoring and control. They identify potential conflicts between stakeholders and present two strategies for resolving these conflicts.

Ambrose, Alder, and Noel (chap. 4) follow by exploring the ethics of the powerful new monitoring technologies available to today's managers. In this chapter, they draw on Locke's conceptualization of natural law to create an ethical model of electronic monitoring that generates rules of moderation and disclosure for monitoring systems.

Next, Kracher and Wells (chap. 5) propose a new way of thinking about selecting individuals to fit today's organizations. Drawing on Gilligan's work on the ethics of care, they consider how caring individuals might make better employees. They consider the current state of the literature on the caring individual and explore some of the steps that would be neccesary to add this to our inventory of selection procedures.

Treviño and Weaver's (chap. 6) essay on punishment in organizations follows. In this chapter, they provide an insightful challenge to the conventional wisdom surrounding organizational punishment. They consider the managerial implications of both punishment and nonpunishment. In doing so, they explore the social context in which punishment occurs and the fairness perceptions that surround it.

The later chapters shift the level of analysis from individuals toward the systems and processes involved in managing organizations. For example, Petrick (chap. 7) discusses the link between organizational integrity and quality. He demonstrates the parallels between building quality products and building ethical organizations.

Next, Cropanzano and Grandey (chap. 8) explore another systemic organizational issue—politics. In this chapter, they compare formalist, utilitarian, and integrative approaches, and provide three suggestions for ethically managing organizational politics.

Seabright and Moberg (chap. 9) then explore the darker side of interpersonal influence processes and the ethical implications of those processes from utilitarian, rights, and justice perspectives. They provide an interesting look at both the descriptive and prescriptive side of interpersonal manipulation.

Griffith, Northcraft, and Fuller (chap. 10) close this part of the book by using Group Support Systems to illustrate a large array of ethical issues that may arise in group and high-tech settings. In particular, they consider the ethical issues that may arise in facilitated settings and provide guidelines for ensuring the ethical integrity of facilitators and their work.

The book concludes with chapter 12, "The Magic Punchbowl: A Nonrational Model of Ethical Management." In this chapter, I propose that ethical decision making is no more a pure, rational, linear process than any other form of managerial decision making. I suggest that, to be able to wed management and ethical theory in meaningful ways, we first need to unfreeze our thinking about how people make ethical decisions in complex organizational settings.

CLOSING

My goal for this book is to initiate what might be termed a "reflect and connect" strategy for business ethics researchers. That is, to challenge readers to reflect on their own and others' histories of exploring ethics issues, and to connect those pursuits with those other fields and, eventually, with the business world itself. Campbell, Daft, and Hulin (1982) are correct to remind us that the creative problem-solving literature suggests that true innovation rarely comes from inside one's own field (cf. Stein, 1974, 1975). Rather, they cited both interaction with other disciplines and contacts with the real world as useful strategies for increasing the likelihood of discovering new and meaningful ideas. This book's purpose is not simply to encourage more research in business ethics. (The aphorism "research not worth doing is not worth doing well" still applies!) The key is to unfreeze our thinking about our own and other theoretical bases and biases, to identify situations in which theory—ethical and managerial—may guide our thinking when exploring both what is and what ought to be, and to ground that work in real organizational settings. The result may be research that means something to academics and practitioners, shaping both theory and practice (Kahn, 1990).

REFERENCES

Bowie, N. E., & Freeman, R. E. (Eds.). (1992). *Ethics and agency theory: An introduction.* Oxford, England: Oxford University Press.

Campbell, J. P., Daft, R. L., & Hulin, C. L. (1982). *What to study: Generating and developing research questions.* Beverly Hills, CA: Sage.

Ciulla, J. B. (1995). Leadership ethics: Mapping the territory. *Business Ethics Quarterly, 5,* 5–28.

Cropanzano, R., & Schminke, M. (in press). Justice as the mortar of social cohesion. In M. Turner (Ed.), *Groups at work: Advances in theory and research.* Mahwah, NJ: Lawrence Erlbaum Associates.

Daft, R. L., & Lewin, A. Y. (1990). Can organization studies begin to break out of the normal science strait-jacket? An editorial essay. *Organization Science, 1,* 1–9.

Davis, M. S. (1971). That's interesting! Toward a phenomenology of sociology and a sociology of phenomenology. *Philosophy of Social Science, 1,* 309–344.

Decker, W. H. (1994). Unethical decisions and attributions: Gains, losses, and concentration of effects. *Psychological Reports, 75,* 1207–1214.

Donaldson, T. (1994). When integration fails: The logic of prescription and description in business ethics. *Business Ethics Quarterly, 4,* 157–169.

Donaldson, T., & Dunfee, T. W. (1994). Toward a unified conception of business ethics: Integrative social contracts theory. *Academy of Management Review, 19,* 252–284.

Fleming, J. (1987). A survey and critique of business ethics research, 1986. In W. Frederick (Ed.), *Research in corporate social performance and policy: Vol. 9* (pp. 1–24). Greenwich, CT: JAI Press.

Forsyth, D. R. (1980). A taxonomy of ethical ideologies. *Journal of Personality and Social Psychology, 39,* 175–184.

Guzzo, R. A., & Shea, G. P. (1990). Group performance and intergroup relations in organizations. In M. D. Dunnette & L. M. Hough (Eds.), *Handbook of industrial and organizational psychology* (pp. 269–313). Palo Alto, CA: Consulting Psychologists Press.

Greenberg, J., & Bies, R. J. (1992). Establishing the role of empirical studies of organizational justice in philisophical inquiries into business ethics. *Journal of Business Ethics, 11,* 433–444.

Kahn, W. A. (1990). Toward an agenda for business ethics research. *Academy of Management Review, 15,* 311–328.

Kohlberg, L. (1984). *The psychology of moral development.* San Francisco: Harper & Row.

Noc, T. II., & Rebello, M. J. (1994). The dynamics of business ethics and economic activity. *American Economic Review, 84,* 531–547.

Payne, S. L., & Giacalone, R. A. (1990). Social psychological approaches to the perception of ethical dilemmas. *Human Relations, 43,* 649–665.

Popper, K. R. (1972). *Objective knowledge.* London: Oxford University Press.

Rest, J. R. (1986). *Moral development: Advances in theory and research.* New York: Praeger.

Rest, J. R. (1994). Background: Theory and research. In J. R. Rest & D. Narvaez (Eds.), *Moral development in the professions: Psychology and applied ethics* (pp. 1–26). Hillsdale, NJ: Lawrence Erlbaum Associates.

Robertson, D. C. (1993). Empiricism in business ethics: Suggested research directions. *Journal of Business Ethics, 12,* 585–599.

Stark, A. (1993). What's the matter with business ethics? *Harvard Business Review, 71,* 38–48.

Stein, M. J. (1974). *Stimulating creativity* (Vol. 1). New York: Academic Press.

Stein, M. J. (1975). *Stimulating creativity* (Vol. 2). New York: Academic Press.

Treviño, L. K., & Weaver, G. R. (1994). Business ETHICS/BUSINESS ethics: One field or two? *Business Ethics Quarterly, 4,* 113–128.

Victor, B., & Stephens, C. U. (1994). Business ethics: A synthesis of normative philosophy and empirical social science. *Business Ethics Quarterly, 4,* 145–155.

Weaver, G. R., & Treviño, L. K. (1994). Normative and empirical business ethics: Separation, marriage of convenience, or marriage of necessity? *Business Ethics Quarterly, 4,* 129–143.

CHAPTER TWO

Fairness as Moral Virtue

Robert Folger
Tulane University

Morality includes fairness as a notable virtue. This chapter contrasts fairness-as-morality (ethical conduct) with the fairness of social and organizational studies. The fairness that those disciplines portray only faintly resembles fairness-as-morality. Their legacy—an anorexic fairness—instead reduces fairness to selfishness. Despite noble efforts to break the stranglehold of economic rationality and self-interest maximization, their version of fairness remains closer to greed and envy than to the moral virtue that can sustain the commonweal.

ORGANIZATIONAL AND MANAGERIAL RELEVANCE

What makes justice as virtue a management topic? If "justice is the first virtue of social institutions" (Rawls, 1971, p. 3), the morality of fairness applies in an organizational context: "while management must satisfy many interests, including those of the shareholders, there is often very little to guard the interests of the public, and even those of the corporation itself, from the self-interest of the managers" (Wilbur, 1997, p. 576). Imagine a totally selfish person as CEO of a large corporation, able to wield power with impunity and with potentially devastating impact. Using externally imposed sanctions to curtail this person's power would require monitoring and guaranteeing punishment severe enough to deter malevolent intent. We might not want to rely exclusively on laws, courts, and the police as countervailing forces.

We might wish that this person had a conscience. We could sleep better at night if this person put some value on other people's well-being, as an internalized moral virtue that motivates other-regarding sentiment to an appropriate, mutually beneficial degree. Fairness, internalized as moral virtue, can augment external sanctions. Given how corporations can affect the local, national, and global community, we sorely need the self-restraint of a managerial regard for fairness.

SOCIAL FAIRNESS AS A MORAL VIRTUE: A CONTRAST WITH TRADITIONAL APPROACHES

Asking only why people dislike unfairly adverse situations deletes the social context of morality and, instead, yields asocial preference. Imagine a person on a deserted island who adopts a moral code about good and bad foods. This person treats certain animals as unclean (based on a dream, not social influence)—a personal code for private behavior rather than a social code for interpersonal behavior (i.e., ruling personal actions despite the lack of other island inhabitants). Similarly, ethicists distinguish between moral values that concern how to treat others and moral values that are irrelevant to social conduct (e.g., gluttony was not proscribed because it was harmful to other people).

The study of fairness can build on that distinction. Suppose the island dweller works hard tending the crops. If a hurricane destroys them, that's personally, but not interpersonally, unfair. Crop destruction by hurricane is personally unfair, whereas destruction by a sadist is socially unfair. This chapter deals with social fairness as moral precepts about the right way to treat other people—a topic that organizational justice scholars have insufficiently addressed, having focused too exclusively on egoistic (selfish) motives to explain fairness.

Self-Centeredness in Accounts of Outcome Fairness: Equity Theory

Are fairness theories too selfish? Traditionally, they distinguish between distributive justice (outcome fairness) and procedural justice (process fairness). Accounts of distributive justice, such as equity theory (Adams, 1965), explained how outcome reactions took fairness into account. Equity theory, however, focuses on personal fairness rather than on social fairness. Interest in other people's outcomes, according to the theory, does not stem from caring about whether other people receive fair treatment. Rather, social comparisons represent a way of determining the fairness of one's own outcomes. The desire not to have one's own outcomes below a fair return rate (e.g., the rate at which comparable others receive outcomes) means experiencing negative emotions about one's own outcomes when they fail to match that rate. If concerns about morality apply only to what the self receives, such concerns indicate little more than selfishness by another name (cf. Walster, Walster, & Berscheid, 1978).

Selfishness in Two Dominant Explanations for Interest in Procedural Justice

People sometimes evaluate the fairness of a procedure separately from the fairness of the outcome from that procedure. For example, they might feel that a legal trial's procedures for evidence presentation were conducted fairly even though the resulting verdict was unfair.

Lind and Tyler (1988) reviewed two approaches regarding concern about procedural justice. One approach (Thibaut & Walker, 1975) says that people want control over resources and benefits. If denied direct control (e.g., choice, veto), people want at least some indirect control. Thus, indirect control—the potential for influence via participatory procedures, or voice (Folger, 1977)—should enhance the perceived procedural justice of decision-making methods, dispute-resolution arrangements, and so on. If fair processes act merely as a proxy for fair outcomes, and fair outcomes as a compromise between unfettered self-interest and the degree of self-interest tolerated by others, then this first account reduces fairness to selfishness in the same way as does the equity account of distributive justice. Preferences among procedures would follow self-interest about the resources presumed obtainable by using each procedure.

Lind and Tyler (1988) criticized this resource control account by citing noninstrumental effects (procedural fairness·perceptions independent from outcomes and perceived control over resources): "It is difficult to see how such effects could be accounted for by explanations that suppose that people view procedures solely as instruments for generating either favorable or equitable rewards" (p. 229). Other such effects refer not to formal, structural properties of decision-making procedures but to the sensitivity of interpersonal conduct by administrative agents. Tyler and Folger (1980) found that citizens' reactions to police varied with the latter's demeanor, regardless of whether the outcome of the encounters (e.g., a potential citation; the potential recovery of stolen property) favored or did not favor citizens' personal interests. Perceived fairness of processes often stems from treatment with dignity, respect, politeness, and concern for rights as much as from controlling material resources, if not more.

Lind and Tyler (1988) explained such findings in terms of a group value model, later called a relational model of authority (Tyler & Lind, 1992). They stressed that people value relations with groups: "The group-value model hypothesizes that in reacting to procedures people are primarily concerned about their long-term relationship to the authorities or institutions that employ the procedures" (p. 140). This explanation implies "some potential limits to the procedural justice effect" because of the "empirical question whether procedural justice concerns affect the treatment of individuals outside the boundary of the group" (p. 123).

Why might concerns about procedural fairness be limited to relations among group members subject to a common authority? According to group-value and relational models, such fairness is tied to personal identity and self-esteem, which, in turn, are heavily affected by relationships with group authorities and other group members. Thus, as the underlying assumption, this explanation posits "that people derive a sense of self-worth from group membership" (Huo, Smith, Tyler, & Lind, 1996, p. 40). Moreover, this explanation "links concerns about [procedural] justice [in particular] to concerns about the social bonds that exist between people and groups, group institutions, and group authorities" (Tyler, 1994, p. 851). As my brackets show, the relational model explores procedural, not distributive, justice. For example, "procedural justice . . . informs people about their social connection to groups and group authorities" (Tyler, Degoey, & Smith, 1996, p. 914). The key features of procedures that a group adopts indicate the group's concern for seeing fairness institutionalized in methods for making decisions. Moreover, such rules or structural features of decision making as well as an authority's demeanor and manner of conduct in the treatment accorded group members can provide messages about the symbolic significance of belonging to the group.

One set of messages involves contrasting positive and negative implications about the self—fair treatment indicating "a positive, respected position within the group" versus unfair treatment indicating "marginality and disrespect" (Tyler et al., 1996, p. 914; see also Tyler, 1994; Tyler & Lind, 1992). A second set contrasts (a) practices that reflect badly on any and all group members and (b) practices that reflect favorably on any and all group members. As Tyler et al. (1996) said, "the use of fair or unfair decision-making procedures in groups also indicates whether members can take pride in their group membership" (p. 914). Both types of messages, therefore, can make someone either feel good or feel bad about being in the group; that is, procedural practices can have implications for variation in personal self-satisfaction.

Selfishness, Outcomes, and Processes

The relational emphasis—connecting perceptions of procedural fairness, group practices, and self-identity—has an odd consequence. Lind and Tyler (1988) invoked that emphasis to criticize Thibaut and Walker's (1975) instrumental control model, which instead emphasized maximizing material self-interest. The motive to acquire material resources differs from the motive to affiliate with a group, so Lind and Tyler's emphasis on affiliative needs extends beyond that narrower, simple-minded, form of self-interest: When Mother Teresa helped the forlorn because of value implications derived from identifying herself as Catholic, for example, such self-interest differed substantially from that of inside traders (whose interests selfishly ignore a larger collective identity).

In the end, however, the relational model simply shifts from material self-interest to esteem (identity-based) self-interest. Either way, self-interest is still a central—perhaps exclusive—concern. What happens if maximizing self-esteem conflicts with others' interests? Relational approaches refer to group-based values but not explicitly to valuing others' welfare.

Identity based on inclusion in a group (and acceptance by it) does not accommodate caring about social fairness as a moral virtue. Thus, the relational model does not attend as fully to social morality as it might: It fails to identify motives that rise above group interests. Only a broader moral base can prevent the Hobbesian "war of all against all," in which one group pits its interests against another group's (e.g., majority opinion against minority rights, as J. S. Mill noted). The social-identity tradition of the relational model traces to in-group versus out-group responses by people who quickly relate more favorably to their own kind even in the most minimally social of situations. It emphasizes achieving self-identity by caring about who the other members of a particular social group are and what they think about one's own identity. It does not emphasize caring about the members of the group as human beings, as ends in themselves, or as the possessors of interests (and requirements for well-being) that might conflict with one's own. The essential characteristic of fairness, on the other hand, is that it addresses how to resolve such conflicts of interest and how to weigh others' well-being in an ethical manner.

Apparently, current theories of justice have less to do with justice or morality than with self-interest, regardless of whether they focus on outcome (distributive justice) or process (procedural justice). Their postulated psychological mechanisms take the perspective of fairness or unfairness experienced firsthand. Their explanations of fairness start by asking why the self—encountering a fair or unfair experience—might care about what happened. Although often described as enlightened or constrained, such a perspective is necessarily grounded in self-interest and, thus, cannot range far from selfishness of one variety or another.

Calling these positions selfish does not impugn their authors (e.g., few were less selfish than Thibaut; Lind and Tyler eschewed self-interest models, rebuking economic-rationality assumptions).[1] Also, my critique of the rela-

---

[1] The Lind–Tyler attack on economic rationality brings to mind one joking way to characterize passionless advocates of "the dismal science": An economist is like a guy who knows 25 ways to make love but has no girlfriend.

tional model applies equally to all other approaches of which I am aware—including my referent cognitions theory (RCT; Folger, 1987, 1993), which likewise addresses why people feel resentful about unfair treatment to their "selves." Lind, Tyler, and others note only two competing accounts of procedural justice effects (control and relational models), but RCT offers another. RCT suggests that procedures (and interpersonal conduct or interactional justice) yield information on responsibility and blame. If someone could and should have acted in a different procedural or interpersonal way, such information about the person's conduct can also foster perceptions of unwarranted deprivation (cf. Folger & Cropanzano, 1998). But, although addressing moral responsibility (see especially Folger, 1993), RCT has similarly failed to escape the bonds of self-interest in its overall thrust. Despite having touched on questions about the morality of another person's conduct, RCT has dealt primarily with self-interested reactions to personal harm (e.g., resentment).

A Focus on Problems for Accounts
That Remain Self-Centered

Next, I introduce an alternative perspective by first depicting anecdotal and experimental evidence seemingly inconsistent with self-interest explanations of fairness. I focus on outrage about violated fairness norms, often resulting in a desire to see violators punished. I examine what can make that incongruent with self-interest, then discuss alternative explanations.

Anecdotal Evidence. What unfairness reactions don't threaten self-identity? Elsewhere (Folger, 1993), I've told of talking to a seatmate on a flight to Dallas. This other passenger, a Cowboys football fan, recounted Tom Landry's firing as coach of the Cowboys. Apparently, Landry saw a news story about it before the owner notified him. Such treatment, of course, involves interpersonal conduct as interactional rather than procedural injustice (governance-structure design). In particular, publicizing someone's termination before personal notification represents unfair conduct that is separate from the decision-making procedure that determined the major material outcome (Landry's job as coach)—one reason for distinguishing procedures from interpersonal conduct, even though both can affect self-esteem as group-based identity.

Certainly, Landry had a right to feel that this demeaning treatment reflects negatively on his Cowboys-affiliated identity. If he were esteemed as part of that organization, why the shabby treatment? But Landry's reaction is not the point (although his lengthy refusal to be inducted into the Cowboy "ring of honor" suggests the strength of his reaction); rather, I consider the passenger as a fan and not a member of the Cowboys organization. His self-identity was certainly not threatened as directly as Landry's, yet he expressed outrage about Landry's mistreatment. He did not express outrage about Landry's firing per se; in fact, he considered it fair and even overdue (believing that Landry's effectiveness had declined dramatically). Hence, to the extent that the fan identified his own fortunes with that of the Cowboys organization and its football team's future success, he experienced nothing but positive consequences from Landry's firing. Still, he seethed. How dare the new owner act this way?

Such cases parallel public outcries about injustice with consequences more symbolic than tangible—such as when anti-Semitic graffiti on a synagogue causes outrage from Gentiles. Some results are as tangible as death itself, such as reports of strangers murdered heinously elsewhere in the world, whose deaths have no direct impact on the hearer (e.g., victims in Bosnia, Biafra, Cambodia, Somalia, or other areas in which people seem to suffer unfairly at the hands of cruel oppressors). Victims often appeal to public outrage in hopes of bringing about change (e.g., reporting on mutilation of women's genitalia in foreign lands). Other cases range from such examples as the outrage about Susan Smith's drowning her children and lying glibly about it, to an incident in which a baseball player spit in an umpire's face (when even people who did not care about baseball sometimes had opinions and heaped scorn on the player). Thus, common experience provides plenty of evidence that people do not have to suffer firsthand as victims in order to recognize injustice and feel moved by it. Moreover, these reactions seem to have as much to do with wrath about someone's breaking the rules as with empathy toward the victim who has suffered from a rule violation. Indeed, people probably feel no empathy toward inanimate objects (e.g., a sacred religious icon), yet still experience outrage and indignation when such objects' defilement constitutes immorality.

Experimental Data in Search of an Expanded Model. In a two-person scenario called a Dictator Game, Player 1 divides some money, deciding how much each player gets. Player 1 chooses privately. Player 2 does not know the identity of Player 1. Some versions also hide Player 1's identity from the experimenter. The standard version treats money as a free good (not earned by work), so neither Player 1 nor Player 2 have distinctive production inputs. With $20 as the amount divided, for example, Player 1's choices range from keeping $20, to splitting it so that the players get the same or different proportions of the money, to giving Player 2 $20. Not surprisingly (from a self-interest standpoint), virtually no one gives Player 2 the entire $20. But, even under strict anonymity, many in the dictator position of Player 1 do not keep all the money.

Kahneman, Knetsch, and Thaler (1986) reported data from a two-part variation, which I use here to illustrate penalties imposed on a person who wrongs someone. In Part I of this study, students as Player 1 participants selected between two options: keeping $18 and giving $2 to the other (anonymous) student, Player 2; or keeping $10 and giving the other student $10. The students knew that after the choices had been made, a small number of them would be picked randomly to receive the amount of money dictated by their choices (Player 2 students were also paid accordingly). Some Player 1 students selected the $18 for themselves, some selected $10; plenty in both categories did not have their names randomly drawn for actual payments.

Part II, in a different class, told students about the Dictator Game instructions given to students in the other class, including that some pairs were not randomly selected for payment. The Part II students got different instructions. They chose either dividing $10 evenly ($5/$5) between themselves and one anonymous Player 1 from the prior class, or dividing $12 evenly ($6/$6) between themselves and another anonymous Player 1 from the prior class. Of course, any Part II student making the $6/$6 choice kept $1 more than someone making the $5/$5 choice. Economic rationality predicts that all students would pick the $6/$6 option, regardless of Player 1's choice in the original Dictator Game.

Information about those prior Dictator choices by the Player 1 students from the other class was provided—and it did make a difference in the allocations of Part II students. Specifically, the Kahneman et al. instructions for Part II always informed the students that choosing the $12 split would cause $6 to go to a Player 1 who—as Dictator—had not actually received any previous money (was not in a randomly selected pair), but who had made the choice of an $18/$2 split, hoping to get a lot of money if his or her pair was among those randomly selected for payment. Each Part II student also learned that, if he or she selected the option of splitting $10, $5 of that amount would go to a Player 1 whose Dictator choice had been a $10/$10 split. In two separate replications, approximately three out of every four students preferred to keep $5 rather than $6 when the former decision meant sharing with someone who also had chosen equal sharing. To put it another way, these students gave up $1 in order to punish a Player 1 in the other class who had been greedy and had tried selfishly to treat another person unfairly (by selfishly dictating the $18/$2 option).

Comments on the Anecdotal and Experimental Anomalies. What do such Dictator results have to do with Tom Landry, Susan Smith, Biafra, and umpires spit upon—or with management and organizations? Both the experimental and the anecdotal evidence show that people react negatively to unfair treatment of others. Relational-model explanations do not address such data, which, instead, call for more emphasis on sanctions as means to preserve the moral order. Of course, wanting to preserve moral order can affect injustice reactions along with reactions influenced by wanting to preserve self-identity against threats to esteem (i.e., the motives can coexist; a response can reflect both). In the examples, however, I think that the motive to uphold a moral order predominates and that the motive to preserve self-esteem plays a reduced or entirely absent role.

Likewise, Camerer and Thaler (1995) noted two explanations for tendencies to "treat others fairly and punish those who behave unfairly" (p. 218). By one account, such tendencies simply reflect the rationality that applies when "long-run concerns outweigh the short-run costs"; this account admits that, although the one-shot play of a single bargaining game technically lacks long-run concerns, "subjects . . . cannot curb their repeated-game impulses" (p. 218). Camerer and Thaler find that implausible: "We prefer to think that people have simply adopted rules of behavior they think apply to themselves and others, regardless of the situation. They leave tips in restaurants that they never expect to visit again not because they believe this is really a repeated game, but because it would be rude to do otherwise" (1995, p. 218).

Moreover, we need not precommit to the details of such a motive. Lerner's (1980) Just World hypothesis, for example, is but one characterization of a general justice motive. Arguments for fairness as loyalty to a moral order come from multiple perspectives, including those invoking evolutionary tendencies (e.g., Cosmides, 1989; Damasio, 1994; de Wall, 1996; Etzioni, 1991; Frank, 1988; Simon, 1990; Wilson, 1993). These all point to the same conclusion: humans have an aversion to other people's unfair conduct. The stakes are too high for unfettered self-interest to prevail by general disinterest; human survival would be problematic without means for individual and collective management of self-restraint regarding interdependencies (cf. Dawes, 1986). Adherence to principles of moral conduct, such as the commitment to honor norms of fair treatment, in itself constitutes a protected social resource.

This collective competence embodied as an aptness for responding to moral principle, especially as that competence involves the capacity to be outraged about violations of norms such as fairness, preserves social welfare in mutually advantageous ways. I explore that theme's implications from two perspectives: ethical philosophy (briefly, in terms of moral development) and managerial and organizational practice. Of course, space constraints dictate that these discussions be short. In other words, I have to exercise self-restraint!

MORAL DEVELOPMENT:
COMMENTARY ON FAIRNESS-AS-VIRTUE

There are philosophical difficulties in arguing for fairness as a moral virtue, but, for simplicity, I ignore problematic issues. Instead, I relate fairness-as-morality to theory and research on stages of moral development (e.g.,

Kohlberg, 1984; see also Rest, 1986), providing convenient distinctions that parallel many made in more technical treatments of moral philosophy (e.g., subvarieties of positions such as egoism; utilitarian, consequentialist, and telelogical ethics; and Kantian or deontic approaches). I refer to fairness as a virtue loosely, for convenience, rather than in a philosophically technical sense of virtue (cf. MacIntyre, 1981).

Kohlbergian Parallels to Egoism, Group Values, and Fairness-as-Virtue

My remarks have had an implicit, sometimes explicit, theme: not all ethical codes are created equal; some are morally superior to others. In particular, most (perhaps all) brands of egoism fall short of common ethical canons. Some of the moral development literature presumes as much, with less- and more-moral stages: The earliest is lower order (morally impoverished) as regards full development. This literature puts egoism on the lowest rung of the ladder. In what sense is fairness-as-virtue an elevated position, perhaps on the top rung?

In Kohlberg's (1984) account of moral development, six stages progress through three levels. Level 1 is egoism. Level 2 is a socially aware utilitarianism (i.e., maximizing the common good constitutes a noble end). Level 3 grounds behavior in adherence to universal principle. I have suggested that fairness-as-morality seeks to avoid egoism. My arguments imply greater attention to at least Level 2 and that even it may lack something found only at Level 3. The following remarks distinguish Level 2 from Level 3 and emphasize the latter as a promising and challenging perspective on fairness that is worth exploring.

Level 1 and Egoism

There are striking parallels between Kohlberg's two stages of Level 1 morality and social/organizational explanations of fairness. At Level 1, people do not treat moral norms as principles of right conduct. Rather, such guidelines are followed only to the extent that they aid self-interest (without regard to others, i.e., egoism). Moral judgments are made on the basis of concrete consequences (e.g., the likelihood of reward or punishment by authorities) rather than for some greater good or because it's the right thing to do.

People at the Stage 2 borders of Level 1 recognize a connection between delaying self-gratification and promoting beneficial payoffs in the long run— the so-called enlightened self-interest orientation similar to Thibaut and Walker's (1975) perspective as characterized by Lind and Tyler (1988). Note that the relational model, in certain respects, might be subject to somewhat similar analysis—at least to the extent of overlap between self-esteem and material self-interest that I noted earlier. Kohlberg's Level 2, however, indicates that the relational approach is nonetheless distinguishable from more narrow-minded forms of egoism.

Level 2 and Group-Oriented Values

Just as the Thibaut–Walker control model does not equate simplistically to egoism, the Lind–Tyler group value/relational model is not a one-to-one match with Kohlberg's Level 2. Even its overlap with Level 2, however, falls short of the Level 3 Kohlberg principles. Level 2 people link moral conduct and group functioning (i.e., group norms and values foster cohesiveness and group well-being). By the Lind–Tyler view, identification-based self-esteem strengthens such attitudes, but social-identity researchers find own-group favoritism as a side effect (perceiving one's own group as superior to others). Ironically, pursuing a Level 2 form of fairness allows mistreating out-groupers (if fairness ideals conflict) because in-groupers consider their own fairness ideals morally superior.

Thus, Level 2 is not quintessentially moral, although it is beyond egoism in fostering the collective greater good: ardor for organization, other in-groups, and nation, along with fealty to leaders, rules, and laws. I criticize such perspectives as inferior to cherished fairness ideals that I think motivate at least some of the people, some of the time, when they act fairly or react with outrage to unfair conduct. Note, however, that widely endorsed ethical philosophies, such as utilitarianism (the greatest good for the greatest number), reflect Level 2 thematic variants.

Level 3 and Fairness-as-Virtue

Level 3 is postconventional in superseding conventions (social norms). Level 3 people follow principles based on what philosophers call a reflective attitude (cf. Rawls, 1971) rather than simply accepting handed-down truths (cf. group values) or merely pursuing unreflective and self-interested desires. This perspective can be consistent with group values, such as those embodied in a nation's legal code (and can even be consistent with forms of constrained/enlightened self-interest), but only as long as such values or aims themselves embody principles of potentially universal application (i.e., you would not only follow such guidelines but also want others to follow them). An all-too-simplistic phrase captures the spirit of this stance: I'll respect X (e.g., a law or social convention) if it respects persons. Respect for persons captures much of the essence of fairness-as-virtue and also shares common roots with such deontic or duty-observing perspectives as Kant's categorical imperative (roughly equivalent to colloquial expressions about the golden rule, and also to apparently universal expressions of religious belief). Although characterized by reference to such terms as *obligation, duty,* and *ought,* the translation of such principles into practice requires considerably more flexible thinking and adaptiveness than does the more straightforward attention to group-based rules or tenets of enlightened self-interest.

ORGANIZATIONAL APPLICATIONS: MANAGING FOR FAIRNESS-AS-VIRTUE

How do fair organizations treat shareholders, customers, employees, and the public? The motive matters—egoistic, collectivistic, or virtuous. I first stress the unfair egoism of "CEO disease." Next comes a deliberately provocative stance on why unified, collective interest is not always the moral high ground (at least, not the highest, to use Kohlberg's metaphor). Other sections on fairness-as-virtue add to these themes in terms of some new concepts.

CEO Disease: The Perils of Egoism at the Top

A *Business Week* article on "CEO Disease" cited dangers from abused power at the top. Symptoms suggest egoism run amok: "can do no wrong, refusing to concede any mistake"; "wants to make every decision but doesn't bother finding out all the details"; "always trying to be one up on counterparts in salary, headquarters, aircraft"; "relishes media attention—not especially for the company but for personal gain." Such egoism fits with statistics on U.S. CEOs as overcompensated, at multiples of average employee pay far beyond those of other countries.

This negative publicity illustrates that self-interest can become self-defeating, also jeopardizing collective interests. Consider gargantuan CEO pay, coupled with massive layoffs. Ironically, the CEOs who are the fastest to boot out potentially resentful layoff victims (e.g., security personnel arrive suddenly, get personal items hastily boxed, and escort offsite with a no-return warning) soon discover that such unfair interpersonal treatment backfires by exacerbating distrust and low morale among survivors (cf. Brockner & Wisenfeld, 1993) as well as negative actions by victims (e.g., bad-mouthing the company to friends, suing, seeking anti-business legislation). Yet some suggestive evidence (Folger, Skarlicki, Bullock, & O'Leary, 1997) indicates that higher rather than lower paid CEOs conduct layoffs more abusively.

Perils of Leading Transformationally: Is All-for-One-and-One-for-All Not Such a Good Idea?

The pitfalls of allegiance to group-based values (e.g., laws, norms, social conventions) parallel the well-known problems with unitary, consolidated thought generally: If all walk the same path, the risks include all falling into the same rut (Groupthink) or off the same cliff (the Challenger explosion). Referring similarly to transformational-leadership foibles, Keeley (1988) described Madisonian federalism as a reaction against leader power: According to Keeley, Madison saw federalism as a way to frustrate majority wishes, curb leadership in the pursuit of collective goals, and protect the interests of the weak against those of the strong. Just as Mill's *On Liberty* argued for checks and balances on majority tyranny, Keeley admonished that a transformational leader's power to unify can yield lockstep rigidity.

Keeley contrasted unitary purpose with mutuality (joint benefit, shared respect). He urged the Madisonian view that government is a social contract for mutual benefit. According to Keeley, organizations operate with sets of agreements, and these exist to further the separate interests of various organizational participants. A collective goal implies unified aims not derived from a coherent weighing of interests with different rank orders (cf. Arrow's impossibility theorem of voting, 1963), whereas mutual benefit can include attention to agreed-upon goals but must also be multipurpose in protecting unshared interests. Obviously, the balance is tricky: It asserts Voltairian freedom ("I do not agree with what you say but respect your right to say it") yet takes into account the need for limits to some minority rights and personal freedoms, as in the injunction against crying fire in a crowded theater. The following notes on principles and metaconcepts expand Keeley and further illustrate nonegoistic, noncollectivistic fairness.

Neither Egoistic nor Collectivistic: Further Implications of Fairness-as-Virtue

Fairness as moral virtue ("it's the right thing to do") entails two general principles and two metaconcepts. These are illustrative, not exhaustive, and they do not explicate fairness-as-virtue rigorously (a task for a longer work). The first principle deals with procedural check-and-balance governance; the second, with constructive conflict as competition restrained by socially sanctioned rules of the game that help keep playing fields level. Both imply limits, constraints, boundaries—rather than unfettered pursuit of singular ends without regard to the morality of means, or unfettered competition that allows destructive conflict and fails to deal with contentiousness in constructive ways. The contours of such boundedness in turn designate the beginnings of freedom, autonomy, and discretion. The first metaconstruct, *bounded autonomy*, indicates the role of those contours in the workplace. The second, the *human covenant*, suggests that a core of protected autonomy deserves universal respect.

Principle: Institutionalized Procedural Designs. Neither self-interest nor collective interest is as single-minded as my superficial critiques of egoism and utilitarian philosophies imply. Anyone can be of two minds (on the divided-self literature, see Prelec & Herrnstein, 1997; Schelling, 1985; Walsh, 1996), with simultaneously nonoverlapping preferences, values, motives, desires, or impulses; the same obviously applies with even greater force in any group, where diversity of interest is almost inevitable. Fairness-as-virtue takes interest diversity as given and asks how fairness deals with dissension. One can agree on means despite strife about ends—a procedural, not a distributive, solution (cf. Folger & Baron, 1996; Folger & Bies, 1989). Organizational examples include open book management, alternative dispute resolution mechanisms, consultative decision making, and other variations on the theme of procedural rights—especially for employees, in light of their otherwise disadvantageously asymmetric power position vis-à-vis the organizational hierarchy.

Principle: Competitive, Minimal Interference. As mentioned earlier, harmonious teams can suffer from Groupthink, which suggests the wisdom of constructive conflict. Wholesome competition cannot survive transformational exhortations about a shared vision, however, without special steps. The marketplace provides a useful analogy: "Moreover, since the efficiency of markets depends on competitiveness, moral inhibitions against engaging in anti-competitive practices (including sabotaging one's rivals) play an important role even if they are viewed only as supplementing the fear of prosecution for violations of antitrust law" (Buchanan, 1997, p. 190). The apparent paradox is that not only stultifying uniformity from noncompetitiveness (e.g., the possible deterioration of product quality from a monopoly producer) but also certain anticompetitor actions in competitive contexts (e.g., sabotaging rivals) equally threaten to undo potential gains from constructive conflict. This idea helps drive home an essential feature of fairness-as-virtue: It is about preserving level playing fields.

Metaconcept: Bounded Autonomy. Simon's (1951) essay on the employment relation provided grounds for a metaconcept to unite the two principles, which jointly limit managerial discretion by procedural check and balance mechanisms and by socially sanctioned rules of the game about level playing fields. Simon's employment-relation analysis in some ways parallels his bounded rationality insights about the limitations of human thought, so I refer to this first metaconcept as *bounded autonomy*. Bounded rationality refers chiefly to limited cognitive capability, but bounded autonomy refers to socially constructed and sanctioned constraints as contours of human freedom. The flip side of constraint is autonomy (residual freedom and discretion)—a reason for pairing *autonomy* with *bounded*. Related pairings include freedom/responsibility, rights/obligations, and authority/accountability.

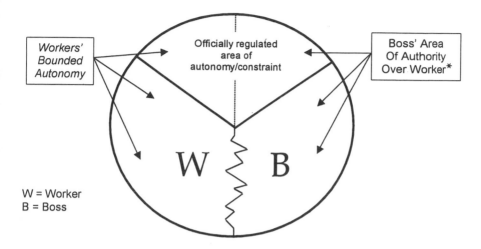

FIG. 2.1. Bounded autonomy. Relative proportions of illustrated areas are arbitrary. The author thanks Judi McLean Parks for this pie chart image.
*This is also the boss's area of bounded autonomy.

Figure 2.1 shows key features of bounded autonomy. Following Simon (1951), it divides Boss (B) and Worker (W) behavioral repertoires (Simon's terms) as pie-segment areas that trichotomize governance: "certain aspects of the worker's behavior are stipulated in the contract terms, other aspects are placed within the authority of the employer, and still other aspects are left to the worker's choice" (p. 195). Figure 2.1 identifies the first as an officially regulated area; it imposes a priori constraints not only on some of W's autonomy but also on B's. In addition to constraints dictated by the terms of a contract (e.g., hours, pay, vacation), others can come from company policies, labor law (e.g., regulations governing overtime pay), and so on. Official rules, accepted in advance, thus establish initial contours of autonomy/discretion for each party.[2]

The remaining two pie wedges indicate additional discretionary areas for B and for W. The jagged line between them shows that each party's discretion ends where the other's begins (cf. "your freedom to swing your fist ends at the start of my nose"). The B portion constitutes an additional part of B's authority over W, beyond the specifics stipulated officially in advance. W

---

[2]Simon's analysis contrasted the uniqueness of the tripartite employment relation of Fig. 2.1 with the type of employment contract that resembles purchases of commodities on the spot market (e.g., buying a tube of toothpaste). Such employment contracts would make the entire pie look like the first bounded area reviewed in my text to this point. A postage stamp purchase, for example, bundles a commodity (the stamp) with a service (letter delivery) in a prespecified way. The other two areas in Fig. 2.1 show how most ordinary employment relations, such as being hired as a full-time employee by a business organization, extend into areas where behaviors are not governed in that same prespecified fashion.

willingly accepts or at least tolerates B's authority to rule over certain matters and to dictate certain behaviors by W within what Simon called the *area of acceptance* (e.g., complying accordingly if B changes some assignments as needed).

An employment relation allows B "to postpone decision . . . [e.g., assignment changes] in order to gain from information obtained subsequently" (Simon, 1951, p. 194). B can wait to see how capable W becomes and what needs doing—rules of the game about B's latitude of authority. In exchange for pay, W allows B postponed (discretionary, contingent) decision making as a management prerogative: "The postponement of choice may be regarded as a kind of liquidity preference where the liquid resource is the employee's time instead of money" (p. 194). B's bounded autonomy comprises B's authority that has been designated by the officially regulated area in advance, plus that which has been postponed for use at B's discretion. W's bounded autonomy also includes a pool of postponed decisions to be exercised at W's discretion. Thus, bounded autonomy refers to implicit and explicit social conventions about where one party's discretion ends and another's begins.

Because workers do not give up total autonomy, their time and efforts are not a completely liquid asset for management. Some demands or some forms of treatment by bosses are tolerated less than others; some are unacceptable. Some reasonable demands may be made with an intolerable disrespect of the worker, another way in which a boss can cross the line between legitimate authority and the worker's autonomy as a basis for dignity. Workers feel that they have rights not only because they are granted officially but also because there are certain things an employer just shouldn't do. But, border disputes can erupt over contested territory, and discretion/ constraint boundaries prove no exception to the rule. The line between B's and W's discretion is fuzzy (jagged in Fig. 2.1) and subject to different perceptions (cf. actor/observer attributional biases). Some involve cherished aspects of autonomy—one source of which is the next topic.

Metaconcept: The Human Covenant. A second metaconcept, the human covenant, relates to the first and links it with the fairness-as-virtue of tacit understandings about how to treat others (cf. Fukuyama, 1995, on trust, and Selznick, 1992, on moral commonwealth; see Fig. 2.2). This "social covenant" of "implied rules that allow us to exist as a society" (Pitts, 1997, p. B-7) has respect for human dignity as an inviolable core germane to unique fairness claims on an irreducible minimum of deserved social treatment. The dignity of human autonomy allows externally imposed bounds only so much before evoking negative sanctions. This idea implies an irreducible pool (liquidity) of "Posted: No Trespassing; Keep Out" discretionary personal control as the core of human dignity. Crossing this line is an ultimate universal affront because "human dignity seems to be

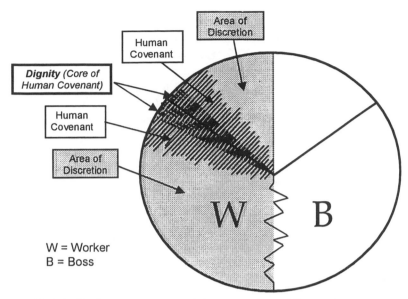

FIG. 2.2. The human covenant. Relative proportions of illustrated areas are arbitrary.

one of the few common values in our world of philosophical pluralism" (Spiegelberg, 1970, p. 62).

Although externally bounded autonomy circumscribes discretionary conduct, belief in an inalienable core of human dignity—the human covenant's centerpiece—exerts countervailing force. "Rank hath its privileges" justifies some managerial authority, for example, but the privileges of rank are subject to dispute if they infringe on the dignity core of the human covenant. Thus the rules of the game, a phrase used with Simon's concept of the employment relation, aptly characterizes the need to regulate contested territory. Sanctioning bodies govern sports; referees blow whistles to signal "out of bounds" violations of sanctioned, official rules; competitors who fail to play by the rules get penalized. Similarly, labor–management relations are subject to legal regulation and agreed-upon boundary constraints on the discretionary autonomy of each side vis-à-vis the other side's bounded autonomy (hence authority) up to that point. The changing nature of modern work (e.g., Baron & Newman, 1996; Cappelli et al., 1997; Rousseau, 1997) has made the boundary lines increasingly fuzzy, however, and has brought implicit psychological contracts to the forefront of the management literature again (e.g., Morrison & Robinson, 1997; Robinson, 1996; Rousseau, 1995). I do not speculate what this resurgence of interest might yield. Rather, I address both sides of the employment relation as discretionary areas circumscribed by the human covenant, which has human dignity at its core. I argue society will judge changes in contract terms—implicit as well as explicit—according to the implications for human dignity.

The contours of an employee's personal autonomy pool of liquidity (postponed exercise of freedom) are partly designated by the norms of the moral community. Employees perceive norm violations as reproachful conduct by organizational authorities (cf. Folger & Cropanzano, 1998). Such conduct is like cheating; it breaks the rules of the human covenant concerning inalienable dignity. Some interpersonal conduct norms might even have roots so shaped by evolution as to be nearly universal. Anthropologists might disagree about the existence of universal norms, but moral sensibility regarding interpersonal conduct seems as readily acquired as language or sight (viz., based on its properties as an evolved biophysical system shaped by adaptive fitness; cf. Cosmides, 1989).

CONCLUSION: FAIRNESS-AS-VIRTUE
AND RESPECT FOR HUMAN DIGNITY

What do respect for persons, agreement about means, and a level playing field share in illustrating fairness-as-virtue? Each hints at gaps in an egoistic or collectivist treatment of fairness, indicating that those approaches (roughly equivalent to Kohlberg's first two levels) fail to account for all that the concept of fairness implies. Note that respect for persons is a Kantian, deontic theme. Similarly, Rawls (1971) emphasized the importance of institutionalizing the types of agreements about means that impartial parties would endorse. He also suggested that, by agreeing on procedurally pure means that structurally placed people in equivalent positions with respect to personal interests (the theoretical fiction of consent from behind a veil of ignorance about one's own endowed capacities instrumental to maximizing such interests—or lotteries as real world examples of procedures deemed fair in advance, regardless of outcomes), the types of solutions sought would give due regard to minority interests. That is a point I meant to convey in referring to a level playing field as a means of competitive minimal interference—that is, people free to compete to the extent that such autonomy does not impinge on others' similar freedoms.

Principled fairness is an elusive concept perhaps best elucidated by the fairness metaphor of rules for playing games. Think about playing a game for money, so that material self-interest adds to the potential for gains and losses in self-esteem. At some point, one of the players says "Unfair—that's cheating." This complaint might be egoistically motivated, in two ways. First, self-interest (for material or psychological gain) might tempt a person to say it manipulatively, perhaps even making a false claim in hopes that it would go undetected. Second, the complaint could be genuine, in the sense of actual belief about having suffered from illegitimate play.

A "not fair!" complaint could also reflect motives related to self-esteem and identity-management concerns such as emphasized by the group value model and other collectivist takes on fairness. But such an orientation has some perverse implications that surely fall short of at least some ideals of fairness. Why not, for example, make a ruling between two players that favors one's own side (the in-group) rather than the opponent's side (the out-group)? Similarly biased impulses would favor family members over mere acquaintances; the former constitute an in-group whose opinions we value more highly and whose approval we court with greater fervor. Both examples illustrate a moral fault line in the collectivist terrain: Conflating fairness with collective interest (or self-esteem based on identification with collective interests and values) does not aim at fairness for all, but only for those with whom we identify—a limited fairness at best.

Lind and Tyler's astute insight showed how fairness can flow from group-related concerns beyond economic self-interest. But fairness perceptions and reactions also derive from principles based on neither such source. "That's unfair" can refer simply to the right way to play a game. Adhering to a game's rules as principled conduct can stem from realizing that not to do so would mean playing a different game! Virtuous fairness is like applying a game's rules to everyone (e.g., principles governing commercial transactions that take into account externalities, such as pollution, and their effect on the public). Respect for persons means respect for all players as stakeholders, including the public at large. Modern corporations can wield vast power, with some international conglomerates loyal to no single state and yet having budgets as big as major world powers. Although players from a multiple stakeholder perspective, most elements of the public at large (and any given individual) constitute a minority whose interests are potentially threatened by such power when abused. External, legal sanctions insufficiently curb abuse. The moral fiber of corporate leaders plays a vital role, so fairness as morality bears close examination.

Kant's second formulation of the categorical imperative called for treating humans as ends in themselves and never as means only—the sense in which humans possess dignity as intrinsic worth and value. As Spiegelberg noted in commenting on the connection of that imperative with the concept of dignity, it contrasts with "price" as "the kind of value for which there can be an equivalent, whereas dignity makes an object irreplaceable" (1970, p. 49). In that sense, Lind and Tyler (1988) were on the right track in contrasting a relational point of view with the control-oriented view that Thibaut and Walker (1975) took when analyzing the basis for concern about procedural justice. By the latter analysis, the interest in procedures is derivative because procedures serve as means for attaining equitable ends. But equity, as Adams' (1965) presentation in terms of equivalent ratios showed, is about price (a fair rate of return on inputs invested) and equivalent value. Procedural rights based on human dignity, however, do not serve merely to promote an equitable distribution of outcomes. They can manifest value independently of such an objective.

I differ from Lind and Tyler in not wanting procedures to serve self-gratification (desire for a valued self-identity based on esteem from a group with which one identifies). I think that a more ultimate source of value is the role of procedures in preserving human dignity. In that sense, procedures are not merely (in part) means for seeking equity as distributive justice, but neither are they ends in themselves. Their principal value—in connection with fairness-as-virtue—derives from an instrumental association with human dignity (e.g., as part of a system of checks and balances maintaining a level playing field and preventing someone's unfair exploitation by others).

I've tried to suggest that fairness-as-virtue calls for principled conduct that rises above ordinary self-interest in seeking to preserve human dignity. Our righteous indignation and sense of outrage should not be evoked only by the psychological damage to the esteem of someone whose dignity has been violated. Rather, the very willingness of someone to pursue such actions (e.g., humiliating another person without just cause, or to a degree that cannot be condoned) should elicit wrath and reproach independently of harm to the person most affected by those actions. In that sense, what also matters is the harm done to principle itself. Violations of human dignity call for rebuke not simply because of the consequences they cause, but also because of the stand against virtue that they take. They oppose the decency, goodness, and civility without which human life becomes solitary, poor, nasty, brutish, and short. Cheaters are to be punished because they cheat, period, not because it looks as if the cheating might help them win or cause someone else to lose. We need not identify with other players to revile the cheater; but we must care about right and wrong, about human dignity— hence, about virtue in fair play. Virtuously granting other people fair treatment means exercising self-imposed restraint that confines autonomy otherwise capable of exploitation. As self-bounded autonomy, fairness thus manifests a discretionary choice: honoring the other's claim to human dignity on a par with the self's claim, even if only to enjoy the ultimate sense of virtue as its own reward.

REFERENCES

Adams, J. S. (1965). Inequity in social exchange. *Advances in Experimental Social Psychology, 2*, 267–299.

Arrow, K. J. (1963). *Social choice and individual values* (2nd ed.). New York: Wiley.

Baron, R. A., & Newman, J. (1996). Workplace violence and workplace aggression: Evidence of their relative frequency and potential causes. *Aggressive Behavior, 44*, 1–26.

Brockner, J., & Wisenfeld, B. (1993). Living on the edge (of social and organizational psychology): The effects of job layoffs on those who remain. In J. K. Murnighan (Ed.), *Social psychology in organizations: Advances in theory and research* (pp. 119–140). Englewood Cliffs, NJ: Prentice-Hall.

Buchanan, A. (1997). Economics and ethics. In *The Blackwell encyclopedia of management* (Vol. 11, pp. 187–191). Oxford, England: Blackwell.

Camerer, C. F., & Thaler, R. (1995). Anomalies, ultimatums, dictators and manners. *Journal Economic Perspectives, 9*(2), 209–219.

Cappelli, P., Bassi, L., Katz, L., Knoke, D., Osterman, P., & Useem, M. (1997). *Change at work.* New York: Oxford University Press.

Cosmides, L. (1989). The logic of social exchange: Has natural selection shaped how humans reason? Studies with the Wason selection task. *Cognition, 31,* 187–276.

Damasio, A. R. (1994). *Descartes error: Emotion, reason and the human brain.* New York: Putnam.

Dawes, R. (1986). *Group identification and collective action.* Paper presented at the Nag's Head Conference on Social Dilemmas, Nag's Head, NC.

de Wall, F. (1996). *Good natured: The origins of right and wrong in humans and other animals.* Cambridge, MA: Harvard University Press.

Etzioni, A. (1991). *A responsive society.* San Francisco: Jossey-Bass.

Folger, R. (1977). Distributive and procedural justice: Combined impact of "voice" and improvement on experienced inequity. *Journal of Personality and Social Psychology, 35,* 108–119.

Folger, R. (1987). A referent cognitions theory of relative deprivation. In J. M. Olson, C. P. Herman, & M. P. Zanna (Eds.), *Relative deprivation and social comparison: The Ontario symposium* (Vol. 4, pp. 33–55). Hillsdale, NJ: Lawrence Erlbaum Associates.

Folger, R. (1993). Reactions to mistreatment at work. In J. K. Murnighan (Ed.), *Social psychology in organizations: Advances in theory and research* (pp. 161–183). Englewood Cliffs, NJ: Prentice-Hall.

Folger, R., & Baron, R. A. (1996). Violence and hostility at work: A model of reactions to perceived injustice. In G. R. VandenBos & E. Q. Bulatao (Eds.), *Violence on the job: Identifying risks and developing solutions* (pp. 51–85). Washington, DC: American Psychological Association.

Folger, R., & Bies, R. J. (1989). Managerial responsibilities and procedural justice. *Employee Responsibilities and Rights Journal, 2,* 79–90.

Folger, R., & Cropanzano, R. (1998). *Organizational justice and human resources management.* Thousand Oaks, CA: Sage.

Folger, R., Skarlicki, D. P., Bullock, J., & O'Leary, B. (1997). [Layoff rationale as a predictor of insensitive dismissal]. Unpublished raw data.

Frank, R. H. (1988). *Passions within reason: The strategic role of emotions.* New York: Norton.

Fukuyama, F. (1995). *Trust: The social virtues and the creation of prosperity.* New York: The Free Press.

Huo, Y. J., Smith, H. J., Tyler, T. R., & Lind, E. A. (1996). Superordinate identification, subgroup identification, and justice concerns: Is separatism the problem; Is assimilation the answer? *Psychological Science, 7,* 40–45.

Kahneman, D., Knetsch, J. L., & Thaler, R. H. (1986). Fairness and the assumptions of economics. *Journal of Business, 59,* S285–S300.

Keeley, M. C. (1988). *A social-contract theory of organizations.* Notre Dame, IN: University of Notre Dame Press.

Kohlberg, L. (1984). *The psychology of moral development.* San Francisco: Harper & Row.

Lerner, M. J. (1980). *The belief in a just world: A fundamental delusion.* New York: Plenum.

Lind, E. A., & Tyler, T. R. (1988). *The social psychology of procedural justice.* New York: Plenum.

MacIntyre, A. C. (1981). *After virtue.* Notre Dame, IN: University of Notre Dame Press.

Morrison, E., & Robinson, S. L. (1997). When employees feel betrayed: A model of how psychological contract violation develops. *Academy of Management Review, 22*, 226–256.

Pitts, L., Jr. (1997, August 1). The apathy to crimes in progress. *The Times-Picayune*, p. B-7.

Prelec, D., & Herrnstein, R. J. (1997). Preferences or principles: Alternative guidelines for choice. In H. Rachlin & D. I. Laibson (Eds.), *The matching law: Papers in psychology and economics* (pp. 293–312). Cambridge, MA: Harvard University Press.

Rawls, J. (1971). *A theory of justice*. Cambridge, MA.: Harvard University Press.

Rest, J. R. (1986). *Moral development: Advances in theory and research*. New York: Praeger.

Robinson, S. L. (1996). Trust and breach of the psychological contract. *Administrative Science Quarterly, 41*, 574–599.

Rousseau, D. (1995). *Psychological contracts in organizations: Understanding written and unwritten agreements*. Thousand Oaks, CA: Sage.

Rousseau, D. M. (1997). Organizational behavior in the new organizational era. *Annual Review of Psychology, 48*, 515–546.

Schelling, T. C. (1985). Enforcing rules on oneself. *Journal of Law, Economics and Organization, 1*, 357–374.

Selznick, P. (1992). *The moral commonwealth: Social theory and the promise of community*. Los Angeles: University of California Press.

Simon, H. A. (1951). A formal theory of the employment relation. *Econometrika, 19*, 293–305.

Simon, H. A. (1990). A mechanism for social selection and successful altruism. *Science, 250*, 1665–1668.

Spiegelberg, H. (1970). Human dignity: A challenge to contemporary philosophy. In R. Gotesky & E. Laslo (Eds.), *Human dignity: This century and the next* (pp. 39–64). New York: Gordon & Breach.

Thibaut, J. W., & Walker, L. (1975). *Procedural justice: A psychological perspective*. Hillsdale, NJ: Lawrence Erlbaum Associates.

Tyler, T. R. (1994). Psychological models of the justice motive: Antecedents of distributive and procedural justice. *Journal of Personality and Social Psychology, 67*, 850–863.

Tyler, T. R., Degoey, P., & Smith, H. (1996). Understanding why the justice of group procedures matters: A test of the psychological dynamics of the group-value model. *Journal of Personality and Social Psychology, 70*, 913–930.

Tyler, T. R., & Folger, R. (1980). Distributional and procedural aspects of satisfaction with citizen-police encounters. *Basic and Applied Social Psychology, 1*, 281–292.

Tyler, T. R., & Lind, E. A. (1992). A relational model of authority in groups. *Advances in Experimental Social Psychology, 25*, 115–191.

Walsh, V. (1996). *Rationality, allocation, and reproduction*. Oxford, England: Clarendon.

Walster, E., Walster, G. W., & Berscheid, E. (1978). *Equity: Theory and research*. Boston: Allyn and Bacon.

Wilbur, J. (1997). Self-interest. In *The Blackwell encyclopedia of management* (Vol. 11, pp. 576–577). Oxford, England: Blackwell.

Wilson, J. Q. (1993). *The moral sense*. New York: The Free Press.

CHAPTER THREE

A Multiple Stakeholder Model
of Privacy in Organizations

Dianna L. Stone
Eugene F. Stone-Romero
University of Central Florida

Seventy years ago Supreme Court Justice Brandeis argued that

> the makers of the Constitution undertook to secure conditions favorable to
> the pursuit of happiness . . . They sought to protect Americans in their beliefs,
> their thoughts, and their sensations. They conferred . . . the right to be let
> alone . . . the most comprehensive of rights and the right most valued by
> civilized men. (*Olmstead v. U.S.*, 1928)

Despite what is implied by Justice Brandeis' argument, the practices of work
organizations have increasingly violated individuals' expectations of privacy.
As a result, there has been a growing conflict in our society between the
needs of social systems for information and individuals' actual or perceived
rights to privacy. The debate about privacy has recently intensified in employment contexts. One reason for this is that organizations need large
amounts of information about individuals (e.g., job applicants, job incumbents) to facilitate decision making. For example, to ensure that job applicants will be successful on the job, many organizations regularly gather
information on job applicants' education, family background, personality,
credit, and medical history. Not surprisingly, critics have become concerned
that the accumulation of information about individuals tends to enhance the
power and authority of organizations at the expense of individuals' actual
or perceived rights to privacy (Gross, 1962; Privacy Protection Study Commission, 1977; Schein, 1976; Shils, 1966; E. Stone & Stone, 1990).

Another reason for the growing conflict about privacy is that advances in technology have outpaced traditional norms and expectations of privacy (Westin, 1967). The proliferation of databases and computer networks has given employers access to personal data that may unfairly stigmatize some individuals and prevent them from achieving their life and career-related goals (e.g., being hired for jobs; Linowes, 1989). For example, the use of integrated information systems often gives decision makers easy access to personal information about individuals (e.g., medical data, credit history, arrest records, family background data) and allows organizations to freely share and disseminate this information. Some critics contend that the practice of networking data may impose permanent "marks or stigmas" on individuals, and unfairly create adverse consequences for them (Wasserstrom, 1984, p. 327). In addition, the expanding power of organizations to collect and disseminate information has overshadowed the ability of individuals to protect their privacy and personal dignity. Finally, some analysts contend that in many cases intrusions into privacy are not only morally offensive but unnecessary, being attributable to little more than the "frivolous self-indulgence of the professionals of intrusion" (Shils, 1966, p. 306).

It is evident from the above that privacy poses a moral dilemma for organizations that have simultaneously an obligation to protect the interests of owners and customers and an ethical responsibility to protect the dignity and welfare of employees. On the one hand, organizations need information to facilitate decision making about employees. On the other hand, however, employees have needs for privacy in order to protect their autonomy and personal freedom (cf. E. Stone & Stone, 1990).

In the late 1970s, the Privacy Protection Study Commission (PPSC; 1977) predicted that technological advances would require organizations to balance their needs for information against employees' expectations of privacy. Despite this prediction, there has been a paucity of research that considers the privacy issue from the perspectives of all relevant stakeholders in organizations, including job applicants, job incumbents, customers, managers, owners, and the public.[1] Thus, a model is needed that (a) examines privacy from a multiple stakeholder perspective, (b) identifies sources of conflicts among stakeholders, and (c) specifies mechanisms for resolving such conflicts. In view of this, the primary purpose of this chapter is to describe a multiple stakeholder model of privacy in organizations. Before introducing and discussing the model, however, it is essential to consider its focus and theoretical bases.

---

[1]The terms *privacy* and *information control* are used interchangeably throughout this chapter. The reason for this is that information control assures privacy. In the case of individuals, it is personal privacy. In the case of organizations, it is privacy of organizational data.

MULTIPLE STAKEHOLDER MODEL OF PRIVACY

The multiple stakeholder model of privacy considered here is based on a compilation of previous theory and empirical research on such topics as work adjustment (Lofquist & Dawis, 1969), behavior in organizations (Porter, Lawler, & Hackman, 1975), the stakeholder theory of organizations (Evan & Freeman, 1988; Freeman & Gilbert, 1987), and privacy in organizational contexts (PPSC, 1977; E. Stone & Stone, 1990). Several aspects of the model deserve note. First, in developing the model, we focused on privacy as information control because information mediates the relationship between individuals and organizations, and is often the primary determinant of organizational decision making. For example, information about job applicants' background and experience is often vital to personnel selection decisions.

Second, our model focuses on the perspectives of three key sets of stakeholders, that is, organizations (e.g., managers, stockholders), individuals (e.g., job applicants or incumbents), and members of the general public (e.g., customers). Each set of stakeholders has a legitimate interest in the data collection and dissemination practices of organizations (cf. Donaldson & Preston, 1995).

Third, our model assumes that stakeholders in organizations often hold multiple roles. For example, sometimes a person performing the role of manager may also be the owner of an organization, and those in the role of employee may simultaneously serve as owners or stockholders in the organization.

Fourth and finally, although information privacy may be an important issue in a variety of organizational contexts (e.g., credit, insurance, government), the scope of our model is limited to privacy in employment contexts. Our multiple stakeholder model of privacy is shown in Fig. 3.1. Major elements of the model are considered in the following paragraphs.

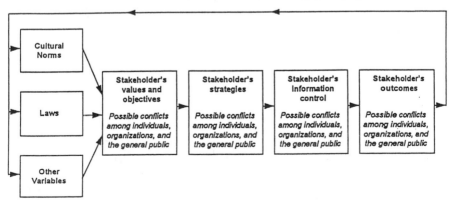

FIG. 3.1. A multiple stakeholder model of privacy.

As noted previously, the model is based on the assumption that information control is a key issue for various stakeholders (the organization, individuals, and other stakeholders). Thus, the model focuses on a number of antecedents and outcomes of information control in organizations. In particular, the model emphasizes that three antecedent variables influence a stakeholder's ability to control information, including environmental variables (e.g., cultural norms, laws), the values and objectives of various stakeholders, and the strategies used by stakeholders. In addition, the model suggests that a stakeholder's ability to control information influences experienced outcomes. Finally, the model stresses that discrepancies between the desired and experienced outcomes of various stakeholders feed back to influence antecedent variables (e.g., the values of stakeholders, stakeholder support for legislation). Given this brief overview of the model, a more detailed explanation of the factors in the model follows.

First, as noted earlier, the model suggests that national cultural norms, laws, and other environmental variables (e.g., economic conditions) affect the values and expectations of various stakeholders (Hall, 1966). For example, national cultural norms may lead individuals to develop expectations of privacy within the employment context. Likewise, national norms influence the values and expectations of work organizations regarding their ability to collect and control information. It merits noting, however, that the values of U.S. organizations do not always mirror American cultural norms because there are many contradictions and inconsistencies in American culture (Trice & Beyer, 1993). For example, although American culture stresses individual rights (e.g., privacy rights), it also emphasizes that managerial action should be rational and based on science. Thus, organizations collect vast amounts of information, often more information than they need, in an attempt to create the illusion of rationality and commitment to rational decision making. As a result, the values and practices of work organizations may often be inconsistent with broader societal norms regarding the rights of individuals. Similarly, extant laws (e.g., the Polygraph Protection Act, the Privacy Act of 1974) may influence the values of both organizations and individuals (e.g., job applicants). However, American cultural norms may also lead individuals to expect that they have rights to privacy when, in fact, no specific law actually guarantees them such rights. For example, although most Americans may perceive they have fundamental rights to privacy, the U.S. Constitution does not explicitly guarantee such rights (Alderman & Kennedy, 1995). Thus, throughout this chapter we refer to expectations of or perceived rights to privacy rather than actual rights to privacy.

Moreover, cultural norms and laws also influence the values and expectations of other stakeholders, including customers. Customers generally value such outcomes as high quality products and services, fair treatment in their dealings with organizations, and ethical behavior on the part of organizational members. For example, customers typically expect to be protected from the harm that can result from immoral behavior by organizations and their employees (e.g., the cover-up of research on nicotine addiction by managers of several U.S. tobacco companies).

Second, the model posits that the values of stakeholders influence the objectives they pursue. For instance, because owners of organizations value profit, a relevant objective is to hire and retain workers who have high levels of motivation, integrity, and job-relevant abilities (Cascio, 1991; Porter et al., 1975). Moreover, the values of job incumbents (e.g., achievement) may motivate them to pursue work-related goals and objectives that enable achievement. Similarly, given that customers often value quality service, they may be more motivated to purchase products and services from organizations that can be trusted to provide it than from organizations that have histories of providing poor service.

Third, the model suggests that stakeholders' values and objectives are a major determinant of the strategies that they use to reach their goals. Because information is vital to the achievement of stakeholders' objectives, they employ various strategies for controlling information. Thus, for example, in the interest of ensuring high levels of worker productivity, an organization may try to (a) collect accurate data about individuals in order to make hiring and placement decisions, (b) use a number of methods to monitor and control employee performance (e.g., supervisory or video surveillance), and (c) establish precise records on all employees for planning and tracking purposes. Likewise, in order to secure high levels of rewards, individuals may try to manage favorable impressions by limiting the amounts and types of information that organizations collect about them (cf. Porter et al., 1975; E. Stone & Stone, 1990). For example, in the interest of preventing embarrassment and securing job offers, job applicants may conceal potentially stigmatizing information (e.g., disability or medical problems) and present themselves in a socially desirable manner (Giacalone & Rosenfeld, 1989; Goffman, 1959; E. Stone, Stone, & Dipboye, 1992). Other stakeholders may also use a number of strategies to obtain information they view as relevant to the achievement of their goals. For example, customers may assess the trustworthiness of an organization and its employees by gathering data from sources that have knowledge about the organization (e.g., other customers, Better Business Bureaus).

Fourth, the model posits that the strategies used by stakeholders influence their capacity to actually control information. The model also suggests that the strategies used by one stakeholder may affect the degree to which another stakeholder can control information. For example, although the use of multiple data-collection methods by the organization (e.g., interviews, background checks, personality inventories) may increase its capacity to control information, the same practices may limit the degree to which individuals can control personal information and protect their privacy. Likewise, if individuals seek to control (e.g., withhold, distort) personal information about themselves in the selection process, they will decrease the extent to which the organization or general public has access to information that may be critical to job performance or public safety (e.g., illicit drug use, prior criminal activity).

Fifth, the model suggests that stakeholders' abilities to control relevant information influences their experienced outcomes. Thus, for example, organizations that have the capacity to control relevant information from job applicants and use the data to make selection decisions may enjoy higher levels of worker productivity than those that do not (Cascio, 1991). However, if the data are invalid (e.g., inaccurate or incomplete), personnel decision making is likely to be adversely affected and personnel selection goals might not be reached. Similarly, if individuals have the ability to control the disclosure of personal information they may experience autonomy. However, if they do not have the capacity to control information they may experience embarrassment or loss of personal freedom.

Sixth, the model suggests that stakeholders compare the outcomes they experience to expected outcomes or objectives (Thibaut & Kelley, 1959).[2] Discrepancies between desired and experienced outcomes are posited to serve as feedback that influences norms, laws, and other relevant variables. In addition, discrepancies may also serve to directly affect values, objectives, and strategies.[3] Thus, for example, an organization might assess the utility of information gathered in the personnel selection process through any of several conventional test validation strategies (cf. Cascio, 1991). To the extent that experienced outcomes (e.g., worker ability levels) differed from expected outcomes (e.g., desired ability levels), corrective action would be taken. Similarly, the model suggests that individuals and other stakeholders evaluate their ability to achieve desired outcomes through controlling information. For example, if job applicants felt that organizational data-collection practices (e.g., polygraph, honesty test) left them in a position of being unable to control personal information, they would feel that their privacy had been invaded (cf. E. Stone & Stone, 1990). Likewise, customers who are unable to obtain information about the trustworthiness of an organization's employees may experience physical harm or psychological damage.

The model identifies potential sources of conflict between and among stakeholders. To illustrate such conflict, we consider the values and objectives-related elements in the model. Assume that an individual has applied

---

[2]In the interest of clarity, all of the relevant paths are not shown in the model.
[3]In the interest of clarity, all of the relevant feedback loops are not shown.

for a job as a school bus driver. In the interest of protecting privacy and getting the job, the individual fails to tell the employer about his or her alcoholism problems and previous convictions for driving while under the influence of alcohol. In this case, the applicant's objective of protecting privacy would be quite inconsistent with the objectives of the organization and members of the general public. Neither would want to have an alcohol-impaired individual driving a school bus.

Of course, conflicts between and among stakeholders are not limited to values and objectives. Conflicts may also arise when stakeholders have competing strategies and abilities to control information. For example, an organization's strategies for collecting information about the performance of individuals (e.g., through the use of video surveillance) may conflict with workers' expectations of privacy. Likewise, workers' values and expectations of privacy may conflict with the general public's desire for information about workers to ensure the health and safety of others. For instance, the public may want to know about the illicit drug use of bus drivers, pilots, police officers, and air traffic controllers.

Although not illustrated in the model, technology affects virtually all of its elements and processes. In particular, the broad availability and low costs of electronic technology (e.g., computers) have motivated the collection and storage of vast amounts of information about individuals (PPSC, 1977). Moreover, the same technology has allowed for the rapid dissemination of this information to individuals within and outside of the organization, reducing the control that individuals have over data concerning them. Along with the unbridled collection and dissemination of information about individuals by organizations comes the possibility that the same individuals will be directly or indirectly harmed (e.g., an individual may become stigmatized when an organization releases information that the person is HIV positive).

Consistent with stakeholder theory (cf. Evan & Freeman, 1988; Freeman & Gilbert, 1987), we believe that, in general, one stakeholder should not be allowed to pursue his or her own interests at the expense of the interests of others. All stakeholders may have legitimate interests in controlling information (e.g., maintaining privacy), and within reason, a balance should be sought among those interests. In instances where stakeholders disagree considerably about the resolution of conflicts, one of several strategies can be used to resolve the disputes.[4] For example, appeals can be made to legal remedies, labor–management agreements, societal norms, or superordinate moral principles. We consider several of these strategies in the section titled "Conflict Resolution Strategies."

---

[4]In the interest of clarity, our model does not contain elements concerned with conflict resolution strategies.

INTERESTS OF VARIOUS STAKEHOLDERS

Having considered the basic logic of our model, we now offer an analysis of the values, interests, and strategies of each of three major groups of stakeholders, that is, the organization, the individual, and other stakeholders.

The Organization as a Stakeholder

Organizations are important stakeholders that clearly value their ability to control information about job applicants and employees. The control of information helps organizations meet a number of key objectives, including enhanced productivity, responsiveness to market changes, and profits. As a result, organizations use a variety of strategies to collect and store data about job applicants and job incumbents (PPSC, 1977; E. Stone & Stone, 1990). We next consider the organization's values, objectives, and strategies for controlling information.

The Organization's Values and Objectives

Organizations value controlling information about job applicants and incumbents for a variety of reasons. In particular, organizations have an obligation to owners and customers to produce profits, provide owners with a return on investments, and deliver quality products and services to customers. In order to achieve these and other objectives, organizations must ensure that there is a dependable level of role performance among employees (Katz & Kahn, 1978). As a consequence, organizations have come under increased pressure to collect large amounts of information about actual and potential employees in order to maintain a productive workforce. Apart from the reasons just noted, the pressure to collect and store vast amounts of data about employees also stems from new legislative reporting requirements (e.g., EEO) and growing organizational concerns about a variety of employee-related issues, several of which are discussed next.

Concerns About Worker Values and Deviant Behavior

Since the 1950s, authors have argued that the growth of organizations and their reliance on mass production technologies and scientific management principles led managers to distrust job applicants and incumbents (Shils, 1966; Whyte, 1957). For example, Shils argued that the ongoing distrust of employees stems from the labor–management disputes that were common in the 1930s. In addition, as the size of organizations increased, there were diminished opportunities for face-to-face contact which, coupled with decreased loyalty among employees, increased the perceived need to collect data about individuals to ensure acceptable worker behavior (PPSC, 1977). These and other factors resulted in the use of human resources management techniques that were motivated (at least in part) by the view of each employee "as an instrument of industrial efficiency whose innermost attitudes and (thoughts) had to be disclosed and assessed since the organization could not count on the employee's resourcefulness, truthfulness or loyalty" (Shils, 1996, p. 296).

More recently, social scientists have argued that there has been a growing deterioration of the moral foundation of our society (Etzioni, 1996; Kahn, 1979). For example, Etzioni noted that since the 1960s there have been disturbing changes in several core values in American society, including a decline in individuals' work values, a decreasing level of respect for authority, and a tendency for society to relax its definitions of deviance. As a result, organizations have experienced a seemingly dramatic rise in criminal activity on the part of workers, including on-the-job drug usage and theft of organizational property. For example, empirical studies suggest that between 5% and 13% of the workforce abuses drugs and alcohol, and 35% to 40% of employees admit to some sort of pilferage on the job (Hollinger & Clark, 1983).

Strategies Used to Control Deviant Behavior. Given that a key objective of organizations is to maximize dependable role performance, the growing incidences and costs associated with employee substance abuse and theft have led employers to experiment with strategies for dealing with these and other problems. One very common strategy is to test both job applicants and job incumbents for drug use and integrity (honesty). Some reports indicate that 26% of companies now use drug tests, and 5,000 to 6,000 firms currently use honesty tests (cf. Sackett, Burris, & Callahan, 1989). Organizations also collect data about job applicants' nonwork behaviors (e.g., credit history, criminal record) in order to screen out those who might be untrustworthy or pose safety risks to current employees or customers. For example, many firms now regularly use a variety of methods to collect data on applicants' lifestyle (e.g., living arrangements), character, and employment history, including background checks, credit reports, and private investigative agencies. In addition, data on nonwork behavior and employment history are often compiled in databases and shared among employer associations. One estimate indicates that such associations (e.g., Employers Mutual Association) check the backgrounds of 150,000 applicants per year and share the data.

Concerns About Negligent Hiring Lawsuits

Organizations also gather large amounts of information about individuals because of the dramatic rise in the number of negligent hiring lawsuits brought against employers (cf. Extejt & Bockanic, 1991) and because companies are increasingly being held liable for injuries or harm caused by their employees (Extejt & Bockanic, 1991). Under the tort of negligent hiring, employers have a duty to protect the health and safety of employees. Moreover, modern agency and tort law have expanded the company's duty to customers and the general public. For example, in a now classic case (*Kendall v. Gore Properties*, 1956), a landlord was held liable when an employee with a history of mental problems murdered a tenant. The landlord was found negligent because he hired the man without a reference check and gave him a key to paint the murdered woman's apartment.

Strategies Used to Prevent Negligence Lawsuits. Given that organizations have a legally mandated objective to protect the safety of employees and customers, employers feel obligated to thoroughly assess applicants' fitness for duty and their potential to behave responsibly on the job. As a result, organizations often collect data about such factors as drinking habits, illicit drug use, mental illness, physical disabilities, risk proneness, and past criminal history through such means as background investigations, drug and alcohol testing, personality assessment, and medical examinations. Moreover, employers argue that extensive data collection is especially important when the job involves high levels of responsibility for the safety and welfare of others (e.g., police officers, firefighters, airline pilots, bus drivers, school teachers).

Concerns About Monitoring the Workforce

As noted previously, the use of scientific management principles led managers to believe that workers could not be trusted to perform their jobs unless they were monitored closely. As a result, organizations began to use supervisory surveillance to ensure that workers performed their jobs effectively. Although employee monitoring is typically used to evaluate work performance and facilitate customer service, some organizations also believe that monitoring is needed to control employee theft and to deter employees from using organizational resources for personal purposes.

Strategies Used to Monitor the Workforce. In order to achieve productivity objectives, most organizations now monitor worker performance using various forms of performance appraisal. However, recent innovations in technology have prompted some companies to use more sophisticated electronic monitoring methods (cf. Alder & Ambrose, 1997; D. Stone, Eddy, & Stone-Romero, 1997). In particular, there has been a rise in the use of video and audio technology to monitor workers' behaviors and interactions with customers and an increased use of computer systems to monitor workers' output (D. Stone et al., 1997). Some reports estimate that over 26 million employees in the United States are monitored using electronic methods (Ross, 1992) and a large number of organizations peruse employees' e-mail, voice mail, and computer network files.

Need to Maintain Employee Records

As noted previously, as organizations grew in size, they substituted employee records for face-to-face contact with individual employees (PPSC, 1977). Records are now used to help organizations make employment-related decisions and efficiently manage the workforce (Kavanagh, Gueutal, & Tannenbaum, 1990). In recent years, the passage of legislation (e.g., EEO) has also made employee record keeping a requirement for most organizations.

Strategies Used to Maintain Employee Records. Given that employee record keeping is needed to help organizations make employment-related decisions, almost all organizations now maintain employee records in manual or computerized files. Furthermore, the extensive availability and low costs of computer technology have made it quite economical for organizations to collect, store, and disseminate large amounts of information about employees. Human resources information systems (HRIS) are now widely used in organizations and are thought to greatly benefit strategic decision making (e.g., compare compensation strategies), and to help firms evaluate human resources policies and practices (e.g., monitor costs of absenteeism; Kavanagh et al., 1990). Note, moreover, that advances in computer networks and the use of the Internet have facilitated the interface between these HRIS and other information systems within and outside organizations. For example, HRIS are often linked to an organization's internal accounting system and may be connected to external health insurance systems, state and federal tax systems (IRS), and other commercial data banks (cf. Kavanagh et al., 1990). In addition, many organizations give employees access to networked systems (e.g., intranets) so that they can easily communicate with coworkers, update personnel records, and select new insurance policies.

As is evident from the discussion, organizations typically collect considerable amounts of data about individuals in order to achieve their business-related objectives. However, as records increasingly displace face-to-face relationships in organizations, individuals have become extremely concerned about their ability to control personal information and protect their privacy (PPSC, 1977; E. Stone & Stone, 1990). Thus, we next consider individuals' values and objectives as stakeholders.

The Individual as Stakeholder

Our model specifies that individuals value controlling information about themselves in order to achieve a number of objectives, including managing favorable impressions and getting numerous job-related outcomes (cf. E. Stone & Stone, 1990). In addition, they use a variety of strategies to ensure that they can control information about themselves and, thus, protect their privacy. In order to better understand the individual as a stakeholder in the system, we now consider the individual's values, objectives, and strategies for controlling personal information.

Individuals' Values and Objectives

As noted previously, individuals value controlling information and protecting privacy for both intrinsic (e.g., enhanced autonomy, improved psychological well-being) and instrumental reasons (e.g., competitive advantages in achieving social and job-related goals; cf. Laufer & Wolfe, 1977; E. Stone & Stone, 1990). Moral and legal philosophers argue that privacy is primarily an intrinsic value (e.g., Fried, 1968; Wasserstrom, 1984). Thus, we first consider the intrinsic value of privacy.

All people have private thoughts, fantasies, and fears. Many of these thoughts are private because they are central to the person's identity and define who he or she is emotionally, cognitively, physically, and relationally (Fried, 1968). Given that others cannot read minds, privacy serves to keep all the world from knowing a person's thoughts. If every thought, word, or deed were made known to others, individuals would undoubtedly experience embarrassment or social disapproval (Wasserstrom, 1984). Through concealing private thoughts from others, people are able to protect their autonomy, personal dignity, self-image, happiness, and emotional well-being (Klopfer & Rubenstein, 1977). Privacy also allows individuals the freedom to think or say things that are unpopular (Fried, 1968).

It is evident that privacy serves to satisfy a number of purely intrinsic objectives for individuals, including protection of the self (Derlega & Chaiken, 1977), development of a sense of autonomy and freedom, and enhancement of happiness or other positive affective states (cf. E. Stone & Stone, 1990). However, prior theory and research on privacy suggest that the ability to maintain control over information is also instrumental to the achievement of a variety of positively valued extrinsic outcomes in work organizations (e.g., social approval, jobs, pay, praise, promotions; cf. E. Stone & Stone, 1990). Moreover, the same literature suggests that privacy is vital to the avoidance of many negative outcomes, including stigmatization, embarrassment, job loss, and demotion (cf. E. Stone & Stone, 1990; Wasserstrom, 1984).

Interestingly, a number of theorists have argued that people lead both public and private lives (Goffman, 1963; Wasserstrom, 1984). Furthermore, because every society has norms about appropriate thoughts and behaviors, when an individual's thoughts or deeds run counter to these norms, the person may be ostracized or sanctioned by others (Jourard, 1966). Thus, societal pressures often lead people to believe that they should be ashamed or embarrassed by personal thoughts or actions that deviate from societal norms (Wasserstrom, 1984). As a result, people attempt to shield their true identity by constructing public images of themselves and often use impression-management strategies to try to accentuate their positive attributes and downplay or cover up their negative attributes (Giacalone & Rosenfeld, 1989; Goffman, 1963; Klopfer & Rubenstein, 1977). Goffman argued that people are stigmatized when their actual identity is discrepant from their virtual identity (i.e., what is expected in society). Thus, in organizational contexts individuals often use a number of strategies to avoid stigmatization and to make themselves appear more attractive to organizations. Such behaviors often allow individuals to project a positive image, which enables them to obtain desirable outcomes (e.g., job offers) and avert negative outcomes (e.g., embarrassment; cf. E. Stone & Stone, 1990; E. Stone et al., 1992).

Strategies Used by Individuals

Given that controlling information enables individuals to achieve valued objectives (e.g., avoiding negative or obtaining positive outcomes), our model indicates that individuals use a number of strategies to control information about themselves (for a comparable view, see E. Stone & Stone, 1990). In particular, the model suggests that individuals use two primary strategies to control information: (a) selectively withholding or disclosing personal information and (b) distorting information about themselves (cf. E. Stone & Stone, 1990). For example, during the job application process, individuals may disclose or emphasize positive information about their previous work experience, skills, or accomplishments, and withhold or omit information about their weaknesses (e.g., deficiencies in job-related skills, previous mental problems; cf. Porter et al., 1975). In addition, they may use nonverbal behavior to mask their privately held feelings. For example, applicants may smile at interviewers in order to hide their anxieties. Similarly, individuals may also protect their privacy by presenting inaccurate data about themselves to others (cf. Porter et al., 1975). For instance, research shows that people tend to overstate (inflate) both their work experience and previous salary levels (Weiss & Dawis, 1960, cited in Cascio, 1991). However, individuals are unlikely to distort information that can be verified easily. The reason for this is that they risk embarrassment or job loss if the organization discovers they have falsified information. Thus, individuals may be less likely to present false information as a means of managing a favorable impression than simply withholding information about deficiencies in job-related skills and abilities.

Individuals' Reactions to the Loss of Information Control

Conflicts between individuals and organizations over information control often stem from the fact that organizational data-collection practices violate individuals' privacy-related norms, values, and expectations. Thus, the consideration of these norms is vital to understanding why individuals react negatively to the loss of control over information. To illustrate this, we consider norms about (a) the types of data that are collected by organizations, (b) the autonomy of individuals in organizational settings, (c) the opportunity for redemption (i.e., release from blame), and (d) the value of justice or fairness in organizations.

Norms About the Types of Data Collected. Each society has norms that specify the amounts and types of information that individuals should exchange with one another (PPSC, 1977; E. Stone & Stone, 1990). For example, research shows that some types of information are considered more private than others (Jourard, 1966; D. Stone, Stone, & Hyatt, 1994; E. Stone, Stone, & Hyatt, 1989). In particular, American cultural norms specify that information about such matters as excretory functions, sex, health, finances, personality, and family background should not be widely shared with others (cf. E. Stone & Stone, 1990). Thus, in general, it is considered inappropriate to question an individual about such matters and to disseminate information about the same matters without the individual's permission. Thus, some organizational data-collection practices violate norms and expectations about the types of data that should be collected from individuals. To the degree that they do, the practices may be viewed as invasive of privacy. There are many types of preemployment tests that violate norms about privacy, including (a) drug testing procedures that require job applicants to produce urine samples while being observed by a laboratory technician, (b) personality inventories that use ambiguous stimuli to assess individuals' motives, values, and interests (e.g., Rorschach, Thematic Apperception Test), and (c) biographical data (biodata) inventories that have items dealing with such sensitive matters as family background and finances (e.g., educational attainment of parents, father's income level). Recent research provides clear evidence about not only the degree to which people value control over various types of data (E. Stone et al., 1983), but also the degree to which various data-collection practices are perceived as invasive of privacy (D. Stone & Behson, 1996; Stone-Romero, Stone, & Eddy, 1995; D. Stone et al., 1994; E. Stone et al., 1989).

Norms About Freedom From Organizational Control. A number of theorists have argued that Americans place great importance on the right of individuals to be free from social and organizational controls (Brehm, 1966; Hofstede, 1991; Trice & Beyer, 1993). Furthermore, American cultural norms dictate that individuals should have a voice in the design and use of any control system that may affect them (Trice & Beyer, 1993). Given these values and norms, individuals are likely to view data-collection practices that unduly restrict their freedom as invasive of privacy. For example, the practice of monitoring the telephone conversations of customer service representatives may be perceived as invasive of privacy because it unduly restricts worker freedom. Moreover, the electronic monitoring of work behavior by organizations is likely to be regarded as invasive because there is always an unseen audience and workers must constantly be on guard against revealing discrediting information (Fried, 1968).

The norm that individuals should have a voice in any control system that affects them is, at least in part, reflected in the widespread use of employee participation programs and involvement systems in U.S. organizations (Trice & Beyer, 1993). Given this norm, individuals may expect that organizations will allow them to participate in any, and all, decisions regarding the uses that are made of information about them. Thus, for example, when organizations release employee information without permission or disseminate employee data via computer networks, employees are likely to perceive that their privacy has been invaded. Recent research provides strong support for this view (e.g., Fusilier & Hoyer, 1980; Tolchinsky et al., 1981).

Norms About Redemption. American culture has been heavily influenced by norms about redemption (i.e., the ability to overcome one's past mistakes or release oneself from blame). Overcoming one's past is a key concern because world history reveals many examples of the stigmatization and persecution of individuals based on such factors as caste, race, sex, age, physical disability, religious beliefs, and mistakes made early in life (Buchanan & Mathieu, 1986; E. Stone et al., 1992). In order to develop a just society, American cultural norms stress that individuals should have the opportunity to rise above their birthright (Wasserstrom, 1984), and the right to forgiveness for previous sins. As a result, the use of some organizational data-collection practices (e.g., biographical data about family and personal background) for personnel selection purposes may be perceived as an invasion of privacy because the practice violates norms about people being able to overcome their past and that of their parents (e.g., the socioeconomic standing of their parents). Recent research shows clearly that many biodata items are viewed as highly offensive to individuals (Mael, Connerly, & Morath, 1996; D. Stone & Jones, 1997; Stone-Romero, Stone, & Eddy, 1995).

American culture also stresses that people should be granted forgiveness for various forms of misconduct; otherwise, one instance of youthful misconduct (e.g., petty theft) might unfairly brand an individual as a misfit or deviant for life (Karst, 1966). As a result, American norms discourage institutions from developing systems that impose permanent marks or stigmas upon individuals (Wasserstrom, 1984). Moreover, many individuals feel that organizations should not have access to information about them that is dated or irrelevant and that might negatively affect their status as a job applicant or incumbent. Thus, individuals may view the permanent storage and dissemination of personal information in databases as nothing more than a contemporary means of affixing a permanent brand of disapproval on the individual, not unlike the scarlet letter A impressed on Hester Prynne by the Puritan clergy (Wasserstrom, 1984). As a result, the accumulation and dissemination of personal data through the use of networked computer systems may threaten privacy because these systems violate norms about redemption or the ability to overcome one's past mistakes.

Norms About Social Justice.   American culture has always valued social justice. Philosophers argue that justice exists when (a) people receive outcomes that are proportional to their contributions (Adams, 1965; Buchanan & Mathieu, 1986) and (b) procedures for the allocation of such outcomes are fair (e.g., Leventhal, 1980). Although there are number of justice principles, several are particularly important with respect to privacy, including the materiality principle and the accuracy rule (Bies, 1993). The materiality principle of justice stresses that each person should be judged according to those factors that have a clear bearing on the issues at hand (Buchanan & Mathieu, 1986). Thus, American cultural norms dictate that organizations should collect only those data about individuals that are directly relevant for a given purpose. For example, in personnel selection, organizations should collect data only about the relevant knowledge, skills, and abilities of job applicants. Moreover, the collection of information about factors that are unrelated to the capacity or willingness of applicants to work in a given role is viewed as invasive of privacy (D. Stone et al., 1994; E. Stone & Stone, 1990).

Among the types of data that are perceived to be of little or no relevance to job performance are those dealing with lifestyle, religious beliefs, living arrangements, risk-taking propensities, and credit history (D. Stone et al., 1994; E. Stone & Stone, 1990). Note, moreover, that some research (Simmons, 1968; D. Stone & Behson, 1996) shows that the perceived relevance of personality data for personnel decision making influences beliefs that the collection of such data is invasive of privacy. A recent California Supreme Court case (*Soroka et al. v. Dayton Hudson Corporation*, 1992) highlights the importance of using only relevant data for selection purposes. In this case, Soroka et al. charged that their privacy had been invaded when Target Stores (a division of Dayton Hudson) screened applicants for the job of security officer using a personality inventory that asked questions about their religious beliefs, sexual behavior, and sexual preferences. The court ruled that personality screening by the defendant violated individuals' rights to privacy.[5]

A second justice principle that may influence expectations of privacy is the accuracy rule. This rule dictates that the allocation of outcomes should

---

[5]Target Stores ultimately settled the claim out of court.

be based on data that are accurate, correct, or truthful (Leventhal, 1980). Thus, American cultural norms dictate that judgments regarding the allocation of outcomes in social and organizational systems should be based on data that are free from error or bias. For example, personnel decisions should be based on data that are reliable and valid. Because the accuracy rule leads individuals to expect that organizations will use accurate information in decision making, they are likely to perceive that their privacy has been invaded if data about them are collected with measures that have high error rates (e.g., unreliable drug tests and honesty tests; cf. E. Stone & Stone, 1990). Likewise, the use of computerized information systems may violate expectations of privacy because individuals may feel they have no means of ensuring the accuracy of data stored in such systems.

Interestingly, 20 years ago the PPSC (1977) argued that organizations often make unwarranted assumptions about the accuracy of data stored in computerized systems. The use of technology tends to enhance the illusion that data in such systems are accurate, and organizations rarely give individuals the opportunity to correct errors or clear up problems that arise from inaccurate data.

As a result of the storage and dissemination of inaccurate data, individuals may be unfairly deprived of various job-related opportunities (e.g., promotions, pay raises, training). Recent surveys highlight the scope and importance of this problem. For example, in a survey, Consumers Union found errors in 48% of reports generated by the "Big Three" credit reporting organizations (i.e., TRW, Equifax, and TransUnion; cited in Piller, 1993). The same survey also noted that 19% of the inaccuracies could have caused denial of credit or job opportunities.

It is apparent from the discussion that individuals react negatively to the loss of control over personal information and use a variety of strategies to control information or protect their privacy in dealing with others. However, social theorists maintain that, even though the rights of individuals, including the right to privacy, are important, the same rights must be balanced continually against the common good (Etzioni, 1996). Thus, in the following section we consider the values and objectives of the general public as a stakeholder.

Other Stakeholders

Numerous stakeholders other than the individual and the organization seek to control information that is viewed as vital to the pursuit of their objectives. Among these are members of the general public, consumers, political action committees, environmental conservation groups, and other special interest groups. In the interest of brevity, we restrict our focus to the values, objectives, and strategies used by members of the general public to control information (hereinafter referred to as the general public).

The General Public's Values and Objectives

The general public often has a considerable interest in obtaining accurate information about organizations and their employees. For example, with such information it may be possible to assess how the actions of organizations and their members may affect the general public. In particular, the general public may need information in order to assess the extent to which customers may be harmed by the behavior of employees (e.g., the public has a need to know if school teachers are likely to sexually molest children). To the degree that available information suggests that organizations or their members are behaving in inappropriate (e.g., illegal, unethical, immoral) ways, the general public can seek change through a number of means, including litigation against the firm, boycotts of the firm's products, or the imposition of sanctions against the firm. An interesting and current example of the general public's interest in accessing information controlled by organizations and their members is the controversy over information held by officials and researchers in tobacco companies on the addictive effects of nicotine and the adverse effects of tobacco products on health. Clearly, the general public has legitimate needs for information regarding the safety of products or services provided by the members of organizations and feels that such information should be made available.

Strategies Used by the General Public

The general public often obtains information about organizations and their employees from data maintained by consumer protection bureaus, better business bureaus, government agencies, and boards responsible for sound professional practice. For example, the State of New York will provide the general public with information about malpractice suits against physicians.

The general public is often a key source of the information that is found in the databases of consumer protection bureaus, government agencies, and so forth. For example, consumers are the source of data on the quality of products and services that are reported in *Consumer Reports* magazine. Moreover, in limited instances the general public is also instrumental in getting government agencies to provide the public with access to information in their databases. For example, as a result of sunshine legislation the general public has access to information used in administering municipal, county, and state governments.

SOURCES OF CONFLICT AMONG STAKEHOLDERS

It should be evident from this discussion that stakeholders often have conflicting values, objectives, and strategies concerning information control and privacy. For example, organizational needs for information about job applicants often conflict with applicants' actual or perceived rights to privacy. Similarly, individual and organizational expectations of privacy often conflict with the public's desire for information needed to avoid harm. Some analysts (e.g., Gross, 1962; PPSC, 1977; Schein, 1976; E. Stone & Stone, 1990; Whyte, 1957) argued that these conflicts have often been resolved in favor of the information needs of organizations. Frequently, society has permitted the highly intrusive data-collection practices of organizations because of the belief that the same practices contribute to the efficient operation of business, and as a consequence, result in the greatest good for the greatest number (Warnock, 1962, cited in Steiner & Steiner, 1991). However, some of the same analysts contended that the utilitarian assumptions about organizational rights have led to the abridgment of many important human rights, among them privacy (Steiner & Steiner, 1991). Thus, we believe that there must be a better balance between the needs of organizations for information and individuals' perceived rights to privacy. At the same time, however, we recognize that an overemphasis on individual rights can sometimes decrease the welfare of the general public (Etzioni, 1996). Thus, we feel that there is a pressing need to balance the rights of individuals against the needs of the general public. However, we also believe that the privacy of individuals should be guarded unless there is a justifiable rationale for doing otherwise. Thus, we agree with Etzioni (1996), who argues that the violation of individuals' rights to privacy should only be tolerated when there is a compelling public need (e.g., need to maintain the safety of children in day care centers or schools).

Given the conflicting values regarding privacy and the needs of social institutions for information, it is not surprising that there are recurring debates about how to best resolve the competing interests of various stakeholders. In order to balance such interests, disputants have sought guidance from legislation, the courts, labor–management agreements, societal norms, and appeals to moral action guides. In addition, some have advocated that conflicts about information control be resolved through consensus-building procedures (cf. Etzioni, 1996). Unfortunately, however, this strategy is unlikely to lead to the acceptable resolution of conflicts if stakeholders have highly divergent values and objectives. Thus, in the section that follows we consider two methods (e.g., legal remedies and appeals to moral goals) that can be successfully used to resolve conflicts among stakeholders.

CONFLICT RESOLUTION STRATEGIES

Legal Remedies

Societies have long used legal means (e.g., laws, the courts) to resolve the competing interests of stakeholders, including conflicts that center on privacy and information control. However, before discussing the use of law as a conflict resolution strategy, we briefly consider the nature of legal and moral action guides. Philosophers maintain that law constitutes a shared system of action guides for regulating social behavior, settling disputes that arise between groups or individuals, reinforcing key norms, and creating harmony within groups (cf. Little & Twiss, 1978). Although laws may be similar to other action guides (e.g., customs) in terms of their prescriptive or directive components, they differ from other action guides in that they are authoritative. Authority is a key legal concept because laws can only be used effectively when there is a final authority beyond which there can be no further appeal (e.g., the Supreme Court). Furthermore, to assure compliance, sanctions are typically imposed upon individuals who violate laws.

Interestingly, many legal action guides have important moral underpinnings in that they are designed to ensure the welfare of persons or groups (e.g., laws against murder). However, many laws have no inherent moral characteristics, and, as a result, are considered relatively weak action guides. Some philosophers argue that "whenever a given practice is required either by custom or law, but forbidden by moral considerations the moral rule takes precedence" (Leiser, 1969, p. 9, cited in Little & Twiss, 1978). A vivid illustration of a moral principle taking precedence over a law is the individual who refuses to kill others while serving in the military.

Although there is no explicit right to privacy guaranteed by the U.S. Constitution, the courts have often been used to resolve privacy-related disputes among stakeholders. For example, in *Griswold v. Connecticut* (1965), the Supreme Court ruled that the right to privacy is a penumbral right emanating from the First, Third, Fourth, Fifth, Ninth, and Fourteenth Amendments to the U.S. Constitution. In addition to privacy rights guaranteed by the Constitution, there are several federal and state laws that are concerned with privacy. At the federal level, the Privacy Act of 1974 regulates the collection and dissemination of information about government employees, whereas at the state level, 25 states have privacy protection statutes or recognize privacy rights (R. Smith, 1992). Despite these laws, there is currently no federal law that can be used to resolve conflicts regarding privacy or information control in the private sector. However, as a result of the Privacy Act of 1974, the U.S. government set up the Privacy Protection Study Commission to assess the value of legal mechanisms for protecting individual rights to privacy. The Commission's 1977 report recommended that private sector employers voluntarily develop fair information management policies and practices (PPSC, 1977). Unfortunately, however, recent surveys show that only one third of all organizations have privacy protection policies, and many employers only develop such policies in reaction to threatened suits by employees or state legislators (H. Smith, 1993). Thus, it appears that, in general, organizations have not heeded the Privacy Protection Study Commission's recommendations regarding the voluntary development of fair information policies. Moreover, with a few notable exceptions (e.g., IBM, General Electric, AT&T), organizations have not typically considered the rights of employees as stakeholders. As a result, the passage of legislation to protect the privacy of private-sector workers may be one viable means of resolving many of the privacy-related conflicts that arise between organizations and individuals.

Although laws may often be a sound method for resolving conflicts about privacy (information control), psychologists and sociologists have argued that unless there is commitment to the underlying values of law, the laws may be set aside and rarely heeded voluntarily (e.g., speed limit laws; Etzioni, 1996; Katz & Kahn, 1978). As a result, privacy laws may induce compliance from organizations, but may not elicit commitment to the core values underlying such laws (i.e., balancing needs of stakeholders; Etzioni, 1996). In addition, organizations that view the generation of profit as their primary goal often find ways of circumventing the law in order to achieve it. Given the many problems connected with legal remedies, Etzioni maintained that laws should be based on moral values and should not serve solely as deterrents to certain types of behavior. Consistent with Etzioni's arguments, we believe that laws will only be an effective means of resolving conflicts concerning privacy when they are based on shared moral values. Thus, in the next section we provide a more detailed discussion of appeals to superordinate moral goals as a means of resolving conflicts about privacy.

Appeals to Superordinate Moral Action Guides

Conflicts about privacy may be resolved through appeals to superordinate moral action guides. A moral action guide is a statement of shared values that is considered superior and "other-regarding" (i.e., concerned with the welfare of others; Little & Twiss, 1978). Moral actions guides have several important properties. First, because they are based upon a shared system of expectations, they provide a viable means of dealing with conflicts among the goals of individuals or groups who often act on the basis of self-interest. Second, because moral action guides are "other-regarding," they require that parties consider how their attitudes, emotions, or actions affect the welfare of others. For example, in most cultures there are moral guides dealing with such issues as murder, rape, perjury, envy, jealousy, greed, anger, and hatred (e.g., the Ten Commandments of Christianity and Judaism). Third, moral action guides tend to take precedence over any conflicting nonmoral action guides; that is, nonmoral action guides (e.g., making profit) are subordinated to moral action guides (e.g., protecting the health and welfare of workers).

Not surprisingly, moral action guides may be an important means of resolving conflicts surrounding privacy in organizations. For example, one current source of conflict stems from organizations collecting large amounts

LIBRARY

of information about job applicants or incumbents without considering the impact of such actions on the welfare of individuals. Organizations often justify their behavior, at least in part, on the utilitarian belief that the data-collection activities of organizations are virtuous because they lead to the greatest good for the greatest number (e.g., employment, economic gain; Steiner & Steiner, 1991). However, moral action guides would consider the impact of an organization's data collection practices on the welfare of all individuals (i.e., job applicants, job incumbents, and the general public). Thus, if the data collection activities of organizations had a negative impact on the well-being of job applicants or incumbents, then moral action guides would dictate that the well-being of individuals would take precedence over the economic interests of organizations, and organizations would be expected to minimize the invasiveness of their data-collection activities.

Moral action guides may also be applied to resolve conflicts between individuals' expectations of privacy and the needs of the general public to be protected from harm. As noted previously, individuals often assert their rights to privacy without considering the impact of their self-interested behavior on the common good. For example, applicants for the job of school bus driver might withhold or conceal information about their alcohol-related problems in order to protect their privacy. However, this behavior might endanger the welfare of the public (e.g., school children, other drivers). An appeal to moral action guides as a means of resolving this conflict would consider the impact on the welfare of others of an individual's attempts to protect privacy; moral action guides would dictate that an individual's rights to privacy should not take precedence over the safety of customers or the public at large. The violation of individuals' expectations of privacy would be tolerated when there was a compelling reason to do so (i.e., protection of the general public's safety and welfare). In short, moral action guides presume that individuals have rights only insofar as those rights do not jeopardize the greater moral order.

CONCLUSION

Our multiple stakeholder model of privacy makes it clear that controlling information is vital to many stakeholders in our society. In addition, because the values of various stakeholders are not always consistent with one another, there are often conflicts between the strategies that they pursue to achieve their goals. As the literature on privacy (cf. Gross, 1962; PPSC, 1977; E. Stone & Stone, 1990; Whyte, 1957) suggests, conflicts between stakeholders have generally been resolved in ways that appear to be consistent with the notion that the economic interests of organizations are more important than the welfare of individuals. We believe that placing the economic interests of organizations above the desires of job applicants or job incumbents for reasonable levels of dignity and autonomy is inconsistent with a number of superordinate moral action guides, including the so-called golden rule that is common to many religions and moral philosophies (e.g., Christianity, Confucianism). At the same time, however, we reject the view that individuals should protect their privacy or use information control strategies in ways that result in harm to others. Thus, strategies for resolving disputes about privacy and information control must be sensitive to the values of all stakeholders. Moreover, to the extent that conflict is resolved by means that allow for stakeholder involvement and rely on appeals to superordinate moral action guides (as opposed, for example, to law), stakeholders are likely to be committed to achieved solutions.

REFERENCES

Adams, J. S. (1965). Inequity in social exchange. In L. Berkowitz (Ed.), *Advances in experimental social psychology* (Vol. 2, pp. 267–299). New York: Academic Press.

Alder, G. S., & Ambrose, M. (1997, August). *Balancing employers' need for information with employees' right to privacy: The role of disclosure and moderation in electronic performance monitoring.* Paper presented at the meeting of the Academy of Management, Boston, MA.

Alderman, E., & Kennedy, C. (1995). *The right to privacy.* New York: Knopf.

Bies, R. J. (1993). Privacy and procedural justice in organizations. *Social Justice Research, 6,* 69–86.

Brehm, J. W. (1966). *A theory of psychological reactance.* New York: Academic Press.

Buchanan, A., & Mathieu, D. (1986). Philosophy and justice. In R. L. Cohen (Ed.), *Justice: Views from the social sciences* (pp. 11–44). New York: Plenum.

Cascio, W. F. (1991). *Applied psychology in personnel management* (4th ed.). Englewood Cliffs, NJ: Prentice-Hall.

Derlega, V. J., & Chaiken, A. L. (1977). Privacy and self-disclosure in social relationships. *Journal of Social Issues, 33,* 102–115.

Donaldson, T., & Preston, L. E. (1995). The stakeholder theory of the corporation: Concepts, evidence, and implications. *Academy of Management Review, 20,* 65–91.

Etzioni, A. (1996). *The new golden rule: Community and morality in a democratic society.* New York: Basic Books.

Evan, W. M., & Freeman, R. E. (1988). A stakeholder theory of the modern corporation: Kantian capitalism. In T. Beauchamp & N. Bowie (Eds.), *Ethical theory and business* (pp. 75–93). Englewood Cliffs, NJ: Prentice-Hall.

Extejt, M. M., & Bockanic, W. N. (1991). Issues surrounding the theories of negligent hiring and failure to fire. *Business and Professional Ethics Journal, 8,* 21–34.

Freeman, R. E., & Gilbert, D. R., Jr. (1987). Managing stakeholder relationships. In S. P. Sethi & C. M. Falbe (Eds.), *Business and society* (pp. 397–423) Lexington, MA: Lexington Books.

Fried, C. (1968). Privacy: A moral analysis. *The Yale Law Journal, 77,* 475–493.

Fusilier, M. R., & Hoyer, W. D. (1980). Variables affecting perceptions of invasion of privacy in a personnel selection situation. *Journal of Applied Psychology, 65,* 623–626.

Giacalone, R. A., & Rosenfeld, P. (1989). *Impression management in the organization.* Hillsdale, NJ: Lawrence Erlbaum Associates.

Goffman, E. (1959). *The presentation of self in everyday life.* Garden City, NY: Doubleday.

Goffman, E. (1963). *Stigma: Notes on the management of spoiled identity.* Englewood Cliffs, NJ: Prentice-Hall.

Griswold v. Connecticut, 381 U.S. 479 (1965).

Gross, M. L. (1962). *The brain watchers.* New York: Random House.

Hall, E. T. (1966). *The hidden dimension.* New York: Doubleday.

Hofstede, G. (1991). *Cultures and organizations: Software of the mind.* London: McGraw-Hill.

Hollinger, R. C., & Clark, J. P. (1983). *Theft by employees.* Lexington, MA: Lexington Books.

Jourard, S. M. (1966). Some psychological aspects of privacy. *Law and Contemporary Problems, 31,* 307–318.

Kahn, H. (1979). *World economic development: 1979 and beyond.* Boulder, CO: Westview Press.

Karst, K. L. (1966). "The files": Legal controls over the accuracy and accessibility of stored personal data. *Law and Contemporary Problems, 31,* 342–376.

Katz, D., & Kahn, R. L. (1978). *The social psychology of organizations* (2nd ed). New York: Wiley.

Kavanagh, M., Gueutal, H. G., & Tannenbaum, S. (1990). *Human resource information systems: Development and application.* Boston, MA: Kent.

Kendall v. Gore Properties, 236 F.2d 673 (D.C. Cir, 1956).

Klopfer, P. H., & Rubenstein, D. I. (1977). The concept of privacy and its biological basis. *Journal of Social Issues, 33,* 52–65.

Laufer, R. S., & Wolfe, M. (1977). Privacy as a concept and a social issue: A multidimensional developmental theory. *Journal of Social Issues, 33,* 22–41.

Leventhal, G. S. (1980). What should be done with equity theory? New approaches to the study of fairness in social relationships. In K. Gergen, M. Greenberg, & R. Willis (Eds.), *Social exchange: Advances in theory and research* (pp. 27–55). New York: Plenum.

Linowes, D. F. (1989). *Privacy in America: Is your private life in the public eye?* Urbana: University of Illinois Press.

Little, D., & Twiss, S. B. (1978). *Comparative religious ethics.* San Francisco: Harper & Row.

Lofquist, L. H., & Dawis, R. V. (1969). *Adjustment to work: A psychological view of man's problems in a work-oriented society.* New York: Appleton-Century-Crofts.

Mael, F. A., Connerly, M., & Morath, R. A. (1996). None of your business. Parameters of biodata invasiveness. *Personnel Psychology, 49,* 613–650.

Olmstead v. U.S., 277 U.S. 438 (1928).

Piller, C. (1993). Bosses with x-ray eyes: Your employer may be using computers to keep tabs on you. *MacWorld, 8,* 118–123.

Porter, L. W., Lawler, E. E., & Hackman, J. R. (1975). *Behavior in organizations.* New York: McGraw-Hill.

Privacy Protection Study Commission. (1977). *Personal privacy in an information society.* Washington, DC: U.S. Government Printing Office.

Ross, S. (1992). Big brother in workplace growing bigger every day. *Reuter Business Report,* 15 September, 11–12.

Sackett, P. R., Burris, L. R., & Callahan, C. (1989). Integrity testing for personnel selection: An update. *Personnel Psychology, 42,* 491–529.

Schein, V. E. (1976). Privacy and personnel: A time for action. *Personnel Journal,* 604–615.

Shils, E. B. (1996). Privacy: Its constitution and vicissitudes. *Law and Contemporary Problems, 31,* 281–306.

Simmons, D. D. (1968). Invasion of privacy and judged benefit of personality test inquiry. *The Journal of General Psychology, 79,* 177–181.

Smith, H. J. (1993). Privacy polices and practices: Inside the organizational maze. *Communications of the ACM, 36,* 105–122.

Smith, R. L. (1992). *Compilation of state and federal privacy laws.* Providence, RI: Privacy Journal.

Soroka v. Dayton Hudson Corp., I Cal. Rptr. 2d. 77 (1991).

Steiner, G. A., & Steiner, J. F. (1991). *Business, government, and society: A managerial perspective* (6th ed). New York: McGraw-Hill.

Stone, D. L., & Behson, S. (1996). Effects of type of inventory and purpose of the request on reactions to personality assessment. *Proceedings of the Eastern Academy of Management,* 59–62.

Stone, D. L., Eddy, E., & Stone-Romero, E. (1997, April). *Scaling of employee monitoring systems in terms of invasion of privacy.* Paper presented at the meeting of the Society for Industrial and Organizational Psychology, St. Louis, MO.

Stone, D. L., & Jones, G. (1997). Perceived fairness of biodata as a function of the purpose of the request and gender of the applicant. *Journal of Business and Psychology, 11,* 313–323.

Stone, D. L., Stone, E. F., & Hyatt, D. E. (1994, April). *Some potential determinants of individuals' reactions to personnel selection procedures.* Paper presented at the meeting of the Society for Industrial and Organizational Psychology, Nashville, TN.

Stone, E. F., Gueutal, H. G., Gardner, D. G., & McClure, S. (1983). A field experiment comparing information-privacy values, beliefs, and attitudes across several types of organizations. *Journal of Applied Psychology, 68,* 459–468.

Stone, E. F., & Stone, D. L., (1990). Privacy in organizations: Theoretical issues, research findings, and protection mechanisms. In G. Ferris & K. Rowland (Eds.), *Research in personnel and human resources management* (Vol. 8, pp. 349–411). Greenwich, CT: JAI Press.

Stone, E. F., Stone, D. L., & Dipboye, R. L. (1992). Stigmas in organizations: Race, handicaps, and physical unattractiveness. In K. Kelley (Ed.), *Issues, theory, and research in industrial and organizational psychology.* Amsterdam: North-Holland.

Stone, E. F., Stone, D. L., & Hyatt, D. (1989, April). Personnel selection procedures and invasion of privacy. In R. Guion (Chair), *Privacy in organizations: Personnel selection, physical environment, and legal issues.* Symposium conducted at the meeting of the Society for Industrial and Organizational Psychology, Boston, MA.

Stone-Romero, E. F., Stone, D. L., & Eddy, E. (1995, May). *The perceived invasiveness of biodata.* Paper presented at the meeting of the Society for Industrial and Organizational Psychology, Orlando, FL.

Thibaut, J. W., & Kelley, H. H. (1959). *The social psychology of groups.* New York: Wiley.

Tolchinsky, P., McCuddy, M., Adams, J., Ganster, D. C., Woodman, R., & Fromkin, H. L. (1981). Employee perceptions of invasion of privacy: A field simulation experiment. *Journal of Applied Psychology, 66,* 308–313.

Trice, H. M., & Beyer, J. M. (1993). *The cultures of work organizations.* Englewood Cliffs, NJ: Prentice-Hall.

Wasserstrom, R. A. (1984). Privacy: Some arguments and assumptions. In F. D. Schoeman (Ed.), *Philosophical dimensions of privacy: An anthology* (pp. 317–332), New York: Cambridge University Press.

Westin, A. F. (1967). *Privacy and freedom.* New York: Atheneum.

Whyte, W. H., Jr. (1957). *The organization man.* New York: Doubleday.

CHAPTER FOUR

Electronic Performance Monitoring:
A Consideration of Rights

Maureen L. Ambrose
G. Stoney Alder
Terry W. Noel
University of Colorado at Boulder

It's not fair. Personal rights go out the window. Aren't these monitoring practices infringing on our rights?
—Anne, monitored worker

Electronic performance monitoring (EPM) has increased significantly since the 1980s. In 1987, the Office of Technology Assessment (OTA) estimated that 6 million workers were electronically monitored. By 1990, this number had grown to 10 million. In 1994, it was estimated that 20 million workers were electronically monitored (Flanagan, 1994). The number of electronically monitored workers is expected to approach 30 million by the year 2000 (DeTienne & Abbott, 1993). Current indications are that sales of software to monitor employees are growing 50% per year (Flanagan, 1994). They had been expected to exceed $1 billion in 1996 (Aiello, 1993).

With this increase has come heated debate about the appropriateness of EPM in the workplace. One dimension of this discussion involves the ethics of EPM; underlying most discussions of electronic monitoring are assumptions about employee or employer rights. In this chapter, we take a rights perspective (Valesquez, 1992) in examining the ethics of EPM. We explicitly examine the impact of EPM on the rights of employees and employers and explore how organizations can reconcile these seemingly conflicting concerns. First, we summarize the debate between opponents and proponents of EPM; then, we discuss the rights that are relevant to EPM. Next, we describe the potential for conflict between employee and employer rights. Finally, we discuss how organizations can manage these areas of conflict.

ELECTRONIC PERFORMANCE MONITORING

Performance monitoring has been critical to organizational effectiveness for centuries (OTA, 1987). Monitoring enables organizations to obtain information that can be used to assess and improve employee performance. Research indicates that effective supervisors tend to monitor their subordinates more frequently than do less effective supervisors (Komaki, 1986; Komaki, Desselles, & Bowman, 1989). Motivated by the variety of benefits that may accrue from monitoring, organizations have sought to improve the effectiveness of their monitoring efforts through the use of electronic technology.

EPM is the use of electronic instruments, such as audio, video, and computer systems, to collect, store, analyze, and report individual or group performance (Nebeker & Tatum, 1993). This technology enables organizations to continuously observe, record, and report a wide range of worker activities with or without the workers' knowledge. Thus, EPM greatly expands both the amount and range of monitoring that organizations can perform and has the potential to permeate nearly all aspects of employees' work lives.

The increasing use of EPM has generated debate among employee advocate groups, business groups, and politicians (Sanders, 1990; OTA, 1987). Employee advocate groups claim that EPM is an oppressive practice that should be eliminated, or at least limited (Bylinsky, 1991; Garson, 1988; Nussbaum & duRivage, 1986; Piturro, 1989; Ross, 1992). Critics contend that EPM invades worker privacy (Bylinsky, 1991; OTA, 1987; Ross, 1992) and increases workers' stress and health problems (Piturro, 1989).

Proponents of EPM counter that monitoring is similar to other widely accepted managerial practices and, if implemented properly, will not created the abuses feared by monitoring's critics. Proponents argue that monitoring is an indispensable tool that organizations can use to increase productivity, improve quality and service, heighten safety, and reduce costs. Advocates also suggest that electronic monitoring increases employee satisfaction and morale by resulting in more objective performance appraisals and improved performance feedback (Angel, 1989; Henriques, 1986a, 1986b).

The intensity of the public debate over EPM is reflected in the legislative arena where senators and members of Congress have attempted to legislate the amount and type of monitoring that organizations may conduct. For example, the Privacy for Consumers and Workers Act, introduced by Senator Paul Simon (D-IL), would allow employers to electronically monitor employees only if they complied with provisions regarding notification, tenure limitations, review of data obtained from monitoring, employee access to data, use of data, and employee privacy (for a complete analysis of the bill, see DeTienne & Alder, 1995). Although no monitoring bills have passed Congress, each attempt to legislate employee monitoring receives increasing support and brings more attention to the issue. The political debate over EPM parallels the public debate over EPM and reflects the widespread disagreement over its benefits and costs.

Despite the attention EPM receives, little progress has been made toward reconciling the different perspectives on monitoring. Semantic confusion may be one reason for this lack of progress. Discussions about EPM commonly group all types of EPM into one general category—as though all monitoring techniques are created equal. There is a wide variety of techniques organizations may use to electronically monitor their workers, including accounting for telephone calls or keystrokes or computer time; using cards and beepers to monitor locations; monitoring computer files; sharing screens on networks; observing telephone calls and using video camera observation (Fickel, 1991). Each of these techniques is designed to monitor different activities and each may raise different concerns. Thus, the practice of considering all forms of monitoring under the general label of EPM may mask important differences and inhibit a constructive discussion about how to reconcile conflicts between opponents and proponents of EPM.

We believe it is useful to categorize the various forms of EPM and then separately analyze these classes. We suggest three broad categories: surveillance, computer monitoring, and eavesdropping. Surveillance includes such monitoring devices as cards, beepers, and video cameras. Computer monitoring includes keystroke or computer time accounting, computer file monitoring, and screen sharing capabilities on networks. Finally, eavesdropping includes techniques such as telephone call observation.

As shown in Table 4.1, three monitoring system characteristics differentiate between the three forms of monitoring: the type of electronic device utilized by the system, the kind of activities captured by the system, and the scope of the monitoring. For example, electronic surveillance uses technology, usually visual equipment, designed to observe employee behavior or track their movements. Employee surveillance is broader in scope than other forms of monitoring and may capture activities that are not performance related. In contrast, computer performance monitoring uses computer hardware and software to record workers' computer-driven activities. Thus, computer monitoring is usually restricted to work-related activities.[1] Finally, eavesdropping uses telephonic equipment to monitor telephone activities through either service observation or call accounting. Under service observation, employee conversations are listened to in real time or recorded for subsequent playback. With call accounting, the monitoring system measures the number, length, and destination of employees' calls. Eavesdropping most often monitors interactions between the firm's employees and its customers.

---

[1]Recently, many employers have begun to monitor employee e-mail. Such monitoring is more likely to capture nonwork-related activities than traditional computer monitoring.

TABLE 4.1
Key Characteristics of the Three Categories of Monitoring

	Surveillance	Computer Monitoring	Eavesdropping
Type of device	Primarily visual	Computer hardware/software	Telephonic
Scope of monitoring	Broad	Narrow	Moderate
Activities monitored	Work/nonwork	Work	Primarily work
Concerns	Invasiveness	Job stress	Invasiveness/stress
Focus of debate	Appropriateness	Utilization	Primarily utilization

Thus, eavesdropping is generally confined to work-related activities. However, if employees make and receive personal calls at work, nonwork activities may also be captured by eavesdropping systems.

Identifying these categories of monitoring is important not so much for their technical differences but because each form of monitoring raises different concerns. This classification scheme helps identify the concerns raised by each form and leads to a more focused analysis and discussion. Because surveillance is more comprehensive and frequently includes both work- and nonwork-related activities, critics are concerned primarily with its potential invasiveness. As a result, debates over electronic surveillance are likely to focus on whether the practice is appropriate regardless of how it is conducted. In contrast, computer performance monitoring is less comprehensive and produces primarily work-related statistical data. Critics of computer monitoring are concerned not with invasiveness, but with its potential to increase production requirements and job stress. However, because organizations have gathered information about work-related statistics for centuries, the key issue is not whether computer monitoring is appropriate, but how the technology may be utilized most appropriately. Finally, since eavesdropping has characteristics of both electronic surveillance and computer monitoring, both appropriateness and utilization issues arise. However, as the scope of monitored activities is more limited than that of electronic surveillance, the intensity of debate is more limited as well.

Another equally important obstacle to resolving the debate over electronic monitoring may stem from the distinction between legal and ethical perspectives. Although a monitoring organization may cover itself legally with relative ease, a host of ethical dilemmas may remain unresolved. The arguments raised by both sides of the debate over EPM have clear ethical overtones. That is, some of the debate centers around what is morally right and wrong rather than what is legally right and wrong. Yet, few efforts have been made to apply ethical theories to the realm of electronic monitoring (see Alder, in press; Hawk, 1994; Ottensmeyer & Heroux, 1991, for exceptions). The relationship between monitoring and ethics clearly merits greater attention. In the remainder of this chapter, we address this need by discussing the ethical implications of considering the rights of employees and employers on each of our three proposed categories of EPM technology. In the next section, we provide a general overview to those rights most relevant to EPM.

RIGHTS

Philosophers have conceptualized rights in a variety of ways (Waldron, 1984). Perhaps the most influential in modern civil societies is the natural law approach outlined by Locke (1690/1952). Locke maintained that rights can be thought of as a guarantee that an individual is due certain considerations by virtue of the fact that he or she is a member of the human race (1967, p. 289). In *The Second Treatise of Government*, Locke identified three fundamental human rights: liberty, life, and property. So influential were Locke's thoughts on rights that Lockean rights have played a central role in our society since its birth. (Jefferson used this Lockean approach in framing the U.S. Constitution, changing the pursuit of property to the pursuit of happiness.) Locke believed these rights were absolute, inalienable, and universal. If a society were to be considered legitimate, these basic rights must be inherent in the design of its institutions.

In the past 200 plus years, U.S. society has expanded the number of rights, adding concepts such as the right to life, the right to die, employment rights, and privacy rights to the list. A similar expansion of rights also has occurred in organizational settings. Discussions of employee rights include the right to due process, the right to organize, the right to meaningful work, the right to good faith and fair dealing, the right to a nonhostile work environment, and so on. In this chapter, we focus on three rights that are especially relevant to electronic monitoring and that flow from Locke's original rights: privacy, health, and property. We briefly discuss these rights next.

Privacy

There are multiple meanings to *privacy*. Des Jardins (1987) noted three general meanings used in legal and philosophical literature: (a) the proprietary relationship that a person has with his or her own name and likeness, (b) the right to be let alone, and (c) the right to control information about oneself. These conceptualizations of the right to privacy can be traced to Locke's right to liberty. However, the right to privacy in organizations goes beyond a right to liberty (Des Jardins, 1987).

Of the three general meanings of privacy, the latter two are most relevant for organizations (Des Jardins, 1987; Stone & Stone, 1990). The right to be let alone, stems from the Supreme Court ruling in *Griswold v. Connecticut* (1965). The Court found that the Constitution guaranteed citizens a zone of privacy around their person that government could not violate. Much of the discussion about privacy in organizations starts with this definition of privacy. Issues associated with this definition of privacy include freedom from polygraphs, surveillance, restrictions of nonwork activities, privacy of personal property at work, and employee appearance (Des Jardins, 1987). However, the terms *zone of privacy* and *the right to be let alone* are vague. This creates difficulty in determining which activities are protected by privacy rights and which are not. In work settings, courts have applied a standard of "an expectation of privacy" (*Simmons v. Southwestern Bell Tel Co.,* 1979). That is, employers have the legal right to monitor employees unless there is an expectation of privacy (e.g., the activities take place in an area generally thought of as private).

The other approach to privacy that is relevant to organizations maintains that individuals have the right to manage and control information about themselves. This control includes both the information that individuals disclose to others as well as the dissemination of information about the individual that is collected by the organization. Organizations have a responsibility to safeguard the information they collect or acquire about their employees (Fox & Ostling, 1979).

Health

The right to a safe workplace stems from Locke's right to life. Werhane (1985) argued that workers have a right to a safe workplace because dangerous working conditions threaten the most basic right: the right to life. DeGeorge (1986) similarly contended that society's mandate to business is to not cause harm to any of those affected by its decisions (p. 416).

However, the right to a safe workplace is a relatively new phenomenon. In the late nineteenth century and early twentieth century, there were few restrictions on employers regarding how they ran their operations. Employees injured on the job had to file a lawsuit against their employer to receive any compensation for their injuries. Employers could not be held liable if they could demonstrate that the employee knew of the job hazards when accepting the job. In the early 1900s, state governments enacted workers' compensation laws that created a fund to provide compensation to workers who were involved in work-related accidents. By 1948, all states had adopted some form of workers' compensation law. However, these laws focused only on the compensation for injuries. They did not focus on the prevention of injuries. The 1970 Occupational Safety and Health Act shifted the focus to prevention. The act's goal is "To assure so far as possible every man and woman in the Nation safe and healthful working conditions and to preserve our human resources."

Property

The right to property was originally identified as a fundamental human right by Locke. The right to property allows individuals to use and dispose of their property (and their own labor) as they see fit. Individuals are free to trade and contract with each other as long as the arrangements are voluntary and do not demonstrably harm others who are not a party to the agreement (Locke, 1967, p. 306). Property rights also allow an employer to set standards for how equipment (e.g., phones, computers, copiers) is used and to assert control over outcomes produced by the machinery.

Employee Rights in Organizations

Whether employees have special rights in the workplace is a subject of substantial debate (Hall, 1987; Machan, 1987; Nuttig, 1987). The modern view of rights maintains that employees need no special rights to govern the employee/employer relationship. Employers' basic private property rights give them full authority to set the terms of employment, and workers are held to be free to choose how and with whom to invest their labor. Thus, employers are free to set working conditions and requirements, and employees are free not to work for a company that engages in activities they find objectionable.

The postmodern approach views rights not just as liberties, but as entitlements. The postmodern approach maintains that an employer's ability to fire or sanction the employee for refusing to submit to organizational processes constitutes coercion. This coercive power overrides the employee's free choice, and employees are forced to accept organizational activities to which they object. The postmodern view suggests employees need special rights (and additional protection, usually from the government) when they enter the workplace.

Collisions between employers' and employees' rights claims are most likely to occur in areas where the concept of rights is applied differently at the organizational and the societal level. When individuals' rights conflict with governmental needs, individual rights generally take precedence. However, in organizations, rights conflicts occur between two individuals—the employee and the employer. Thus, there is not a clear priority of one individual's right over the other's.[2] For example, an employee's right to privacy—to control information about him or herself (e.g., not answering questions about past misdeeds)—may conflict with an employer's property

---

[2]In general, courts have upheld employers' rights to control their property and set standards as they see fit. However, there is a large body of case law that identifies when the employees' rights prevail. A detailed discussion of this area is clearly beyond the scope of this chapter.

rights—to set the conditions of employment (e.g., use integrity tests in selection).

Rights claims differ depending on where we are trying to exercise our rights. There is a continuum between one's public and one's private life. One does not shed the mantle of privacy completely upon walking through the organization's doors. On the other hand, one does not expect to be free of being monitored to the same degree at work as at home. Part of being a member of an organization is submitting to some degree of observation as part of the employment contract.

Similarly, health rights claims vary between home and work. We expect to be free of health-endangering influences on our own property (or at least to make the choice for ourselves about the hazards to which we are subjected). We may ask our guests and family members not to smoke, may choose to use only nontoxic forms of pest control, or restrict activities we find stressful. But, when we enter the workplace, we may agree to work in a factory where there is the risk of radioactive contamination or where the pressures of production are severe. Thus, we forfeit some control over things that may adversely affect us. These trade-offs and tensions can be analyzed as illustrated in Table 4.2.

EPM AND RIGHTS

Most discussions of electronic monitoring center around one or more of the rights identified earlier. The most frequent concerns raised by critics of monitoring are that the practice invades employee privacy, increases their stress, and, consequently, threatens their health (Piturro, 1989). On the other hand, management groups argue that monitoring is a legitimate tool that organizations can use to increase productivity, improve quality and service, and reduce costs.

As pointed out previously, most discussions about EPM do not distinguish between the various forms of monitoring. This tendency masks important differences. Each type of monitoring has different characteristics that may make privacy, health, and property rights particularly salient. In this section, we discuss the relationship between each form of EPM and the three basic

TABLE 4.2
Strength of Perception of a Rights Claim

Private Life	Work Life
Employee privacy strong	Employee privacy weak
Employee health strong	Employee health weak
Employer property weak	Employer property strong

rights to privacy, health, and property. We discuss which rights concerns are more or less salient for each form of monitoring.

Surveillance

Monitoring techniques included under the category of surveillance are those electronic devices that permit supervisors to visually observe workers' behavior and track their movements. The most common form of electronic surveillance is video camera observation. From employees' perspective, the predominant concern with electronic surveillance is their right to privacy. In a 1987 report to Congress, the OTA concluded that monitoring raises serious concerns because it can be abused and may invade employee privacy.

We suggest that the employees' concern for privacy may be more salient when they are subjected to electronic surveillance than when they are subjected to eavesdropping or computer monitoring. As support for the argument that EPM violates employee privacy, opponents of monitoring cite examples of employers who have gone beyond reasonably acceptable means to monitor their employees' behavior. For example, these stories may involve organizations that place hidden video cameras in employee dressing rooms and locker rooms and broadcast worker activities over in-house cable channels.

This covert surveillance may be perceived by employees as violating their right to privacy both because of their right to be let alone and because of their right to control information about themselves. Employees may have an expectation of privacy in locker rooms, bathrooms, and their personal offices. Moreover, employees may feel their privacy is violated if they are unable to control when and how the surveillance information is collected and its subsequent use.

Clearly, close supervision and visual observation of sensitive nonperformance related areas, like rest rooms and locker rooms, can make employees feel as though their privacy has been eroded and as though their dignity has been compromised (Aiello, 1993). However, employers claim that their right to conduct electronic surveillance stems from property rights. Electronic surveillance protects the employer's property from theft, helps guard against other illegal activity, and may even help protect the organization's members. For example, cameras and video monitors in remote places can improve a company's security and provide its employees some measure of protection from violent crime (Testimony of R. J. Barry, 1993). Electronic surveillance can also be an effective tool in the fight against employee theft. The retail industry realized a savings of $1.3 billion in reduced shrinkage in one year through the use of alarm cables, electronic surveillance, and video surveillance ("Retailers use high tech," 1993).

Legally, electronic surveillance has been permitted by the courts as long as employees do not have an expectation of privacy. For example, in *Marrs v. Marriot Corp.* (1992), an employee sued for invasion of privacy based on the fact that he was being secretly videotaped while breaking into another employee's desk. The district court ruled in favor of the employer because there was no reasonable expectation of privacy in an open space. Similarly, the court ruled against the employer in *Doe v. B.P.S. Guard Services, Inc.* (1991), stating that an invasion of privacy did occur when the employer conducted videotaped surveillance of models' dressing rooms. However, even if an employer stays within the legal limit of the law, employees may feel that their privacy is violated. For example, surveillance of private offices, which may be legal, may violate an employee's sense of a zone of privacy. Thus, for electronic monitoring, legal and ethical concerns are not the same.

Computer Monitoring

Computer performance monitoring is the use of computer hardware and software to collect, store, analyze, and report individual or group actions or performance (Nebeker & Tatum, 1993). Computers can record and report a wide range of computer-driven activities. Thus, unlike electronic surveillance, which permits visual monitoring of employee behavior, and electronic eavesdropping, which permits auditory monitoring of employee conversations, computer monitoring facilitates the monitoring of employee performance based largely on statistics. Computer monitoring systems provide supervisors with performance data such as work speed, work completed, and error rate. Computer performance monitoring has been widely used in many industries, including insurance, communications, telemarketing, transportation, banking, and retailing. The National Institute of Occupational Health and Safety (NIOSH) estimates that two thirds of all video display terminal users are electronically monitored (Nussbaum & duRivage, 1986).

From the employees' perspective, the primary rights concern with computer monitoring is one of health: increased stress and related health problems. Critics contend that computer monitoring leads to work speedups and an overemphasis on quantitative measurements, which increase workers' stress and health problems (Piturro, 1989). Computer monitoring has been referred to as an "electronic whip" that turns the workplace into an "electronic sweatshop" (Garson, 1988; Nussbaum & duRivage, 1986).

Empirical research that investigates employee responses to computer performance monitoring indicates that, under some conditions, computer monitoring may accelerate the pace of work, increase stress, and decrease health (Nine to Five, 1984; Nussbaum & duRivage, 1986; Ross, 1992; Smith, Carayon, Sanders, & Legrande, 1992). Aiello (1993) investigated the impact of electronic monitoring in several telecommunication organizations and found that, due to monitoring standards, directory assistance operators felt they could not provide the high quality service they wanted to (Aiello, 1993).

The Massachusetts Coalition on New Office Technology surveyed 700 employees from 49 companies and found that 81% felt monitoring made their job more stressful (Ross, 1992). Smith et al. (1992) similarly compared the attitudes of monitored workers to those of unmonitored workers and obtained three important results. First, 81% of the monitored employees reported being depressed, as opposed to 69% of those not monitored. Second, of those monitored, 72% felt extreme anxiety, compared to only 57% of those who were not monitored. Finally, 57% of employees who were monitored by the number of keystrokes they entered complained of sore wrists, a ratio double the rate of unmonitored workers who experienced sore wrists. Thus, empirical evidence indicates that computer performance monitoring may create stress and health problems for employees.

Organizations may justify computer monitoring on the basis of property rights. Because productivity is a derivative of property, organizations may do anything to enhance production, short of physical coercion. Thus, to the extent that computer monitoring facilitates improved productivity and organizational performance, it may be justified on the basis of ensuring the organization gets the performance for which it pays.

Empirical work demonstrates that organizations may obtain positive results from electronic monitoring (Aiello, 1993; Griffith, 1993). For example, in a controlled experiment, Nebeker and Tatum (1993) found database operators who were aware that their performance was being recorded and were given performance feedback to be more productive than workers who were either not monitored or were unaware that they were being monitored. Significantly, this increased productivity did not come at the expense of increased stress, reduced satisfaction, or lower quality.

There are privacy rights issues with computer monitoring, too, although we suggest these are not as salient.[3] For example, employees may feel they are unable to control the performance information that the computer collects about them. Employee groups argue that an appeals process or method of correcting erroneous computer performance monitoring information is needed.

There is little legal precedent for computer performance monitoring concerns. There is no case law addressing the health issues associated with computer monitoring, although stress-related injuries and repetitive motion injuries are among the fastest growing categories of workers' compensation

---

[3]The recent rise in in e-mail increases the privacy concerns associated with computer monitoring. Most employees view e-mail much as they do personal phone calls: they expect the communication to be private. However, the courts deal with e-mail significantly differently than they do with telephone communication. Thus far, the courts have held that employers may monitor e-mail—even if they have told employees the communication is private. We view the monitoring of e-mail as more similar to eavesdropping than to other forms of computer monitoring.

claims. Thus, for health, employees' may feel their rights have been violated even when the employer is behaving lawfully. On the privacy front, the court held (*Barksdale v. IBM*, 1985) that the employer's "observation and recording of the number of errors the plaintiffs made in the tasks they were instructed to perform can hardly be considered an intrusion on the plaintiff's solitude or seclusion or other private affairs or concerns" (p. 1383).

Eavesdropping

Electronic eavesdropping includes those devices that permit supervisors to silently listen to conversations between employees and customers. Thus, the most common forms of electronic eavesdropping are telephone call observation and telephone call accounting. Use of electronic eavesdropping is widespread. For example, the OTA (1987) estimated that employers listened to more than 400 million telephone calls between employees and customers each year.

From the employees' perspective, electronic eavesdropping raises many of the same concerns associated with both surveillance and computer monitoring, but to a lesser degree. Specifically, electronic eavesdropping may be expected to raise privacy issues to a greater degree than computer monitoring of work-related activities, but to a lesser extent than electronic surveillance. Similarly, electronic eavesdropping may be expected to have a stronger relationship with stress and health problems than electronic surveillance, but a weaker relationship with these problems than would computer monitoring. For example, employees are likely to feel that their privacy has been invaded if their supervisor listens to their private telephone conversations. However, their felt sense of invasion is likely to be stronger if that same supervisor observes their bathroom or locker room activities. Similarly, employees may experience increased stress if their supervisors listen to their calls. However, these same employees are likely to experience a greater degree of stress if their work is subjected to the continuous evaluation made possible by computer monitoring. Thus, employees may claim that electronic eavesdropping violates both their right to privacy and their right to health.

Employers may invoke the concept of property rights in two ways to justify electronic eavesdropping. The first argues that, as with computer monitoring, electronic eavesdropping may enhance performance. This argument is most applicable when the monitored interaction is work related. For example, telephone call observation provides organizations with a way to ensure that their customer service representatives provide customers with accurate information and quality service. When GE implemented a telephone surveillance system for customer service calls, its customer satisfaction rate increased to 96% (Bylinsky, 1991). AT&T, MCI, and Pacific Bell have obtained similar customer service improvements through telephone call observation use of electronic monitoring (CWA calls monitoring "menace," 1993; Testimony of J. Gerdelman, 1993). Thus, electronic eavesdropping may be an integral aspect of an organization's training programs (Bylinsky, 1991; Testimony of J. Gerdelman, 1993) and is clearly within the employer's property rights.

The second justification for electronic eavesdropping addresses the employers' right to control their property. Because the employer owns the telephone and pays the telephone bill, the employer has a right to ensure that the phone is being used for business purposes. Monitoring telephone usage allows employers to ensure that their equipment is not being used inappropriately. Thus, telephone monitoring may also be an effective way to enhance productivity by focusing individuals on business-related, rather than personal, phone calls. For example, a California insurance company realized a 300-hour drop in monthly telephone usage and a productivity increase equal to 7.5 labor weeks per month after using a call accounting system for one month. This productivity improvement resulted in a 15%, or $81,000, monthly cost savings (Tucker, 1992).

Legally, the courts have held that employers may monitor phone calls that pertain to business, but not personal calls. The employer may monitor the call long enough to determine if it is a business or personal call. If it is a personal call, the employer must cease monitoring (*Watkins v. L. M. Berry & Co.*, 1983). The law here seems to be consistent with employees' expectations of ethical behavior.

RULES FOR CREATING ETHICAL MONITORING SYSTEMS

In the previous section, we demonstrated that each type of monitoring raises ethical concerns because each has the potential to violate one or more employee rights, whereas restricting its use may violate employers' rights. We also note that the legal standard to which an employer is held may not satisfy the employee's expectation of ethical behavior. This gap is important for several reasons. First, employees who feel employers have violated their rights—even if the legal standard is met—are likely to feel unfairly treated. These perceptions of unfair treatment may translate to decreased satisfaction, commitment, and performance and increased intentions to quit, increased grievances, and theft. (See Cropanzano & Greenberg, 1997, for a review of the organizational fairness literature.) Second, research demonstrates that when subordinates believe their superiors are behaving unethically, the subordinates are more likely to engage in unethical behavior themselves (Brenner & Molander, 1977; Posner & Schmidt, 1984; Vitell & Festervand, 1987). Finally, when individuals believe they have been treated unethically, they are more likely to seek legal recourse (Bies & Tyler, 1993). Thus, it is clear that following the legal guidelines for EPM is not enough for employers.

Managers need also be concerned about employee perceptions of ethical behavior.

In this section, we argue that the apparent conflict between employee and employer rights can be resolved by considering both the needs of the employer and the concerns of the employee. We suggest that two elements are key to this resolution: moderation and disclosure.

The Rule of Moderation

Electronic technology provides organizations with the ability to monitor a large range of areas and worker activities, many of which are not performance related. As a result, moderation may be one key to creating ethical monitoring systems. We suggest employers should use moderation for two dimensions of monitoring: activities monitored and performance standards. First, organizations must decide with workers' rights in mind what tasks and areas to monitor. Second, the health-related concerns with monitoring arise because monitoring results in increasingly difficult performance standards and production quotas. By focusing on employees' perceptions of rights and by using moderation, employers may be able to balance the ethical concerns associated with monitoring.

Moderation in What Is Monitored. Activities in the workplace range from those that are clearly task related (e.g., answering customer questions during working hours) to those that are clearly not task related (e.g., using the bathroom during a scheduled break). A number of researchers and theorists note that organizations need to identify the tasks that are most important to successful job performance and restrict monitoring to these activities (Carayon, 1993; Grant & Higgins, 1989; Susser, 1988). Ambrose and Alder (1996) argued that monitoring will be considered fairer if it is restricted to performance-related activities than if it includes nonperformance-related activities that may be considered an invasion of privacy. Others indicate that close supervision of personal activities may be resented by workers because it erodes their privacy and compromises their dignity (Aiello, 1993; Marx, 1992). Monitoring personal, nonperformance-related activities and areas, such as employee rest rooms or the number of trips to the bathroom, may be considered unethical because it ignores individuals' right to privacy. Thus, moderation—monitoring performance relevant activities—is critical to ethical monitoring.

The use of moderation for electronic surveillance suggests that organizations may conduct electronic surveillance but must restrict it to nonsensitive areas and avoid surveying areas that reasonable individuals may consider private, such as a locker room stall. Clearly, there may be conditions, such as high amounts of employee theft, when business necessity calls for monitoring such areas. In such instances, disclosure, which is discussed in the next section, becomes critical to ethicality.

Moderation is also important when conducting electronic eavesdropping and computer monitoring. For example, employers may legitimately claim the right to listen in on telephone calls between employees and customers because such conversations play an integral role in organizational productivity and performance and are not generally considered private conversations. Organizations may not legitimately claim a right to eavesdrop on their employees' private conversations because employees may legitimately claim a right to privacy in private, personal matters. Moreover, the use of information by the employer from these private conversations violates employees' rights to control information about themselves. As noted earlier, the courts allow monitoring for business purposes only. This is consistent with employees' perceptions of their rights. However, we suggest that, if organizations are going to monitor conversations, disclosure is also critical from a rights perspective.

Similar conclusions may be drawn regarding computer monitoring. Monitoring work-related computer-driven activity, such as data entered or errors, may be considered legitimate. Monitoring that intrudes on private matters, such as reading private e-mail, may be considered an invasion of employee privacy. In sum, the rule of moderation indicates that electronic surveillance, electronic eavesdropping, and computer monitoring should all be restricted to business-related, nonsensitive, and nonpersonal activities, tasks, and areas.

Moderation in Monitoring-Related Performance Standards. EPM systems are generally developed to assess worker performance against a set of performance standards. However, monitoring can also be used to establish, enforce, and steadily increase performance. Smith et al. (1992) pointed out that because monitoring-related standards are sometimes based on the capabilities of machinery rather than on scientific grounds, monitoring may result in excessive and unrealistic standards. When monitoring results in, or is used in connection with, unfair or excessively difficult performance standards, increased employee stress and health problems may result (Smith et al., 1992). Indeed, criticisms of monitoring often focus not on the monitoring itself but rather on the performance standards and quotas enforced by monitoring. For example, Nussbaum and duRivage (1986) argued that monitoring will result in production quotas and speedups that are "chillingly reminiscent of management practices in nineteenth century garment industry sweatshops" (p. 18).

Empirical research similarly indicates a relationship between performance standards and employee reactions to monitoring. Aiello (1993) found that almost 25% of monitored directory assistance operators cheated in order to reach monitoring-based standards. The Massachusetts Coalition on New Office Technology similarly discovered that 65% of those surveyed felt they could not do a quality job because monitoring-related practices forced them to work too fast (cited in Ross, 1992). Nebeker and Tatum (1993) demonstrated that the dissatisfaction and stress commonly associated with monitoring comes about when monitoring is used in connection with unrealistic standards.

We suggest that monitoring that results in, or is used in connection with, unrealistic or excessively difficult performance standards may be considered unethical because it violates individuals' right to health. Thus, moderation in performance standards is another key to ethical monitoring. Moderation in this sense is most relevant to computer monitoring and indicates that organizations may conduct computer monitoring, but must not use it to increase performance standards or to enforce unrealistically difficult standards of performance, such as an excessively fast average strokes per minute rate. Moderation in this sense is also applicable to electronic eavesdropping, to the extent that such monitoring is conducted to enforce time-per-call or call handling standards.

The Rule of Disclosure

Silent or covert monitoring in which supervisors monitor employees without their knowledge is conducted by numerous organizations. One survey found that only 31% of the companies that conduct computer monitoring or searches of employee computers, voice mail, e-mail, or networking communications notify their employees (Piller, 1993). Silent monitoring may be the most controversial aspect of monitoring systems because critics of the practice claim it is tantamount to spying and creates an atmosphere of mistrust. Practitioners and academics alike have suggested that disclosure, particularly informing employees when they are monitored, is key to effective and ethical monitoring (Laabs, 1992; Picard, 1994; Susser, 1988).

In the modern view of rights, individuals are free to trade and contract with each other as long as the arrangements are voluntary. Disclosure is particularly critical from a rights perspective of ethics because it is critical to volunteerism. Property rights permit organizations to utilize employee resources as productively as possible, as long as the employee is not coerced into remaining in the relationship. Thus, it would appear that organizations have the right to electronically monitor their employees. However, it can be argued that coercion does not consist solely of physical force. Rather, the concept of volunteerism indicates that, unless employees are given a chance to choose the conditions they will be subjected to, there is some degree of coercion via deceit. In the case of silent monitoring, no volunteerism exists because employees have not been given the chance to make an informed choice about whether they are willing to be monitored. Thus, disclosure—informing employees when they are monitored and how the information obtained will be used—is essential to ethical monitoring. Monitoring that is conducted without the knowledge or express consent of workers denies them their right to avoid monitoring.

The modern view of rights suggests that as long as an organization informs workers when they are being monitored, there is no coercion. Consequently, the organization is respecting the rights of its employees. If monitoring becomes overly stressful or noxious, the employee may quit the job and seek employment elsewhere. However, the postmodern view of rights suggests that several factors, including labor market conditions, may impair an employee's probability of actually obtaining employment elsewhere. An employee may strongly object to monitoring, yet perceive little real opportunity to change the situation. Such an employee is likely to remain in the current position despite strong negative feelings to monitoring. Thus, although an organization may inform its workers when they are being monitored, the degree to which employees can truly choose whether to submit to monitoring may be severely limited by external factors. However, both views maintain that an ethical organization must inform prospective employees that it performs electronic monitoring, what type(s) of monitoring it conducts, and how the information obtained from monitoring is used by the organization. The modern view believes truthful disclosure is adequate. The postmodern view sees truthful disclosure as a necessary, but not sufficient, condition for maintaining individual's rights.

Although both the modern and postmodern views of rights believe disclosure is a necessary condition for ethical monitoring, disclosure alone may not alleviate employee concerns. We suggest that it is not enough for employees to know that they are monitored; they also need to know why they are monitored. Research from organizational justice demonstrates that individuals respond more positively when they are provided with explanations for decisions (Brockner, Grover, & Reed, 1990; Greenberg, 1991, 1993; Konovsky & Cropanzano, 1991). Employers need to be sensitive to employees' rights concerns and be able to provide a convincing justification (e.g., high theft) when their monitoring practices may be perceived as violating employee rights. Disclosure coupled with an explanation for why employees are monitored will be more effective than disclosure alone.

CONCLUSION

Managers are most likely sensitive to the legal requirements imposed by EPM. However, focusing on what one can and cannot legally do does not address the underlying ethical concerns associated with EPM. Underlying the debate is a belief about employee and employer rights. To address these concerns directly, we must explicitly consider this conflict of rights and how best to manage it. We believe attributes allow both employers and employee concerns to be addressed: moderating monitoring and disclosing monitoring. Employers need to carefully identify what they need to monitor and why. They need to clearly convey this information to their employees. In this way, organizations may retain their right to monitor yet simultaneously respect individuals' rights to health and privacy.

REFERENCES

Aiello, J. R. (1993). Computer-based work monitoring: Electronic surveillance and its effects. *Journal of Applied Social Psychology, 23*, 499–507.

Alder, G. S. (in press). Ethical issues in electronic performance monitoring: A consideration of deontological and teleological ethics. *Journal of Business Ethics.*

Ambrose, M. L., & Alder, G. S. (1996, August). *Computerized performance monitoring and organizational fairness: The relationship between system attributes and perceptions of fairness.* Paper presented at the meeting of the Academy of Management, Cincinnati, OH.

Angel, N. F. (1989, November). Evaluating employees by computer. *Personnel Administrator,* 67–72.

Barksdale v. I.B.M., 620 F. Supp. 1380, 1383. (W.D.N.C. 1985).

Bies, R., & Tyler, T. R. (1993). The "litigation mentality" in organizations: A test of alternative psychological explanations. *Organization Science, 4*, 352–366.

Brenner, S. N., & Molander, E. A. (1977). Is the ethics of business changing? *Harvard Business Review, 50*, 57–71.

Brockner, J., Grover, S., & Reed, T. (1990). When it is especially important to explain why: Factors affecting the relationship between managers' explanations of a layoff and survivors' reactions to the layoff. *Journal of Experimental Social Psychology, 26*, 389–407.

Bylinsky, G. (1991, November 4). How companies spy on employees. *Fortune, 124*(11), 131–140.

Carayon, P. (1993). Effects of electronic performance monitoring on job design and worker stress: Review of the literature and conceptual model. *Human Factors, 35*, 385–395.

CWA calls monitoring "menace." (1993, June 24). *Communications Daily, 13*(121), 3–5.

Cropanzano, R., & Greenberg, J. (1997). Progress in organizational justice: Tunneling through the maze. In C. L. Cooper & I. T. Robertson (Eds.), *International review of industrial and organizational psychology.* New York: Wiley.

DeGeorge, R. T. (1986). *Business ethics* (2nd ed.). New York: Macmillan.

Des Jardins, J. R. (1987). Privacy in employment. In G. Ezorsky (Ed.), *Moral rights in the workplace* (pp. 127–142). Albany: State University of New York Press.

DeTienne, K. B., & Abbott, N. T. (1993). Developing an employee centered electronic monitoring system. *Journal of Systems Management, 44*, 12–15.

DeTienne, K. B., & Alder, G. S. (1995). The privacy for consumers and workers act: Panacea or problem? *Managerial Law, 37*, 1–32.

Doe v. B.P.S. Guard Services Inc., 945 F. 2d 1422, 1427. (8th Cir. 1991).

Fickel, L. (1991). Don't look now, but . . . : A new crop of network products is forcing a debate over workplace monitoring. *Infoworld, 13*, 50–55.

Flanagan, J. A. (1994). Restricting electronic monitoring in the private workplace. *Duke Law Journal, 43*, 1256–1281.

Fox, J. G., & Ostling, P. J. (1979). Employee and government access to personnel files: Rights and requirements. *Employee Relations Law Journal, 5,* 70.

Garson, B. (1988). *The electronic sweatshop.* New York: Simon & Schuster.

Grant, R., & Higgins, C. (1989). Monitoring service workers via computer: The effect on employees, productivity, and service. *National Productivity Review, 8,* 101–112.

Greenberg, J. (1991). Using explanations to manage impressions of performance appraisal fairness. *Employee Responsibilities and Rights Journal, 4,* 51–60.

Greenberg, J. (1993). The social side of fairness: Interpersonal and informational classes of organizational justice. In R. Cropanzano (Ed.), *Justice in the workplace: Approaching fairness in human resource management* (pp. 79–103). Hillsdale, NJ: Lawrence Erlbaum Associates.

Griffith, T. L. (1993). Monitoring and performance: A comparison of computer and supervisor monitoring. *Journal of Applied Social Psychology, 23,* 549–572.

Griswold v. Connecticut, 381 U.S. 479. (1965).

Hall, B. (1987). Collective bargaining and workers' liberty. In G. Ezorsky (Ed.), *Moral rights in the workplace* (pp. 161–170). Albany: State University of New York Press.

Hawk, S. R. (1994). The effects of computerized performance monitoring: An ethical perspective. *Journal of Business Ethics, 13,* 949–957.

Henriques, V. E. (1986a, July 14). Computer monitoring: Boon to employee and manager? *Computerworld, 20.*

Henriques, V. E. (1986b, December). In defense of computer monitoring. *Training, 23,* 120.

Komaki, J. L. (1986). Toward effective supervision: An operant analysis and comparison of managers at work. *Journal of Applied Psychology, 71,* 270–279.

Komaki, J. L., Desselles, M. L., & Bowman, E. D. (1989). Definitely not a breeze: Extending an operant model of effective supervision to teams. *Journal of Applied Psychology, 71,* 522–529.

Konovsky, M., & Cropanzano, R. (1991). The perceived fairness of employee drug testing as a predictor of employee attitudes and job performance. *Journal of Applied Psychology, 76,* 698–707.

Laabs, J. J. (1992). Surveillance: Tool or trap? The use of electronic surveillance equipment to monitor employee performance. *Personnel Journal, 71,* 96.

Locke, J. (1952). *The second treatise of government.* T. Peardon (Ed.). Indianapolis, IN: Bobbs Merrill. (Original work published 1690)

Machan, T. R. (1987). Human rights, workers' rights, and the "right" to occupational safety. In G. Ezorsky (Ed.), *Moral rights in the workplace* (pp. 45–50). Albany: State University of New York Press.

Marrs v. Marriot Corp., 830 F. Supp. 274. (D. MD. 1992).

Marx, G. T. (1992). The case of the omniscient organization. *Harvard Business Review, 90,* 12–31.

Nebeker, D. M., & Tatum, C. B. (1993). The effects of computer monitoring, standards, and rewards on work performance, job satisfaction, and stress. *Journal of Applied Social Psychology, 23,* 508–536.

Nine to Five, Working Women Education Fund. (1984). *The 9 to 5 national survey on women and stress.* Cleveland, OH: Author.

Nussbaum, K., & duRivage, V. (1986). Computer monitoring: Mismanagement by remote control. *Business and Society Review, 56,* 16–20.

Nuttig, K. (1987). Work and freedom in capitalism. In G. Ezorsky (Ed.), *Moral rights in the workplace* (pp. 97–104). Albany: State University of New York Press.

Office of Technology Assessment. (1987). *The electronic supervisor: New technology, new tensions.* Washington, DC: U.S. Government Printing Office.

Ottensmeyer, E. J., & Heroux, M. A. (1991). Ethics, public policy, and managing advanced technologies: The case of electronic surveillance. *Journal of Business Ethics, 10,* 519–526.

Picard, M. (1994, February). Working under an electronic thumb. *Training, 31,* 47–51.

Piller, C. (1993, July). Bosses with X-ray eyes: Your employer may be using computers to keep tabs on you. *Macworld, 10,* 118–130.

Piturro, M. C. (1989). Employee performance monitoring . . . or meddling? *Management Review, 78,* 31–33.

Posner, B. Z., & Schmidt, W. H. (1984). Values and the American manager: An update. *California Management Review, 26,* 202–216.

Retailers use high tech to fight high cost of theft; security: Sophisticated new video surveillance and alarm systems will aid stores tomorrow, one of the busiest shopping days of the year. (1993, December 25). *Los Angeles Times,* p. D1.

Ross, S. (1992, September 15). Big brother in workplace growing bigger every day. *Reuter Business Report,* 11–12.

Sanders, A. L. (1990, January 8). Reach out and tape someone. *Time, 135,* 55.

Simmons v. Southwestern Bell Tel Co., 452 F. Supp. 392, 396 (W. D Okla 1978), *aff'd,* 611 F. 2d 342. (10th Cir. 1979).

Smith, M. J., Carayon, P., Sanders, K. J., & LeGrande, D. (1992). Employee stress and health complaints in jobs with and without electronic performance monitoring. *Applied Ergonomics, 23,* 17–28.

Statement before the subcommittee on Employment and Productivity, Committee on Labor and Human Resources, United States. 103rd Cong., 1st Sess. (June 22, 1993; testimony of J. Gerdelman).

Statement on behalf of security companies organized for legislative action (SCOLA) regarding S.984 the Privacy for Consumers and Workers Act before the Senate Labor and Human Resources Subcommittee on Employment and Productivity. 103rd Cong., 1st Sess. (June 22, 1993; testimony of R. J. Barry).

Stone, E. F., & Stone, D. L. (1990). Privacy in organizations: Theoretical issues, research findings, and protection mechanisms. *Research in Personnel and Human Resources, 8,* 349–411.

Susser, P. A. (1988). Electronic monitoring in the private sector: How closely should employers supervise their workers? *Employee Relations, 13,* 575–598.

Tucker, T. (1992). Keeping tabs: Call accounting saves money and more. A lot more. *Teleconnect, 10,* 94–100.

Velasquez, M. G. (1992). *Business ethics: Concepts and cases* (3rd ed.). Englewood Cliffs, NJ: Prentice-Hall.

Vitell, S. J., & Festervand, T. A. (1987). Business ethics: Conflict, practices, and beliefs of industrial executives. *Journal of Business Ethics, 6,* 111–122.

Waldron, J. (1984). *Theories of rights.* New York: Oxford University Press.

Watkins v. L. M. Berry & Co., 704 F. 2d 577. (11th Cir. 1983).

Werhane, P. (1985). *Persons, rights, and corporations.* Englewood Cliffs, NJ: Prentice-Hall.

CHAPTER FIVE

Employee Selection and the Ethic of Care

Beverly Kracher
Deborah L. Wells
Creighton University

Consider the following:

Scenario 1: A project manager has been asked by the vice president above her to submit team reports to him in a timely fashion. She is the kind of manager who feels irresponsible when she does not carry through. So, she ensures that, once team reports are submitted to her, the reports are expeditiously given to the vice president. This project manager is conscientious.

Scenario 2: A sales manager has been directed by his company to use a particular incentive system. He is to split 15% of a sale between himself and the person who makes the sale. The sales manager periodically gives the sales people the entire 15% commission rather than taking half for himself. When asked why he does this, he replies, "Look, we're all in this together. I make good money because I work with good people. It's not a big deal. I'm just trying to show them how proud I am of them and give them an incentive to keep working hard." By being altruistic and by extending himself on a regular basis, this manager ensures trust and loyalty in workplace relationships.

Scenario 3: A grassroots committee in a company has been working with their custodians to institute a recycling program. The committee chair discusses the recycling program with the director of environmental services, who refuses to go along with the program. When the chair reports to the rest of the recycling committee about the director's refusal, she focuses on the need to maintain relationships and to look to the future. Rather than deprecate the director, she invites committee members to brainstorm on plans to persuade the director to accept the recycling program. At the end of an hour, the committee decides on a positive plan and is hopeful of success. The committee chairperson shows sportsmanship. She is an active participant in the workplace and gracious in defeat.

Scenario 4: A manager thinks that being decent to his subordinates is important. He thinks that they deserve to be listened to and to be taken seriously. He thinks they deserve to work in a healthy environment that promotes their abilities and helps them find satisfaction and fulfillment. Inside and outside of meetings, he watches the way his subordinates respond to his comments with their voices and body language. He tries to meter his voice to show his cooperation and dedication. He thinks it is important to be considerate and courteous.

Scenario 5: A manager sees herself as part of a community, as a member of a group working toward a common end. She goes to meetings and actively contributes. She answers her mail and takes her phone calls. She has the sense she must contribute even when her job description does not dictate it. She helps out when workers are sick; she volunteers to help with ad hoc projects. She does what she can.

* * *

The managers described in the examples exist; the anecdotes are true. Organizations need to hire good managers such as those in these scenarios. Our thesis is that organizations can get good managers by selecting organizational citizens who embody a caring attitude. This chapter explains effective managerial selection decisions, defines what it means to be caring, shows how the ethic of care relates to organizational citizenship, suggests ways for selecting caring managers, and recommends further courses of research in this area.

CORE JOB FUNCTIONS AND CONTEXTUAL ACTIVITIES

Managers perform certain day-to-day tasks, duties, and responsibilities that make a direct contribution to fulfilling the organization's basic purpose, usually to produce goods of some sort or services. These tasks, duties, and responsibilities are codified in the organization's collection of job descriptions (Borman & Motowidlo, 1993). Managers who fail to perform the functions central to their jobs, or inadequately perform them, will be asked to improve at performance evaluation time and may eventually be terminated for ongoing performance deficiencies (Miner & Brewer, 1976).

Managers also engage in on-the-job behaviors beyond mere performance of the tasks, duties, and responsibilities that are the central focus of their jobs. Borman and Motowidlo (1993) referred to these as "contextual activities," and they described them as activities that ". . . can either help or hinder efforts to accomplish organizational goals by doing many things that are not directly related to their main task functions but are important because they shape the organizational, social, and psychological context that serves as the critical catalyst for task activities and processes" (p. 71). For example, they exhibit cooperation or a lack thereof, maintain cheerful or not-so-cheerful attitudes, and contribute positively or negatively to the overall workplace climate. Thus, the universe of job activities consists of a core set of tasks surrounded by contextual behaviors. Contextual activities are often not codified in organizational job descriptions, and therefore, managers may not be rewarded for performing them or disciplined for failing to perform them (Borman & Motowidlo, 1993).

CONTEXTUAL ACTIVITIES AND ORGANIZATIONAL CITIZENSHIP

These contextual activities include what is known as *organizational citizenship behavior* (OCB; Borman & Motowidlo, 1993). As described by Organ (1988), "Organizational citizenship behavior represents individual behavior that is discretionary, not directly or explicitly recognized by the formal reward system, and that in the aggregate promotes the effective functioning of the organization" (p. 4). Organ (1988) suggested a number of categories of behaviors that good organizational citizens exhibit: altruism, conscientiousness, sportsmanship, courtesy, and civic virtue. Clearly, the concept of organizational citizenship itself addresses behaviors that most organizations would see as additive in nature. In truth, the total realm of contextual activities can stretch from positive voluntary actions that add value to the organization, to simply failing to make additive contributions, to actually wreaking havoc and mayhem with the physical, financial, and human resources of the organization. This wide disparity in contextual activities may be viewed as a continuum, anchored at one end by organizational citizenship behaviors and at the other end by criminal behaviors, as illustrated in Fig. 5.1.

SELECTING MANAGERS: UNDERLYING LOGIC

The traditional model of effective managerial selection is based on the premise of maximizing person–job fit. The knowledge, skills, abilities, and other characteristics (KSAOs) of the job candidate should match as closely as possible what is needed to perform the tasks, duties, and responsibilities of the job (Chatman, 1989; Schneider, 1978). A Venn diagram, shown in Fig. 5.2, provides a good, simple representation of this principle. The greater the overlap between the circles, the better the fit (Heneman & Heneman,

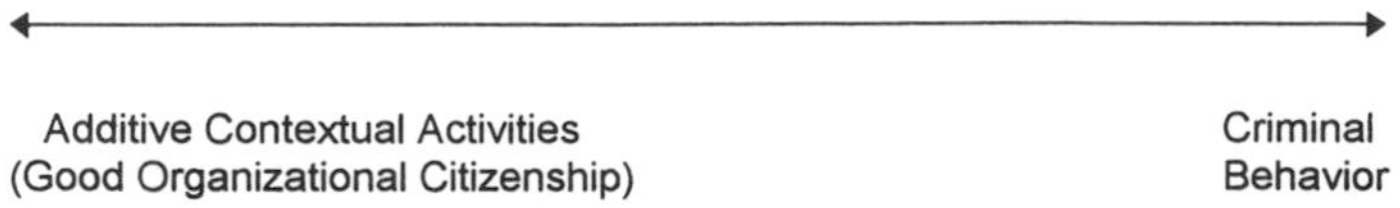

Additive Contextual Activities   Criminal
(Good Organizational Citizenship)   Behavior

FIG. 5.1. Continuum of contextual work activities.

1994). The end result of a good person–job fit is better job performance (Caldwell & O'Reilly, 1990).

To discover the degree of overlap between the two domains illustrated in Fig. 5.2, the selection decision makers need two sets of information. They must discover as much as possible about the KSAOs of the job applicant and as much as they can about the true requirements of the job. In order to know the job candidate, the hirer uses such selection techniques as analysis of information on application blanks, analysis of other biographical information appearing on resumes or vitae, information gleaned in interviews, reference reports, scores or results from tests or profiles, and assessment center results (Gatewood & Feild, 1990). To obtain information about the job, job analyses are conducted and the results are recorded as some type of inventory of tasks, duties, and responsibilities (Harvey, 1990), commonly referred to as job descriptions.

The focus of job analysis, and thus of job descriptions, is on the tasks or duties performed by the manager on a day-to-day basis, rather than on contextual activities, including organizational citizenship. The focus on tasks and duties is a practical one, motivated by two forces: a desire to predict future performance of core job responsibilities (de Wolff, 1993), and legal compliance. Supreme Court decisions interpreting Title VII of the 1964 Civil Rights Act and the guidelines written to help employers comply with Title VII provide additional impetus for task-based analysis of jobs. To minimize discrimination against minorities, the hirer must focus on judging an applicant's ability to perform the tasks, duties, and responsibilities of that job (Uniform Guidelines, 1978). The broader afield the criteria for decision making range, the greater the possibility for discrimination. It has been maintained that selection decisions, to be maximally defensible, cannot be based on nontask-related characteristics of the individual, including race, gender, age, or ability to perform discretionary activities (i.e., OCBs) not part of the core of the job.

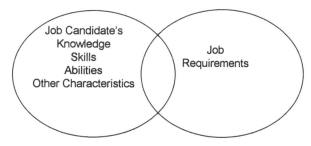

FIG. 5.2. The person–job fit model of effective employee selection.

GETTING ORGANIZATIONAL CITIZENSHIP
TO BE PART OF THE JOB

As long as companies select managers based on the particular tasks and duties of a job, there is a significant hurdle to being able to select good organizational citizens. An obvious solution to this problem is to formalize those behaviors now defined as OCBs by adding them to the description of expected responsibilities. Of course, by doing so, they would no longer classify as OCBs, which are by definition not part of the core job responsibilities. However, for convenience, we continue to refer to this constellation of activities as OCBs.

We are not the first to argue for the expansion of the traditional view of jobs. Borman and Motowidlo (1993) stated this position quite clearly when they argued ". . . that selection criteria should embrace a domain of organizational behavior broader than just task activities; they should also include contextual activities" (p. 71). Nash (1993) argued that relationship-enabling characteristics must be taken into account in hiring, training, and assessing subordinates in order for managers to promote ethical conduct and good business decisions. Making OCBs part of performance expectations and codifying them in the organization's job descriptions, other documentation, and in policies and practices, such as performance appraisal, legitimize their inclusion as selection criteria. There is currently no reason to believe that doing so would place subgroups of applicant populations at a disadvantage (i.e., result in an adverse impact) in the selection process (Bowen, Ledford, & Nathan, 1991). In particular, although Gilligan (1987) argued that women articulate a concern for maintaining healthy relationships, she does not claim that women think one way and men another. Furthermore, there is no definitive study that proves women are more concerned than men with relationships (Derry, 1996; Larrabee, 1993). There is currently no reason to believe that gender discrimination will occur as a result of selecting for organizational citizenship.

SELECTION FOR CORE JOB FUNCTIONS

Human resource decision makers can determine, using an assortment of techniques, whether a job candidate can perform the tasks, duties, and responsibilities that are core job functions. A work sample approach (Asher & Sciarrino, 1974), for example, might be used when hiring a secretary. Job candidates would be asked to generate correspondence using a personal computer and word processing software. They might take typing tests and be asked to provide samples of work done previously. These are all direct indicators of how successfully the applicant will be able to perform this core job function.

For some types of jobs, successful performance depends on being able to do something much less tangible than typing an error-free document. When a job requires persuading a customer to buy a home or a car, being a visionary thinker, or being a good manager of people, it is harder to ferret out who, among a set of candidates, will be the best at it. Tests of cognitive and leadership abilities, personality and interest inventories, peer assessment, assessment centers, and other methods (Cascio, 1991a) have been used as selection techniques for jobs that call for abstract abilities less demonstrable than motor skill-related activities. Choosing job candidates to best perform contextual activities (i.e., be good organizational citizens) presents a similar selection challenge.

SELECTION WITH CONTEXTUAL ACTIVITIES IN MIND

Picking candidates who would perform adequately at contextual activities has not, for the most part, focused on selecting who would ultimately be the best organizational citizens. Instead, efforts have focused on eliminating applicants who might engage in criminal activities that have plagued some workplaces— employee pilfering, stabbings, shootings, assaults, and embezzlement—all activities that fall at the right end of the Fig. 5.1 continuum. To eliminate the potential felon from the applicant pool, employers have resorted to polygraph testing, integrity testing, honesty testing, personality testing, analysis of biodata, integrity interviews, and background and credit checks (Jones & Terris, 1991; Roberson, 1986). With the exception of personality-oriented integrity tests (Ones, Viswesvaran, & Schmidt, 1993; Sackett, Burris, & Callahan, 1989) and certain personality characteristics tests (Barrick & Mount, 1991), most techniques are useful for lopping off the worst of the job candidate pool, but not for selecting good organizational citizens. It is possible that selection methods suggested by the ethic of care perspective can fill the void left by existing selection techniques that focus on contextual activities. To explain why we believe this is true, the sections that follow will describe the caring person, the importance of caring managers, and how they can be selected.

CARING PEOPLE

The sense of care to which we refer was first characterized in the contemporary literature by Gilligan (1982).[1] Our position is that caring people have

---

[1]We do not assert that Gilligan was the first to focus on the ethical perspective she describes. Among others, Aristotle (trans. 1985) and David Hume (1748/1983) proposed ethical systems that stressed many of the same concepts Gilligan does. However, in contemporary literature, Gilligan was the first to package certain concepts and wrap them under the name "the ethic of care." For a better understanding, see Reich's (1995) historical overview of the concept of care and his description of contemporary ethic of care.

a relational way of understanding themselves and hold a particular moral perspective that motivates them to maintain caring relationships.

Caring people see the world through a lens of relationships. They define themselves in terms of their relationships with other people and with their environment. Noddings (1984) took the mother–child relationship as one paradigm of this relational orientation. Others have used voluntary relationships, such as friendship or citizenship, to exemplify the caring orientation (Friedman, 1989; Liedtka, 1996). In each case, individuals are thought to be interdependent and connected to each another. That is, they have the attitude expressed by the phrase, "We are all in this together, whether we like it or not." With regards to business people, Nash wrote (1993), "If you are relationship-oriented, you automatically measure and motivate yourself with reference to the state of affairs between you and the other person, be it customer, employee, shareholder, supplier, distributor, or the public" (p. 110).

When caring people who view the world through a lens of relationships think about what to do in a situation, they do not think in abstract terms such as, "What should I do for a friend?" or "How should I treat a customer?" Instead, caring people concretize (Noddings, 1984). Concretization is an awareness of particulars. Caring people capable of concretization have the ability to put other people at the center of their attention and to understand each individual's unique perspective and special situation. Caring people can mentally put others on their agenda for that person's own sake. By definition, caring people are not egoists; that is, they are not people who are motivated only out of self-interest. They are also motivated for others. They care for the other persons, they do not merely care about them (Noddings, 1984). In doing so, caring people are prepared to worry about, have concern for, and respond on another's behalf (Little, 1995; Reich, 1995). They ask, "What should I do for my friend Sam?" or "How should I treat this customer Annabel?"

Caring people concretize through receptive listening, that is, by listening to other people's voices. Voices are linguistic expressions of how individuals see the world and of who they want to be (Gilligan, 1982). People's voices can be heard in their writing and in their oral communication. For example, when I tell you about an argument I had with my boss, I voice my underlying views about myself and my boss through intonations, particular word usage, and so on. There are different paradigms, that is, different ways of understanding one's self and one's world, so there are different voices.

Receptive listening is a good tool for caring people who try to concretize different voices because it is not based on the assumption that each person

---

In addition to Gilligan, Noddings (1984) and many other philosophers and social scientists made important contributions to the ethic of care literature. See Puka's (1994) moral development compendium to reference many of these works.

is like everyone else. Receptive listening involves putting one's own paradigm aside and being able to receive other voices, that is, see others for who they are. Receptive listening allows the caring person to particularize and, thus, concretize other people. For example, when you, as a caring person, hear me tell a story about an argument with my boss, you are able to put your own beliefs aside about my boss, me, and how our relationship should be. You do not assume that all bosses, all subordinates, and all boss–subordinate relationships are alike. You are able to hear my voice and to understand from my perspective what is happening in the situation. You are able to concretize, that is, to see me as a particular subordinate with particular needs.

A lens of relationships and a concretized way of knowing supports a morality of relationships and responsibility. Caring people try to do no harm. They voice their moral problems by talking about attachment and detachment, or staying together or not. Under this framework, caring people understand that autonomy means freedom to maintain caring relationships where people are valued for their own sakes. Caring people find freedom or personal autonomy problematic when autonomy is understood as being free from restraint in order to act independently. This sense of autonomy is problematic because it does not presuppose that individual people are, at their cores, related to each other.

Caring people see that maintaining relationships requires accepting moral responsibilities. Caring people have broad moral domains because, whether relationships arise at the interpersonal or social level, moral responsibilities (ethics) matter. Moreover, caring people do not think in terms of universal moral responsibilities, but of responsibilities contingent on the particular people in the particular situation. For example, the responsibilities I have to one of my coworkers is not the same as the responsibilities I have to a different coworker because each friend has unique needs and desires. If two coworkers are in the hospital in my town, I may have the responsibility to visit only one because only she wants visitors when she is sick; if the second coworker hates visitors when she is ill, it is inappropriate to talk about a responsibility to visit her.

In summary, caring people have been characterized by their perspective on the world. They have a relational, interdependent orientation. They understand themselves through their relationships with other people and the world. They tend to use receptive listening to understand others. They concretize by putting other people on their agenda and seeing them for the unique people they are. Caring people are concerned for others. They seek to do no harm. They understand freedom as the freedom to develop and maintain relationships with others. They understand morality or ethics as the art of maintaining caring relationships. Caring people do not tend to think in terms of universal moral obligations. They see morality everywhere and think that their moral responsibilities arise from their particular relationships.

It is not enough to have a caring perspective in order to be a caring person. A perspective must also motivate action (Gilligan, 1982; Koehn, 1994; Noddings, 1984). One reason for selecting for caring people when hiring managers is the way caring people act.

WHY ORGANIZATIONS SHOULD SELECT
FOR CARING MANAGERS

The concept of a caring person is useful for selecting good managers. Caring people are good citizens (Ferguson, 1984). Corporations need good organizational citizens who are, according to Organ (1988), conscientious, altruistic, sportsmanlike, courteous, and who have civic virtue. We believe that the scenarios at the beginning of this article can be used to demonstrate that being a good organizational citizen makes sense if viewed in light of an ethic of care.

Scenario 1: Conscientious Managers. Caring managers are primarily concerned about maintaining strong, enabling relationships in the workplace. They are interested in fulfilling their role responsibilities, for example, relaying reports, because they see that it builds strong, trusting relationships.

Scenario 2: Altruistic Managers. Caring people are able to put others on their agenda and thus, by definition, are altruistic. Caring managers think about the particular people they supervise (concretize). They create incentive programs to fulfill the specific needs of their subordinates, sometimes forsaking their own interests. However, caring managers are aware of their capacities and are able to calibrate their level of care to the situation (Moberg, 1994).

Scenario 3: Managers Who Are Good Sports. Caring managers are able to listen to the concerns of particular upper level managers (through concretization and receptive listening) and think of creative ways to handle upper management's rejection of a proposal. Caring managers realize that maintaining relationships with upper level managers requires enabling: behaviors that include soothing tempers, boosting confidence, fueling pride, preventing frictions, and mending ego wounds (Moberg, 1994). Caring managers must preserve the possibility of future caring if they can.

Scenario 4: Courteous Managers. Caring managers are interested in maintaining healthy relationships. They have a broad moral domain in that actions seen as outside the scope of morality by most people are seen by them as important ways to maintain enabling relationships. Caring people worry about being courteous and honest because they think that these behaviors build trust and respect.

Scenario 5: Managers With Civic Virtue. Caring managers understand themselves as part of a community. They enjoy the freedom to maintain relationships. Caring managers automatically help their colleagues and subordinates when they are in need. They actively contribute to their organizations even when their job descriptions do not dictate it. Caring managers do what they can.

In addition to being good organizational citizens, there are two other reasons why organizations should seek out caring managers. First, the business world is becoming increasingly interconnected and interdependent (Wicks, Gilbert, & Freeman, 1994). Business deals are done across the world using telephones, e-mail, and faxes. Strategic alliances are on the upswing (Bergsman, 1996; Lanciault & Wintersteller, 1996). Businesses, governments, and citizen groups seek each other's help to create healthy, sustainable communities (Stafford & Hartman, 1996). Understanding the connections that bind us together, regardless of culture and regardless of institution, is now essential when doing business. By nature, managers who hold individualistic views and an isolated view of their businesses will find that they are at a disadvantage in this new world environment. Such managers will even find that they are ineffective in their business dealings (Wicks, Gilbert, & Freeman, 1994; Nash, 1993). Caring managers, by nature, understand themselves and their world relationally. Their paradigm is one of interdependence and interconnectedness. They are more trusting of others and interested in maintaining relationships (Dobson & White, 1995). Caring managers fit into the new world environment and, thus, are advantageous for business.

Second, businesses today experience instability and exist in unpredictable environments (Bassi, Benson, & Cheney, 1996; Malone, Morton, & Halperin, 1996). The strength of caring managers is in their responsiveness and adaptability in such a world (Nash, 1993). Caring persons, by the very fact that they are caring, are prepared to listen receptively and be responsive to different voices in a situation. They concretize and seek to understand the particular others. This way of knowing allows them to discover what is relevant rather than impose preconceived notions about people and their environment into a situation. They are able to adapt to unpredictable situations and act in relevant fashions, in a way a principled person is not.

In summary, organizations should select for caring managers. By selecting caring managers, organizations get good citizens. Caring managers have worldviews that are appropriate to the contemporary business scene. Caring managers are responsive, adaptable, and open.

HOW TO SELECT FOR CARING MANAGERS

Earlier in this chapter we stated that, with the exception of some personality-based integrity tests and certain personality characteristics tests (Barrick & Mount, 1991; Sackett, Burris, & Callahan, 1989), most selection techniques aimed at contextual activities allow us to make but a rough cut aimed at eliminating potential criminals among job candidates. But, we have argued that some contextual activities, specifically, organizational citizenship, are relevant hiring considerations. Businesses should try to hire good organizational citizens by selecting for caring managers. How can business select for caring managers? Two interesting approaches that deserve discussion have come to the forefront.

First, Gilligan and her research team have developed a voice-centered, relational interview method for doing psychological research (Brown, Tappan, Gilligan, Miller, & Argyris, 1989). This method is an attempt to capture the relational voice, that is, a perspective of connection to and attachment with others. In such interviews, comments are taped and notes are taken. During the interview process, the interviewer does not merely ask a set of predetermined questions. The interviewer initiates a discussion and then follows the lead of the interviewee, seeking to learn about the interviewee. After the interview, the interviewer listens to the audiotapes and reads the transcripts of the interview four times. The first time, the interviewer listens for plot—to the who, what, where, when, and why of the events voiced by a distinct individual. The second time, the interviewer listens to body—to the interviewees' expressions of what they think of themselves. The third time, the interviewer listens to the way relationships are described—from the perspective of the interviewee. The fourth time, the interviewer listens to the way relationships are described—from the perspective of the social and cultural context (Brown & Gilligan, 1992; Twohey & Volker, 1993).

The voice-centered interview method allows an interviewer to distinguish whether an interviewee understands relationships in narrow distorted ways, as opportunities for abuse, subordination, or violence; or as ways to become more healthy, satisfied, and free (Brown & Gilligan, 1992). The voice-centered interview method can help an interviewer determine whether interviewees are caring or not, as well as their level of care perspective.

There are three difficulties with using the voice-centered interview for managerial selection. The first is its inefficiency. The task of listening to audiotapes and transcripts of 30 to 45 minute interviews four times is extremely time consuming and, therefore, costly on a per capita basis (W. Pinch, personal communication, August 2, 1996). Because the overall utility of any selection technique is affected by its cost (Cascio, 1991b), this problem must be addressed before the voice-centered interview can be used in any significant way in a business context.

The second difficulty relates to the skill level required of the interviewer. The person charged with interpreting interview feedback needs to be highly trained to be sensitive to the cues used to pick up the voice actually being expressed by the interviewee. This means that a relatively small number of persons would be qualified to administer the voice-centered interview. It would be costly for individual companies to have such trained people on their staffs; it is likely that a consultant would have to be employed instead, and this would be costly, too.

The third difficulty with the voice-centered interview as a selection method is a legal problem. Defensible selection procedures ensure procedural justice by using uniform selection techniques across all candidates (Gatewood & Feild, 1990; Heneman & Heneman, 1994). But, the voice-centered interview would have us ask different questions of each interviewee, because it involves pursuing discussions with individual candidates in whatever direction they might lead.

This procedural justice problem was reduced to some extent when Skoe refined the voice-centered interview (Skoe & Diessner, 1994; Skoe & Marcia, 1991). Skoe's method, called the Ethic of Care Interview (ECI), uses a structured, rather than open-ended, interview format, and provides a scoring scale for the interviewer. The ECI consists of four interpersonal moral dilemmas (one self-generated and three prescribed). After each dilemma is described, the interviewee must answer the questions, "What should [name of the hypothetical person facing the dilemma] do? Why?" (Skoe & Diessner, 1994, p. 276). The interviewer then interprets the content of test takers' responses to determine their levels of care perspective, using a 5-point scale: 1, *caring only for self to ensure survival*; 1.5, *some acknowledgment of responsibility to others*; 2, *caring as self-sacrificing for others*; 2.5, *transition from conventional to reflective care perspective*; and 3, *caring for both self and others.*

The ECI takes approximately 30 minutes to administer and about the same amount of time to score. The interview protocol is not proprietary, so there is no per capita fee for its use. It is both time and cost efficient, requires less training on the part of interviewers (although they would have to have some training to do the content analysis called for by the method), and does not suffer from the procedural justice problem that Gilligan's original voice-centered interview does.

AGENDA FOR FUTURE RESEARCH

Future Generations of the ECI

If, as we have argued, we should hire good organizational citizens who encompass a caring attitude, the methods for identifying who they are must undergo further development. Although the ECI shows promise, it needs to become even easier to use. A test must be devised that measures mature caring attitudes in the same way Rest (1979) developed a group-administered, computer-scored test to measure mature justice attitudes. This could be accomplished by doing what Yacker and Weinberg (1990) did for their Moral Orientation Scale: They provided a set of potential responses to the interpersonal dilemmas and presented the responses in a multiple-choice format, so that administrators could use it effectively with even less training. The ECI must undergo further scrutiny. Still in the early stages of development, it has been used in research contexts only and not to predict future behavior in the direct sense that employee selection procedures must do. The reliability of assessment made using this technique needs to be established. Studies must be conducted to confirm the construct validity of the measure and to explore its criterion-related validity (i.e., its accuracy in predicting OCBs) in an employee selection context.

Exploring the Relationship Between Caring and OCB

Earlier in this chapter, we made the case that a caring perspective is exhibited in OCBs. Once it is possible to reliably and validly measure the degree to which individuals hold a caring perspective, the relationship of care to OCB should be empirically explored. There is some precedent for believing that moral orientation has an effect on motivation and behavior (Staub, 1986). Establishing the link, quantitatively, between a caring perspective and organizational citizenship behavior will be necessary to justify its use in an employee selection context.

Exploring Different Notions of Caring
and Parallel Constructs

Personality inventories that have scales for measuring caring and related constructs do exist. For example, the Occupational Personality Questionnaire has a caring scale (Sweetland & Keyser, 1986); the Adult Personality Inventory has a caring scale (Conoley & Impara, 1995), and the California Psychological Inventory has a scale for empathy (Murphy, Conoley, & Impara, 1994). Although the titles of these scales are intriguing, the scales measure emotions. This stops short of characterizing care in the Gilligan sense, that is, as having an overarching ethical attitude or perspective. However, these measures of caring, empathy, and so on, may ultimately have a role to play in fleshing out a complete picture of the caring managerial candidate. Further conceptual analysis of a perspective of care must be completed in order to clarify the picture of a caring manager. Empirical testing needs to be conducted to discover the relationship of the emotions of caring, empathy, and so on, to a caring orientation. Such testing will reveal the value of existing personality scales as part of a battery of assessment tools that could be used to find caring managers.

Alternatives to Selection

Consistent with the time-honored nature versus nurture debate, there have always been two ways for organizations to get employees to exhibit desired behaviors: either select people who already know how to behave in the desired way or train them. Sometimes, it isn't possible to hire people who can do, right at the moment of hiring, the exact things that they are wanted to be able to do on the job at a later date. So, hire people who represent the best raw material available, and train or develop them to meet specifications. This may also be true of caring. Because caring is a perspective (a way of seeing the world) and not a stable dispositional characteristic like a personality trait, there should be ways to train people to have a caring perspective and to implement it in their behavior. For example, the University of Minnesota School of Nursing has developed a learning model that uses role playing, clinical experiences, and discussions of cases to help instill a strong sense of caring and justice in their nursing students (Duckett & Ryden, 1994). The success of this and other training programs should be documented and disseminated.

Innovative teaching techniques should also be explored. For example, Wells and Kracher (1993) advocated a technique called DESC (Describe the situation, Express how you feel, Specify what can be done, and state rewarding Consequences from the change; Bower & Bower, 1976) for assertiveness training to help victims bring about a change from sexually harassing behavior. Because assertive communication may be needed to act on one's caring perspective, for example, to persuade your boss to maintain a long standing relationship with a vendor regardless of contractual or efficiency concerns, DESC is a valuable technique. Furthermore, DESC could be adapted to bring about a more caring attitude on the part of employees. DESC could be used during training sessions to help people understand and manage a particular ethical problem from a caring perspective. They could be taught how to describe objectively a problematic situation brought about or exacerbated by a noncaring manager; how to express to the manager the feelings of those involved; how to specify what could be done instead (by a caring manager in the same situation); and how the rewarding consequences would be achieved that way. The DESC model may be a valuable technique for inducing a mature caring perspective (a transition from Level 1 care through Level 2 and on to Level 3), as described by Gilligan and measured by Skoe.

Finally, there may be ways other than training to develop a caring perspective in a manager. The organizational challenge will be to find internal structures, policies, and mechanisms that can nurture a caring environment and promote and sustain caring managers (Wicks, 1996).

CONCLUSION

This chapter explored what organizations can do to hire good managers. Our thesis, that organizations can get good managers by selecting organizational citizens who convey a caring perspective, was supported by defining what it means to be caring, showing how being a good organizational citizen makes sense if we view the behavior in light of an ethic of care, and suggesting ways for selecting caring managers.

REFERENCES

Asher, J., & Sciarrino, J. (1974). Realistic work sample tests: A review. *Personnel Psychology, 27*, 519–533.

Barrick, M. R., & Mount, M. K. (1991). The big five personality dimensions and job performance: A meta-analysis. *Personnel Psychology, 44*, 1–26.

Bassi, L. J., Benson, G., & Cheney, S. (1996). The top ten trends. *Training & Development, 50*(11), 28–42.

Bergsman, S. (1996). Strategic alliances: Tying the knot for a stronger future. *National Real Estate Investor, 30*, 87–93.

Borman, W. C., & Motowidlo, S. J. (1993). Expanding the criterion domain to include elements of contextual performance. In N. Schmitt & W. C. Borman & Associates (Eds.), *Personnel selection in organizations* (pp. 71–98). San Francisco: Jossey-Bass.

Bowen, D. E., Ledford, G. E., Jr., & Nathan, B. R. (1991). Hiring for the organization, not the job. *Academy of Management Executive, 5*, 35–51.

Bower, S. A., & Bower, G. H. (1976). *Asserting yourself: A practical guide for positive change.* Reading, MA: Addison-Wesley.

Brown, M. L., & Gilligan, C. (1992). *Meeting at the crossroads.* New York: Ballantine.

Brown, M. L., Tappan, M. B., Gilligan, G., Miller, B. A., & Argyris, D. E. (1989). Reading for self and moral voice: A method for interpreting narratives of real-life moral conflict and choice. In M. J. Packer & R. B. Addison (Eds.), *Entering the circle: Hermeneutic investigation in psychology* (pp. 141–164). Albany: State University of New York Press.

Caldwell, D. F., & O'Reilly, C. A., III. (1990). Measuring person–job fit with a profile comparison process. *Journal of Applied Psychology, 15*, 648–657.

Cascio, W. F. (1991a). *Applied psychology in personnel management* (4th ed.). Englewood Cliffs, NJ: Prentice-Hall.

Cascio, W. F. (1991b). *Costing human resources: The financial impact of behavior in organizations.* Boston: PWS-Kent.

Chatman, J. A. (1989). Improving interactional organizational research: A model of person-organizational fit. *Academy of Management Review, 14*, 333–349.

Conoley, J. C., & Impara, J. C. (Eds.). (1995). *The twelfth mental measurements yearbook.* Lincoln, NE: Buros Institute.

de Wolff, C. J. (1993). The prediction paradigm. In H. Schuler, J. L. Farr, & M. Smith (Eds.), *Personnel selection and assessment* (pp. 253–261). Hillsdale, NJ: Lawrence Erlbaum Associates.

Derry, R. (1996). Toward a feminist firm: Comments on John Dobson and Judith White. *Business Ethics Quarterly, 6,* 102–109.

Dobson, J., & White, J. (1995). Toward the feminine firm: An extension to Thomas White. *Business Ethics Quarterly, 5,* 464–478.

Duckett, L. J., & Ryden, M. B. (1994). Education for ethical nursing practice. In J. R. Rest & D. Narvaez (Eds.), *Moral development in the professions* (pp. 51–69). Hillsdale, NJ: Lawrence Erlbaum Associates.

Ferguson, K. (1984). *The feminist case against bureaucracy.* Philadelphia: Temple University Press.

Friedman, M. (1989). Feminism and modern friendship: Dislocating the community. *Ethics, 99,* 275–290.

Gatewood, R. D., & Feild, H. S. (1990). *Human resource selection.* Chicago: Dryden.

Gilligan, C. (1982). *In a different voice.* Cambridge, MA: Harvard University Press.

Gilligan, C. (1987). Moral orientation and moral development. In E. F. Kittay & D. T. Meyers (Eds.), *Women and moral theory* (pp. 19–33). Totowa, NJ: Rowan & Littlefield.

Harvey, R. J. (1990). Job analysis. In M. D. Dunnette & L. M. Hough (Eds.), *Handbook of industrial and organizational psychology* (2nd ed., Vol. 2, pp. 71–163). Palo Alto, CA: Consulting Psychologists Press.

Heneman, H. G., & Heneman, R. L. (1994). *Staffing organizations.* Middleton, WI: Mendota House.

Hume, D. (1748/1983). In J. B. Schneewind (Ed.), *An enquiry concerning the principles of morals.* Indianapolis, IN: Hackett Publishing.

Jones, J. W., & Terris, W. (1991). Selection alternatives to the preemployment polygraph. In J. W. Jones (Ed.), *Preemployment honesty testing* (pp. 39–52). New York: Quorum Books.

Koehn, D. (1994). With a different ear: Hearing Gilligan anew. *Southwest Philosophy Review, 10,* 77–86.

Lanciault, D., & Wintersteller, E. (1996). Strategic combinations. *Oil & Gas Investor* (Special Report Supplement, Third Quarter), 6–10.

Larrabee, M. J. (Ed.). (1993). *An ethic of care: Feminist and interdisciplinary perspectives.* New York: Routledge.

Liedtka, J. M. (1996). Feminist morality and competitive reality: A role for an ethic of care? *Business Ethics Quarterly, 6,* 179–200.

Little, M. O. (1995). Seeing and caring: The role of affect in feminist moral epistemology. *Hypatia, 10,* 117–137.

Malone, T. W., Morton, M. S. S., & Halperin, R. R. (1996). Organizing for the 21st century. *Strategy & Leadership, 24,* 6–10.

Miner, J. B., & Brewer, J. F. (1976). The management of ineffective performance. In M. D. Dunnette (Ed.), *Handbook of industrial and organizational psychology* (pp. 995–1029). Chicago: Rand McNally.

Moberg, D. J. (1994). An ethical analysis of hierarchical relations in organizations. *Business Ethics Quarterly, 4,* 205–220.

Murphy, L. L., Conoley, J. C., & Impara, J. C. (Eds.). (1994). *Tests in print IV: Vol. 1.* Lincoln, NE: Buros Institute.

Nash, L. L. (1993). *Good intentions aside: A manager's guide to resolving ethical problems.* Boston: Harvard Business School Press.

Noddings, N. (1984). *Caring.* Berkeley: University of California Press.

Ones, D. S., Viswesvaran, C., & Schmidt, F. L. (1993). Comprehensive meta-analysis of integrity test validities: Findings and implications for personnel selection and theories of job performance [Monograph]. *Journal of Applied Psychology, 78,* 679–703.

Organ, D. W. (1988). *Organizational citizenship behavior: The good soldier syndrome.* Lexington, MA: Lexington Books.

Puka, B. (Ed.). (1994). *Moral development* (Vol. 6). New York: Garland.

Reich, W. T. (1995). Care. In W. T. Reich (Ed.), *Encyclopedia of bioethics* (pp. 319–344). New York: Simon & Schuster.

Rest, J. (1979). *Development in judging moral issues.* Minneapolis: University of Minnesota Press.

Roberson, C. (1986). *Preventing employee misconduct: A self-defense manual for businesses.* Lexington, MA: Lexington Books.

Sackett, P. R., Burris, L. R., & Callahan, C. (1989). Integrity testing for personnel selection: An update. *Personnel Psychology, 42,* 491–529.

Schneider, B. (1978). Person–situation selection: A review of some ability-situation interaction research. *Personnel Psychology, 31,* 281–297.

Skoe, E. E., & Diessner, R. (1994). Ethic of care, justice, identity, and gender: An extension and replication. *Merrill-Palmer Quarterly, 40,* 272–289.

Skoe, E. E., & Marcia, J. E. (1991). A measure of care-based morality and its relation to ego identity. *Merrill-Palmer Quarterly, 37,* 289–304.

Stafford, E. R., & Hartman, C. L. (1996). Green alliances: Strategic relations between businesses and environmental groups. *Business Horizons, 39,* 50–59.

Staub, E. (1996). A conception of the determinants and development of altruism and aggression: Motives, the self, and the environment. In C. Zahn-Waxler, E. Cummings, & R. Iannotti (Eds.), *Altruism and aggression: Biological and social origins* (pp. 135–164). New York: Cambridge University Press.

Sweetland, R. C., & Keyser, D. J. (Eds.). (1986). *Tests: A comprehensive reference for assessments in psychology, education, and business.* Kansas City, MO: Test Corporation of America.

Twohey, D., & Volker, J. (1993). Listening for the voices of care and justice in counselor supervision. *Counselor Education and Supervision, 32,* 189–197.

Uniform Guidelines on Employee Selection Procedures. (1978). 29 C.F.R. Part 1607.

Wells, D. L., & Kracher, B. J. (1993). Justice, sexual harassment, and the reasonable victim standard. *Journal of Business Ethics, 12,* 423–431.

Wicks, A. C., Gilbert, D. R., & Freeman, R. E. (1994). A feminist reinterpretation of the stakeholder concept. *Business Ethics Quarterly, 4,* 476–497.

Wicks, A. C. (1996). Reflections on the practical relevance of feminist thought to business. *Business Ethics Quarterly, 6,* 523–531.

Yacker, N., & Weinberg, S. L. (1990). Care and justice moral orientation: A scale for its assessment. *Journal of Personality Assessment, 55,* 18–27.

CHAPTER SIX

Punishment in Organizations: Descriptive and Normative Perspectives

Linda Klebe Treviño
The Pennsylvania State University

Gary R. Weaver
University of Delaware

Punishment is an often used but infrequently studied management tool. We define *punishment* as "the manager's application of a negative consequence or withdrawal of a positive consequence from someone under his or her supervision" (Treviño, 1992, p. 649). Given this definition, punishment may include relatively mild actions, such as verbal reprimands, as well as more serious actions, such as withholding a pay raise or bonus, suspending or even terminating an employee. The discussion here begins with a brief review of the once-conventional behaviorist view of punishment in organizations. We then contrast this to current empirical research and theory, which has placed greater emphasis on the context surrounding punishment events and on participants' and observers' cognitive and affective states. Finally, we introduce normative views of punishment adapted from philosophical and criminological writings about punishment in society. These views suggest new ways of thinking about punishment in organizations and new venues for future empirical research.

DESCRIPTIVE/EMPIRICAL PERSPECTIVES

Behaviorism and Organizational Behavior

For many years, the organizational behavior literature represented punishment in organizations from a behaviorist learning theory perspective (Skinner, 1953). Behaviorist-based punishment studies focused on the punishing stimulus and the behavioral response of the punishment target. Behaviorism treated cognitions as scientifically unknowable and, therefore, unworthy of study. Basic principles derived from behaviorist research provided the conventional wisdom about how managers should (and should not) use punishment (e.g., Luthans & Kreitner, 1985). The focus was on the supervisor–subordinate dyad and, in particular, on the subordinate's behavioral reactions to punishment. Managers were advised to refrain from punishing subordinates unless absolutely necessary because punishment would produce unwanted negative side effects (e.g., sabotage). Instead of punishment, managers were advised to use positive reinforcement. Where punishment was unavoidable, managers were to follow a series of principles based on operant conditioning research, principles that would increase the likelihood of behavior change without producing negative side effects. For example, managers were told to be sure that the punishment was timely so that the punished employee would connect the punishment with the undesirable behavior.

Beyond Behaviorist Approaches

Questioning of the conventional wisdom probably began with a celebrated paper by Solomon (1964) in which he reviewed the research on punishment and proposed that Skinner had created a "legend" that punishment didn't work. Skinner (1953) wrote that, in the long run, punishment is disadvantageous to both the punished organism and the punishing agent. Solomon argued that Skinner's conclusions were not based upon the research evidence and had failed to take into account a number of complexities, including the kind and intensity of punishment used, the kinds of subjects, and a number of other factors (cf. Newman, 1985). He called for additional research.

Similarly, in the management literature, Arvey and Ivancevich (1980) observed that "the topic of punishment has received essentially no attention from organizational researchers" (p. 123). They also highlighted the lack of empirical evidence to support the conventional wisdom. Based on key insights learned in various areas of organizational research, they outlined a number of research propositions that pointed toward efforts to come. For example, they explored the importance of the quality of the relationship between the punisher and the punished person as well as the importance of offering a rationale or explanation. In recent years, theorizing and empirical research on punishment in organizations have begun to look more broadly at the social setting surrounding punishment and at the role of cognitions and affect in explaining reactions to punishment (Arvey & Jones, 1980; Ball & Sims, 1991). This is consistent with the general trend toward a more cognitive–affective approach to the study of organizational behavior and toward more complex understandings of the interaction between individual behavior and social context.

Justice Perspectives. The social and organizational justice literatures suggest that subordinates' reactions to punishment are based on justice evaluations that consider both the outcomes (distributive justice) of punishment and the processes by which outcome decisions are made (procedural justice). The underlying thesis argues that employees assess the justice of punishment, and that their reactions to punishment need not be negative if the punishment is perceived to be fair. For example, verbal expressions, such as, "I had it coming," "I asked for it," or "I deserved it," suggest that an individual has taken responsibility for misconduct and has concluded that punishment was justified.

Ball, Treviño, and Sims (1992, 1993, 1994) proposed and found that affective and behavioral reactions to punishment of punished subordinates' are based on evaluations of the distributive and procedural justice characteristics of disciplinary events. In their study, punished subordinates and their supervisors were asked to complete surveys about the same punishment incident. Supervisors were asked to report on the subordinate's postpunishment performance and organizational citizenship behaviors. Punished subordinates reported on their perceptions of the incident and their subsequent attitudinal reactions. The studies (Ball et al., 1993, 1994) find that a distributive characteristic of the punishment, harshness, negatively influenced subsequent performance, perceptions of both distributive and procedural justice, trust in the supervisor, and organizational commitment. Harshness was defined as the subordinate's perception that the punishment was too severe given what others had received and too severe given the misconduct.

Subordinates' perceptions of the procedural aspects of the punishment were also important. Subordinates' perceptions of control—that they had input and that their input was considered—positively influenced citizenship behaviors and satisfaction with the supervisor. Perceptions of arbitrariness (lack of adherence to organizational rules) negatively influenced perceptions of procedural and distributive justice. Perceptions that the punishment was adequately explained also positively influenced perceptions of procedural justice. Perceptions that the supervisor used a constructive, counseling approach with the subordinate positively influenced trust in and satisfaction with the supervisor, and negatively influenced subordinate intentions to leave. In several studies by Baron (1988), destructive approaches to criticism resulted in anger as well as lower goals and self-efficacy. Finally, in the research by Ball and colleagues, the subordinate's perception that the supervisor's demeanor was negative was inversely associated with trust in and satisfaction with the supervisor. In summary, these findings suggest that justice evaluations are extremely important to subordinates' reactions to punishment. Also, they suggest that supervisors can avoid potential negative side effects of punishment by

- matching the severity of the punishment to the severity of the misconduct and making it consistent with what others have received,
- providing the subordinate with input into the punishment decision-making process,
- using a constructive counseling orientation and avoiding negative emotional displays in interactions with the subordinate around the disciplinary event,
- explaining adequately the punishment in a way that clearly ties it to the misconduct,
- following organizational rules.

Clearly, taking justice concerns into account has contributed to our understanding of subordinates' reactions to punishment. This research has provided support for a justice perspective on punishment in organizations. Understanding reactions to punishment requires an examination of how punished employees make sense of what has happened to them and points to an emphasis on cognition in punishment research.

In a broader application of the justice perspective on punishment, Treviño (1992) proposed that punishment in organizations should be conceptualized as a social phenomenon rather than merely a dyadic incident involving a supervisor and a subordinate. When punishment is conceptualized in these broader social terms, observers' evaluations of punishment become important. Based on theorizing and research from the social, organizational, and criminal justice literatures, Treviño (1992) proposed that organizational observers expect wrongdoers to be punished; organization members are disappointed or even outraged when wrongdoers are not disciplined, feeling as if they, rather than the wrongdoers, have been punished. Observers' cognitive, affective, and behavioral reactions are more positive when they perceive that misconduct in the organization is punished fairly. What observers consider to be fair is sometimes surprising. Treviño and Ball (1992) found that observers responded most positively when punishment of ethical rule violators was severe, and they considered the severest punishment (dismissal with legal action) to be the most fair. A number of studies have supported the idea that if observers perceive punishment and other negative outcomes to be fair, they are more likely to express satisfaction, trust, commitment, and lower turnover intention, and their motivation and work performance are likely to be higher (Alexander & Ruderman, 1987; Brockner, DeWitt, Grover, & Reed, 1990; Brockner, Grover, Reed, DeWitt, & O'Malley, 1987; O'Reilly & Puffer, 1989; O'Reilly & Weitz, 1980; Schnake, 1986).

These findings support the notion that punishment can usefully be thought of as a social phenomenon—providing important learning for the entire social group. Moreover, unpunished wrongdoing is a source of moral outrage and perceptions of injustice in the social group. This concern with the broader implications of punishment for larger organization units and for people's sense of justice and injustice further distinguishes recent work in organizational punishment from earlier textbook accounts. Recognition of this broader range of issues also contributes to our ability to provide managers with realistic and useful advice.

A recent qualitative study of managers' reactions to their own experiences with punishment (Butterfield, Treviño, & Ball, 1996) finds that managers are actually quite aware of these justice concerns. Seventy-six managers were interviewed and asked to discuss an "effective" and an "ineffective" punishment incident. The results suggested a number of justice-related concerns. First, managers took subordinates' justice reactions into account when deciding whether and how much to punish the subordinate. Also, in support of a more cognitive approach, managers talked about the fact that employees sometimes accepted responsibility for their misconduct and expected to be disciplined for what they did. Furthermore, managers recognized the social implications of punishment. They were aware that their other subordinates expected them to punish misconduct and that doing so was perceived to be fair. Managers also expressed their own justice concerns when making decisions about whether and how to punish. They discussed issues of equity and severity as well as constructiveness, privacy, and timing. Interestingly, they talked most about the importance of following prescribed punishment procedures. Managers seemed to be more concerned about procedural justice than they were about the distributive issues that appear to be most important for punished subordinates' attitudes and behaviors (Ball et al., 1993, 1994).

Expansion of punishment research to include the broader social environment, justice concerns, and the manager has contributed significantly to our understanding of punishment from a descriptive–empirical perspective. Yet, many questions remain about how managers can balance individual learning, satisfaction, and justice evaluations with work group learning and justice evaluations, and with managers' own needs and concerns. Additional research will be needed to address these complex issues. For example, the punished employee and the work group may react differently to specific punishments. Are there circumstances under which the manager should be concerned more with the particular employee or with the group? Or, is there some ideal level of punishment or approach to punishment that produces the best combination of reactions from punished subordinates and observers?

Social Context Issues. Future research on punishment should consider broadening the focus even more. For example, most of the research has focused on formal punishment within established hierarchical structures. However, much punishment actually occurs more informally as when whistleblowers are ostracized by work group members, or when supervisors use informal means to bring deviant subordinates into line (Fortado, 1994).

In such instances, contextual factors, such as organizational culture, informal norms, and peer-based modes of punishment, may be more important than formal punishment procedures. Furthermore, various forms of self-discipline on the part of employees may make extensive punishment regimes unnecessary in an organization. Grey (1994), for example, argued that the well-defined career tracks in professional accounting firms constitute an internalized system of organizational discipline. Again, more research is needed to understand these alternative approaches to punishment and reactions to them from subordinates, observers, and managers themselves.

Furthermore, research has seldom considered why particular punishment practices are adopted in organizations. Research might, for example, consider how organizational technologies affect systems of punishment. Do certain systems of production make certain modes of punishment necessary, possible, or impossible? Do organizational technologies influence the impact that different modes of punishment have within organizations?

Similar questions may be raised about the impact of extra-organizational context on punishment practice. For example, how do punishment practices diffuse across organizational fields? Consider how the U.S. government recently played an active role in influencing organizations to adopt specific disciplinary practices. Under guidelines imposed in 1991 by the Congressionally chartered U.S. Sentencing Commission, organizations have financial incentives for efforts taken to ensure compliance with the law by the organization and its members. Courts are allowed to adjust fines levied for organizational violations of federal law by a factor of up to 80, with the extent of adjustment dependent on the kinds of actions a firm has taken in order to ensure legal compliance. A firm's adoption and application of well-defined penalties for employees who contribute to illegal organizational behavior serves to mitigate the fines to which the offending organization is subject. This requirement of discipline is coupled with other organizational structures and policies (e.g., investigatory offices and procedures), which together constitute the outlines of a disciplinary system.

Finally, cross-cultural differences in individual behavior and societal culture also suggest important new questions about punishment, especially in light of increasing globalization of business. Cultures differ in their standards of justice, members' attachment to organizations, attributions of responsibility, and beliefs about status, authority, and power. For example, national cultures vary in the degree to which they emphasize individualism or collectivism. Individualism subordinates collective purposes to personal goals (Triandis, 1984, 1989; Triandis, Brislin, & Hui, 1988), while collectivism does the opposite. In terms of the implications for punishment in organizations, individualism, with its emphasis on autonomy and competitiveness, encourages an adversarial approach to conflict, whereas collectivism, with its emphasis on collective purposes and group harmony, encourages a conciliatory approach to conflict within the group (Trubinsky, Ting-Toomey, & Lin, 1991). These differences have several implications for the practice of punishment in organizations. First, persons from individualistic cultures may respond more positively to punishment that addresses personal interests, whereas collectivists may respond more positively to punishment that appeals to group norms and interests (Bontempo, Lobel, & Triandis, 1990). Further, where punishment occurs within collectivist societies, it is more likely to be aimed at reaffirming or reestablishing group harmony than is characteristic in individualistic cultures. Also, collectivist organizations more commonly may direct punishment toward groups (e.g., work groups, departments) rather than toward individuals.

Cultures also differ in what is referred to as *power distance.* A culture's power distance "indicates the extent to which a society accepts the fact that power in institutions and organizations is distributed unequally" (Hofstede, 1980b, p. 45). High power distance reveals a culture's acceptance of inequality and respect for the bounds of social status or class. High power distance is reflected in hierarchical organizational relationships, such that organizational superiors are treated as irreproachable and entitled to their organizational power. By contrast, low power distance cultures minimize inequalities and de-emphasize status and class roles (Hofstede, 1980a, 1980b). These differences in attitudes toward authority, power, and status can affect the degree to which an organization member is seen as entitled to levy punishment or liable to receive punishment. They also indicate potential variation in the degree to which punishment decisions may be challenged by organization members. Future research on how punishment in organizations relates to national culture could be extremely helpful to global businesses that are attempting to create human resource practices that can cross national borders or that are, at least, sensitive to cultural differences.

In summary, empirical research on punishment in organizations has followed the more general transition of social science research away from early twentieth century behaviorist models and toward increasing emphases on cognition, affect, and the complex interactions of individuals with their social context. Although selected aspects of this broader perspective have received empirical attention (e.g., justice-based reactions to punishment), much thinking in these new areas remains to be tested.

BRIDGING DESCRIPTIVE/EMPIRICAL
AND NORMATIVE PERSPECTIVES

The recent focus on justice in understanding reactions to punishment offers a bridge between descriptive/empirical approaches and normative/prescriptive perspectives because a justice approach to punishment indicates that many parties are concerned about the ethics of punishment (what is right) as well as its instrumental outcomes (what works). Ideas about actual and idealized punishment practices have long occupied social theorists and philosophers. We next turn to some of these as a means of further developing theoretical insights, which may inform future research. Attending more consciously to normative issues may bring to light previously ignored assumptions and may open the door to important venues for further research and greater understanding (Weaver & Treviño, 1994). Because our primary interest here is in informing future empirical research, we do not consider how empirical research might inform normative thinking about punishment in organizations. Nevertheless, we acknowledge that empirical and normative theories may inform each other. This clearly has occurred in regard to societal-level questions of punishment (cf. Braithwaite & Pettit, 1990; Duff & Garland, 1994; Garland, 1990).

Management researchers have not explicitly discussed the normative question of what constitutes just punishment in organizations, perhaps assuming that such concerns were more properly the domain of philosophers and social theorists. For example, empirical researchers often seek to evaluate the effectiveness of various modes of punishment in organizations. But, against what criteria is effectiveness to be judged? What is the point of punishment in organizations—to achieve managerial goals? What about the goals of labor or of society in general? Although these kinds of questions often have been debated in the context of societal crime and punishment, they rarely are explicitly considered in reference to punishment in organizations.

But, normative claims are not entirely alien to descriptive/empirical theories of punishment in organizations, although they are generally assumed rather than openly stated. Consider how the conventional wisdom about punishment in organizations admonished managers not to punish because it wouldn't produce the outcomes they desired—a strictly instrumental- rather than justice-oriented rationale. Management researchers were quick to accept this conventional wisdom, despite its lack of empirical support in work organizations. This acceptance may have occurred because the prescriptions generated by the conventional wisdom were consistent with the underlying assumptions and accepted management values of the human relations movement and its characteristic concern for good relationships between managers and subordinates (see Lawrence, 1987). Prescriptions to avoid punishment and to focus on positive reinforcement were acceptable to management scholars who believed that managers should be engaged in developing their subordinates toward self-actualization. On the other hand, these underlying assumptions and values were not voiced or consciously addressed. In fact, the prescriptions were presented in instrumental terms consistent with a managerial ideology; "avoid punishment because it won't achieve the outcome you desire," not "avoid punishment because it has problematic ethical status or because it is inconsistent with the normative principles of the human relations movement." If pressed to express their beliefs, researchers in the human relations school may have viewed punishment as highly manipulative and, thus, unethical. But, they did not need to reject punishment as a form of control on ethical grounds. Rather, they could argue against punishment on grounds of ineffectiveness without having to face the conflict between their supposed scientific objectivity and their normative beliefs.

NORMATIVE–PRESCRIPTIVE PERSPECTIVES ON PUNISHMENT

We have grouped the normative–prescriptive perspectives on punishment into four general categories: consequentialist, retributive, expressive, and reintegrative. Each suggests important issues and venues for empirical research on punishment in organizations. Furthermore, we consider normative critiques of punishment practices and their implications for empirical research on alternatives to punishment.

Consequentialist Theories of Punishment

Consequentialist theories judge the propriety of punishment in terms of its consequences; put simply, a system of punishment is justified if it generates a better set of consequences than any feasible alternative. Various consequentialist theories differ in terms of what they judge to be good consequences. For classical utilitarians (e.g., Bentham, 1789/1970; Mill, 1863/1971), the good consequences to be achieved are defined in terms of societal happiness or welfare, but other consequentialist standards are possible. In general, consequentialist views are considered forward looking; that is, punishment is justified by its instrumental contribution to some future state of affairs. For example, in popular discussions of punishment, the presumed effectiveness of punishment in incapacitating offenders and deterring others constitutes the consequentialist justification for criminal punishment.

The early management literature adopted the behaviorist understanding of punishment in organizations. With its emphasis on questions of effective punishment and counterproductive side effects, this approach, at least implicitly, embodies a consequentialist view of punishment. Punishment is justified if it achieves the manager's desired outcomes. If the normative rationale for punishment is—as management writings presume—to control, change, or deter actions for organizational ends, it is appropriate for empirical inquiry to focus on the effectiveness of punishment as a means or mechanism of behavioral control, change, or deterrence. But, this is a particularly narrow consequentialist view because organizational ends may conflict with the needs of the individual or of society. What is deemed to be a positive outcome for a particular manager or organization may represent a negative outcome for society as a whole. Therefore, consequentialist theories require a broader perspective on the consequences that matter. A particular manager's need to control a particular subordinate's conduct may pale in comparison with the potential consequences for the work group, the organization, and the society. Previous research that has broadened the study of punishment beyond the superior–subordinate dyad, then, would seem to be on the right track. But, in addition to organizational observers, consequences for societal observers need to be considered, especially given that practices internal to an organization can affect its overall societal legitimacy.

Critics of the consequentialist outlook typically argue that it takes an unjustifiably manipulative approach, treating the offender as an object of others' wishes rather than as a subject worthy of respect. In the extreme, critics claim that consequentialism justifies punishment of innocents for the sake of some good consequence. Not surprisingly, current consequentialist views of punishment therefore limit what may be done for the sake of beneficial consequences (e.g., no punishment of innocents; Hart, 1968). But even with those limits, consequentialism is still criticized on grounds that the offender is not treated with respect as an agent capable of making moral choices, but rather is treated as an object whose moral choices can be ignored for the sake of producing some consequence judged beneficial by others.

In organizational contexts, one might reject these criticisms on the grounds that work organization members to some degree surrender claims to respectful treatment on joining an organization. However, empirical research discussed earlier suggests that organization members expect fair treatment for themselves and others. So, regardless of the outcome of philosophical debates about the propriety of consequentialist punishment, organizations still need to account for their members' nonconsequentialist justice expectations. Although some kinds of justice expectations may be held in abeyance (e.g., it may be fair to distribute some resources within organizations in ways that are unfair outside organizations; it may be fair procedurally for the military to use different means of discipline than are used in civilian life), not all such concerns are left at the door upon entering an organization. Future empirical research should consider the conditions under which organization members leave some, but not other, justice expectations at the door when they join a work organization.

Retributive Theories of Punishment

The most prominent nonconsequentialist views of punishment are retributive theories. Whereas consequentialist views are essentially forward looking—justifying punishment by future consequences—retributive views are backward looking, justifying punishment on the grounds that an offender's past actions deserve a particular punishment, as when someone argues that convicted murderers deserve to die. Thus, from a retributive perspective, punishment constitutes the just desert appropriate to an offense. To some theorists, retribution is required as a kind of balance for improper actions (cf. Ellis, 1995; von Hirsch, 1985). For others, retribution is needed because offenders take unfair advantage of others who do not violate the behavioral standards of a social system, and punishment proportional to that unfair advantage removes the advantage (Murphy, 1973).

Social justice theorists (Hogan & Emler, 1981) acknowledged the importance of retributive justice concerns and their work informed Treviño's (1992) arguments about the importance of observers' justice evaluations of organizational punishment. People in groups are motivated to maintain social cohesion, and rule violations threaten that cohesion. Group members desire punishment and believe it is just because, when rules have been violated, punishment serves to reinforce the standards and symbolizes the value of conformity to the rules (Blau, 1964). Punishment also makes an example of the rule violator and contributes to the perception of the organization as a place where people get their just deserts (Lerner, 1970). Failure to punish rule violators leaves the behavioral standards open to question and the social order unbalanced. Empirical research based on a retributive justice perspective should consider how organizational observers think about the appropriate match between offenses and punishments, and how they attribute responsibility to offenders.

Expressive Theories of Punishment

Normative theorizing also has focused on the expressive role of punishment (e.g., Feinberg, 1970). At the individual level, punishment may be seen as an expression of outrage and blame (Tunick, 1992), or an expression of the sense that something wrong has been done (von Hirsch, 1985) and should be denounced (Primoratz, 1989). At the collective level, expressive theories have represented punishment as an expression of a community's solidarity in the face of challenge or threat. Expressive theories emphasize the entity issuing the punishment rather than the punishment recipient. Such an outlook is neither traditionally consequentialist nor conventionally retributive; it is not retributive because it looks at and justifies punishment in forward-looking fashion (as opposed to looking back to the offender's action), but yet it is not typically consequentialist because it is the punishment act itself that fulfills the cognitive or affective purpose of punishment rather than some consequence of punishment distinct from the act itself (Duff & Garland, 1994, p. 8).

For punishment in organizations, expressive theories suggest attention to punishment's effects on the affective and cognitive status of managers and observers and suggest a research agenda focused not on the outcomes and justice of punishment but rather on how punishers and observers make sense of a particular incident (Weick, 1979), and their emotional reactions to it. This is similar to the approach taken by Butterfield et al. (1996) in their study of managers' reactions to effective and ineffective punishment incidents.

Reintegrative Reform Theories of Punishment

Punishment also has been justified by a penitential and educative role that reintegrates offenders into a community (Duff, 1986; Hampton, 1984; Reitan, 1996). If we assume a community of individuals united by some set of values, offenses against those values either create a gulf between the offender and that community or reflect a preexisting gulf. Punishment can bridge that gulf, restoring individuals to community by removing the stigma attached to offenders (Reitan, 1996) or by awakening a sense of morality within the offender (Hampton, 1984). When punishment viewed this way is successful, the offender will come to see the punishment as a form of penance (Duff, 1986). Although in a broad sense such views are consequentialist, it is cognitive and affective rather than behavioral consequences that are the focus of attention. But, this time, it is the offender's cognitive and affective reactions that are the focus. We are not aware of any organizational research that has taken this educative, reintegrative perspective. However, given the importance of knowledge workers in loosely structured organizations held together by shared values, future approaches to understanding punishment may benefit from considering reintegrative theories. Can punishment be used to restore the offender to community and to remove any stigma? What approaches to punishment make reintegration effective? Do different forms of punishment vary in information carrying capacity and educative success?

Punishment in this reintegrative sense is thought to require a set of characteristics related to concepts of interactional justice that are discussed in organizational research (Bies, 1986; Bies-Moag, 1986). For example, to be successfully reintegrative and educational, punishment should be carried out with respect and without malice or revenge (Reitan, 1996). This suggests the need for additional empirical research on the interactional aspects of punishment in organizations to complement earlier work by Baron (1988, 1990) and Ball et al. (1994).

Alternatives to Punishment and Alternative Roles of Punishment

Reintegrative theorists acknowledge that conventional punishments in society typically do not achieve reintegrative, penitential, or educative results, but use this as a basis for proposing reforms (Duff, 1986). They ask whether these results can be achieved by other means. The same issue arises in organizations; reintegration may be more achievable by forgiveness, for example, than by punishment, though forgiveness of an offender may risk violating the justice expectations of other organization members unless forgiveness is ritualized in the organizational culture. Similar implications arise from other normative critiques of conventional punishment practices. Might morally desirable consequences be achieved by means other than conventional punishments? What alternative forms might exist for expressing societal or group disapproval of certain actions? How might punishment practices be altered so that people indeed receive their just deserts rather than an underservedly mild or harsh punishment? Applied to an organizational context, each critique suggests an empirical research program aimed at discovering optimal ways to achieve the normatively based purpose of punishment.

The possibility of effective alternatives to punishment also suggests that existing punishment practices may embody latent organizational roles removed from their manifest, official rationale. Rusche and Kircheimer (1939), for example, argue that criminal punishment practices reflect labor market conditions; regimes of punishment constitute means for economic systems to adjust to changing economic conditions, which affect the relative supply of labor and employment. Punishment may also function to divert attention from issues over which key actors in a society or organization are powerless (Matheisen, 1974). We might think similarly about organizational punishment practices. In the manner of scapegoating, punishment constitutes a kind of symbolic management, which reassures organizational members and constituents that something is being done about an organizational problem (Pfeffer, 1981). In this way, punishment also may serve to reinforce existing distinctions of power and status within organizations. Along these lines, future research should consider the more latent roles played by punishment in organizations.

CONCLUSION

Research on punishment in organizations has advanced significantly in recent years through attention to justice cognitions, affect, and the broader social context within which punishment occurs. Our analysis of the descriptive–empirical research suggests that this work needs to expand even more to include more macro-organizational issues (e.g., organizational culture, technology, and culture) and even extra-organizational issues (e.g., national culture, interorganizational fields).

In addition, we took the opportunity to consider a number of normative perspectives on punishment and to consider how they might inform descriptive–empirical work. A number of ideas emerged. A focus on conse-

quentialist theories suggested the need to consider a broader set of consequences than has been considered in the past and the need to understand
more deeply the kinds of justice expectations organization members hold.
Retributive theories led to a whole set of research questions about observers'
reactions to punishment, responsibility attributions, and how observers think
about the appropriate match between offenses and punishments (Treviño,
1992). Expressive theories focused attention on affect, in particular, the affect
of the punisher, which has only begun to be studied empirically (Butterfield
et al., 1996). Reintegrative reform theories pointed to concerns that have
not been addressed in organizational research as far as we know. They
suggested particularly interesting research questions about what punishment
practices might work best if reintegration were the goal. Finally, the normative literature suggests that we should also consider alternatives to punishment and the latent roles punishment may play in organizations.

REFERENCES

Alexander, S., & Ruderman, M. (1987). The role of procedural and distributive justice in organ-
 izational behavior. *Social Justice Research, 1,* 177–198.
Arvey, R. D., & Ivancevich, J. M. (1980). Punishment in organizations: A review, propositions,
 and research suggestions. *Academy of Management Review, 5,* 123–132.
Arvey, R. D., & Jones, A. P. (1985). The use of discipline in organizational settings: A framework
 for future research. In B. Staw & L. L. Cummings (Eds.), *Research in organizational behavior*
 (Vol. 7, pp. 367–408). Greenwich, CT: JAI.
Ball, G. A., & Sims, H. P., Jr. (1991). A conceptual analysis of cognition and affect in organizational
 punishment. *Human Resource Management Review, 1,* 227–243.
Ball, G. A., Treviño, L. K., & Sims, H. P., Jr. (1992). Understanding subordinate reactions to
 punishment incidents: Perspectives from justice and social affect. *Leadership Quarterly, 3*(4),
 307–333.
Ball, G. A., Treviño, L. K., & Sims, H. P., Jr. (1993). Justice and organizational punishment:
 Attitudinal outcomes of disciplinary events. *Social Justice Research, 6*(1), 39–67.
Ball, G. A., Treviño, L. K., & Sims, H. P., Jr. (1994). Just and unjust punishment: Influences on
 subordinate performance and citizenship. *Academy of Management Journal, 37*(2), 299–322.
Baron, R. A. (1988). Negative effects of destructive criticism: Impact on conflict, self-efficacy,
 and task performance. *Journal of Applied Psychology, 73,* 199–207.
Baron, R. A. (1990). Countering the effects of destructive criticism: The relative efficacy of four
 interventions. *Journal of Applied Psychology, 75,* 235–245.
Bentham, J. (1789/1970). *An introduction to the principles of morals and legislation* (J. H.
 Burns & H. L. A. Hart, Eds.). London: Methuen.
Bies, R. J. (1986). The predicament of injustice. In B. M. Staw & L. L. Cummings (Eds.), *Research
 in organizational behavior* (Vol. 9, pp. 290–318). Greenwich, CT: JAI.
Bies, R. J., & Moag, J. S. (1986). Interactional justice: Communications criteria of fairness. In
 R. J. Lewicki, B. H. Sheppard, & M. H. Bazerman (Eds.), *Research on negotiations in
 organizations* (Vol. 1, pp. 43–55). Greenwich, CT: JAI.
Blau, P. M. (1964). *Exchange and power in social life.* New York: Wiley.
Bontempo, R., Lobel, S., & Triandis, H. (1990). Compliance and value internalization in Brazil
 and the U.S. *Journal of Cross-Cultural Psychology, 21,* 200–213.

Braithwaite, J., & Pettit, P. (1990). *Not just deserts: A republican theory of criminal justice.* Oxford, England: Oxford University Press.

Brockner, J., DeWitt, R. L., Grover, S., & Reed, T. (1990). When it is especially important to explain why: Factors affecting the relationship between managers' explanations of a layoff and survivors' reactions to the layoff. *Journal of Experimental Social Psychology, 26,* 389–407.

Brockner, J., Grover, S., Reed, R., DeWitt, R. L., & O'Malley, M. (1987). Survivors' reactions to layoffs: We get by with a little help for our friends. *Administrative Science Quarterly, 32,* 526–541.

Butterfield, K. D., Treviño, L. K., & Ball, G. A. (1996). Punishment from the manager's perspective. A grounded investigation and inductive model. *Academy of Management Journal, 39,* 1479–1512.

Duff, R. A. (1986). *Trials and punishments.* Cambridge, England: Cambridge University Press.

Duff, R. A., & Garland, D. (1994). Introduction: Thinking about punishment. In R. A. Duff & D. Garland (Eds.), *A reader on punishment* (pp. 1–143). Oxford, England: Oxford University Press.

Ellis, A. (1995). Recent work on punishment. *The Philosophical Quarterly, 45,* 225–233.

Feinberg, J. (1970). The expressive function of punishment. In *Doing and deserving: Essays in the theory of responsibility* (pp. 95–118). Princeton: Princeton University Press.

Fortado, B. (1994). Informal supervisory social control strategies. *Journal of Management Studies, 31*(2), 251–274.

Garland, D. (1990). *Punishment and modern society.* Chicago: University of Chicago Press.

Gorovitz, S. (Ed.). (1863/1971). *Utilitarianism: Text with critical essays.* Indianapolis, IN: Bobbs-Merrill.

Grey, C. (1994). Career as a project of the self and labor process discipline. *Sociology, 28,* 479–498.

Hampton, J. (1984). The moral education theory of punishment. *Philosophy and Public Affairs, 13,* 208–238.

Hart, H. L. A. (1968). Prolegomenon to the principles of punishment. In H. L. A. Hart (Ed.), *Punishment and responsibility* (pp. 1–27). Oxford, England: Oxford University Press.

Hofstede, G. (1980a). *Culture's consequences: International differences in work-related values.* Beverly Hills, CA: Sage.

Hofstede, G. (1980b). Motivation, leadership and organization: Do American theories apply abroad? *Organizational Dynamics, 9,* 42–63.

Hogan, R., & Emler, N. P. (1981). Retributive justice. In M. J. Lerner & S. C. Lerner (Eds.), *The justice motive in social behavior* (pp. 125–143). New York: Plenum Press.

Lawrence, P. (1987). Historical development of organizational behavior. In J. Lorsch (Ed.), *Handbook of organizational behavior* (pp. 1–9). Englewood Cliffs, NJ: Prentice-Hall.

Lerner, M. J. (1970). The desire for justice and reactions to victims. In J. Macauley & L. Berkowitz (Eds.), *Altruism and helping behavior* (pp. 205–229). New York: Academic Press.

Luthans, F., & Kreitner, R. (1985). *Organizational behavior modification and beyond.* Glenview, IL: Scott, Foresman.

Mathiesen, T. (1974). *The politics of abolition.* New York: Wiley.

Murphy, J. G. (1973). Marxism and retribution. *Philosophy and Public Affairs, 2,* 217–243.

Newman, G. (1985). *The punishment response.* New York: Harrow & Heston.

O'Reilly, C. A., III, & Puffer, S. M. (1989). The impact of rewards and punishments in a social context: A laboratory and field experiment. *Journal of Occupational Psychology, 62,* 41–53.

O'Reilly, C. A., III, & Weitz, B. A. (1980). Managing marginal employees: The use of warnings and dismissals. *Administrative Science Quarterly, 25,* 467–483.

Pfeffer, J. (1981). Management as symbolic action. *Research in Organizational Behavior, 3,* 1–52.

Primoratz, I. (1989). *Justifying legal punishment.* Atlantic Highlands, NJ: Humanities Press.

Reitan, E. (1996). Punishment and community: The reintegrative theory of punishment. *Canadian Journal of Philosophy, 26*, 57–82.

Rusche, G., & Kirchheimer, O. (1939). *Punishment and social structure.* New York: Columbia University Press.

Schnake, M. E. (1986). Vicarious punishment in a work setting. *Journal of Applied Psychology, 71*, 343–345.

Skinner, B. F. (1953). *Science and human behavior.* New York: Macmillan.

Solomon, R. L. (1964). Punishment. *American Psychologist, 19*(4), 239–252.

Treviño, L. K. (1992). The social effects of punishment in organizations: A justice perspective. *Academy of Management Review, 17*(4), 647–676.

Treviño, L. K., & Ball, G. A. (1992). The social implications of punishing unethical behavior: Observers' cognitive and affective reactions. *Journal of Management, 18*(4), 751–768.

Triandis, H. C. (1984). A theoretical framework for the more efficient construction of culture assimilators. *International Journal of Intercultural Relations, 8*, 301–330.

Triandis, H. C. (1989). The self and social behavior in differing cultural contexts. *Psychological Review, 96*, 506–520.

Triandis, H. C., Brislin, R., & Hui, C. H. (1988). Cross-cultural training across the individualism-collectivism divide. *International Journal of Intercultural Relations, 12*, 269–289.

Trubinsky, P., Ting-Toomey, S., & Lin, S. (1991). The influence of individualism-collectivism and self-monitoring on conflict styles. *International Journal of Intercultural Relations, 15*, 65–84.

Tunick, M. (1992). *Punishment: Theory and practice.* Berkeley: University of California Press.

von Hirsch, A. (1985). *Past or future crimes: Deservedness and dangerousness in the sentencing of criminals.* New Brunswick, NJ: Rutgers University Press.

Weaver, G. R., & Treviño, L. K. (1994). Normative and empirical business ethics: Separation, marriage of convenience, or marriage of necessity. *Business Ethics Quarterly, 4*(2), 129–143.

Weick, K. (1979). *The social psychology of organizing.* New York: Random House.

CHAPTER SEVEN

Building Organizational Integrity and Quality With the Four Ps: Perspectives, Paradigms, Processes, and Principles

Joseph A. Petrick
Wright State University

The vast research literature in the fields of managing organizational integrity (De George, 1993; Ethics Resource Center, 1994; Le Clair, Ferrell, & Fraedrich, 1998; Paine, 1997; Petrick & Quinn, 1997; Solomon, 1992b) and organizational quality (Bounds, Dobbins, & Fowler, 1995; Evans & Lindsay, 1996; Lindsay & Petrick, 1997; Vroman & Luchsinger, 1994) are often unintegrated in business, education, and management practice. Yet, they exhibit points of parallel convergence that merit conceptual integration in research activities and demonstrate usefulness to practicing managers (Collins & Porras, 1994; Kotter & Heskett, 1992; Posner & Schmidt, 1992).

Too often, however, ethics development and quality improvement initiatives emerge only after a major crisis occurs within a company, in an industry, or as a global disaster (Allinson, 1993; Halfon, 1989; Taylor, 1985). At that time, the reactive, piecemeal task of fixing the problem is delegated to middle managers and technical experts. What is needed at the outset is integrated strategic leadership that simultaneously develops organizational integrity and quality systems to leverage their reciprocal benefits (Bounds et al., 1994; Lindsay & Petrick, 1997).

Quality initiatives obtain their operational power to reduce costs, improve competitiveness, and generate customer value by relying on the soundness of management processes (Bottorff, 1997). Piecemeal quality initiatives will not be sustained without committed integrity at work, and organizational integrity efforts are more likely to be endorsed when linked with quality processes (Bounds et al., 1995; Stahl, 1995). To honor customer demands, courageously acknowledge performance gaps, truthfully monitor process improvements, cooperatively engage in teamwork, and resolutely improve product/service quality while reducing costly variations in a fair manner requires competencies in both ethics and quality at the individual and collective levels (Axelrod, 1984; Paine, 1996; Sims, 1992; Thompson, 1995). The quality capability (QC) and integrity capacity (IC) of firms are both key determinants of organizational performance (Lindsay & Petrick, 1997; Paine, 1994; Petrick & Quinn, 1997; Waters, 1988).

To accelerate the development of those dual capabilities, this chapter focuses on four conceptual parallels useful in the design of organizational integrity and quality efforts. Here, I focus on the marketing mix metaphor of the four Ps (*product, price, promotion,* and *place*) and adapt it to the expanded managerial responsibility for handling the new integrity/quality mix of four Ps (*perspectives, paradigms, processes,* and *principles*). A sharpened awareness of the relationships among the new four Ps can facilitate the implementation of organizational integrity and quality systems by practicing managers and guide scholarly efforts toward more focused, fruitful research projects.

PERSPECTIVES ON ETHICS AND QUALITY
(*THE FIRST P*)

The diverse perspectives adopted or meanings attached to ethics and quality affect managerial decision making by directing attention to different organizational performance areas. Simplistic, narrow interpretations of the domains of integrity and quality produce distorted moral judgments (e.g., believing that a quick, ethics pep talk at work is all that is required to resolve morally complex issues) and suboptimize organizational systems (i.e., advance the interests of one work unit at the expense of the whole organization; Ciulla, 1995; Deming, 1982; Denison, Hoojiberg, & Quinn, 1995). To disclose the perspective dimensions of integrity and quality, therefore, some preliminary generic definitions of key concepts are in order.

First, *ethics* can be defined as the systematic descriptive and normative study of moral awareness, judgment, character, and conduct at all levels of individual and collective activity (Martin, 1995; Rest, 1986). To engage in the study of ethics, however, does not mean that one has integrity. *Integrity* can be defined as the individual and collective process of repeated alignment of moral awareness, judgment, character, and conduct in an appropriate context that demonstrates balanced judgment and promotes sustained moral development (Carter, 1996; McFall, 1987; Petrick & Quinn, 1997). Organizational integrity entails sustained and collective action along four dimensions—judgment, system, process, and development. Each of these dimensions is subsequently treated and affected by the new four Ps. Finally, according to the American National Standard Institute (ANSI) and the American Society for Quality (ASQ), *quality* is the totality of features and characteristics of a product or service that bears on its ability to satisfy given needs (American National Standard Institute/American Society for Quality, 1978; Garvin, 1988).

Although these generic definitions are useful for an overview, they do not pinpoint the five subtle parallel perspectives on ethics and quality that shape managerial judgment in building organizational integrity and quality, as presented in Table 7.1.

In Table 7.1, the Type I *virtue-based* approach to ethics regards moral accomplishment as due to the amount, kind, and degree of cultivated virtue at the individual and collective level (e.g., the extent of individual and organizational justice exhibited in resolving disputes; Moberg, 1997; Slote, 1992; Solomon, 1992a). Ethics initiatives that emphasize character education and organizational readiness to act ethically (i.e., the development of personal and organizational trust, honesty, and justice), reflect this Type I perspective (Kramer & Tyler, 1995; Kupperman, 1989; Murphy, 1993). In a parallel way, the first quality viewpoint emphasizes the *ingredient-based* Type I perspective (Evans & Lindsay, 1996). From this perspective, differences in quality amount to differences in some desired ingredient or input into the product (e.g., milk with butterfat content is regarded as having better quality than milk without butterfat; Garvin, 1988). The difficulty for organizational managers with relying exclusively on the Type I perspective is that ethical character and quality attribute traits may simply be unnecessary, counterproductive, or contextually inappropriate, rather than sure signs of superior desirability.

The Type II *duty-based* approach to ethics emphasizes using proper methods, doing one's duty, adhering to traditional moral rules, respecting rights, and abiding by contractual agreements (e.g., obeying the golden rule or keeping a promise despite adverse organizational consequences; Donaldson & Dunfee, 1994; Dworkin, 1978; Etzioni, 1988; Rawls, 1971). The moral trump card status imputed to this approach by some religious and secular ethicists has often led to the relative neglect of other moral perspectives. The second quality viewpoint emphasizes the *process-based* Type II per-

TABLE 7.1
Perspectives on Ethics and Quality

	Type I	Type II	Type III	Type IV	Type V
Perspectives on ethics	Virtue-based	Duty-based	Result-based	Context-based	Integrity-based
Perspectives on quality	Ingredient-based	Process-based	User-based	System-based	Value-based

spective (Garvin, 1988). This perspective identifies quality as conformance to supply requirements, operational variances, and specification standards. On the design side, this has led to reliability engineering and, on the manufacturing side, to statistical quality control (Lindsay & Petrick, 1997). The difficulty for organizational managers with relying exclusively on the Type II perspective is that a rigid adherence to existing duties will stifle progress in improving overly controlling systems, neglect future opportunities for system change, trivialize adverse consequences of narrow righteousness, promote an extreme sense of due process entitlement and litigious defensiveness, and fail to peacefully resolve ideological and religious duty conflicts (e.g., religious wars; Glendon, 1991, 1994).

The Type III *result-based* approach to ethics regards maximizing beneficial results and minimizing costs for the largest number of individuals as the highest good (i.e., the end justifies the means; Brandt, 1992; Sen & Williams, 1982). Cost–benefit impact statements attached to proposed government regulations, for example, are result-based tactics to anchor and counterbalance duty-based mandates. Likewise, the third quality viewpoint focuses on the *user-based* perspective (Type III; Garvin, 1988). According to this approach, the goods and services that best meet or exceed customer expectations have the highest quality (e.g., books on bestseller lists are high quality because of their sales). The difficulty with organizational managers relying exclusively on Type III perspectives is that they encourage satisfying expectations by any means, avoiding critical evaluation of initial expectations, and discriminating inadequately among customer satisfaction, ethical desirability, and quality standards. For example, books on bestseller lists are clearly preferred by a majority of readers, even though few would agree that they represent the most ethically desirable or highest quality literature available.

The Type IV *context-based* approach to ethics maintains that the nature and extent of supportive environments influence the morality of actions (e.g., extra-organizational regulations, professional association standards, and organizational ethics development systems [OEDS] shape moral action; Cooke & Szumal, 1993; Petrick & Manning, 1990; Victor & Cullen, 1988). Similarly, the *system-based* perspective (Type IV) quality can be defined as the design outcome of externally adapted resources and internally integrated processes (e.g., optimally designed internal system stability within acceptable ranges of variation that meet external international certification standards). The difficulty for organizational managers with relying exclusively on Type IV perspectives is that they depend on the impersonal framework of contextual systems without internalized commitment to principles, offer conflicting views of adequate contextual support, and waste energy and disrupt traditional operational continuity in envisioning future system changes without practical guidance for implementation within current constraints.

The Type V *integrity-based* approach to ethics regards the sustained balancing of virtues, duties, results, and contexts within the constraints of internal and external forces as essential to ethics and, specifically, judgment integrity. *Judgment integrity* is the balanced use of all four types of ethics approaches in the analysis and resolution of moral issues (Petrick & Quinn, 1997). Likewise, the fifth quality viewpoint emphasizes the *value-based* Type V perspective (Garvin, 1988). This perspective identifies quality as the highest degree of excellence possible at an acceptable price, and defines quality as the control of variation at an acceptable cost that enhances customer value (Bounds, Yorks, Adams, & Ranney, 1994; Stahl, 1995). The Type V quality approach provides quality results within price-cost and related constraints (e.g., a $2,000 belt, no matter how well designed, constituted, or made, would not be a quality product, for it would not be perceived as a good value and would, therefore, find few buyers). When this approach is used regularly, managerial and organizational judgment integrity increases and precludes simplistic and unbalanced decisions from prevailing.

It is important, therefore, for managers to be aware of their perspectives regarding ethics and quality, if both organizational integrity and quality capacities are to be simultaneously advanced. Organizational integrity is multidimensional and complex; it will not be achieved by isolated ethics interventions that rely exclusively on Type I through Type IV perspectives. Organizational integrity requires the collective capacity to handle multidimensional moral complexity through balanced judgment and weighted inclusion of all perspectives (Petrick & Quinn, 1997).

PARADIGMS IN ETHICS AND QUALITY (THE SECOND P)

In addition to increasing awareness of their perspectives on ethics and quality, managers need to be aware of their paradigms of ethics and quality in designing organizational structures and accountability systems (Petrick & Manning, 1993). The units held accountable for organizational ethics and quality determine whether responsibility resides within a single detection unit or is a companywide strategy for continually improving system integrity. *System integrity* is the strategic alignment of all ethics policies, processes, and practices to ensure commitment to constant performance within acceptable ranges of variation that meet current standards, exceed expectations, and enhance organizational learning and reputation (Fombrun, 1996; Petrick & Quinn, 1997).

The prospects for achieving system integrity are dependent on the paradigms of ethics and quality adopted by managers, as illustrated in Table 7.2. In Table 7.2, two parallel old and new paradigms of organizational ethics and quality are depicted, with only the last new paradigm leading to system integrity. In the first form of the old paradigm, damage detection, organiza-

TABLE 7.2
Paradigms of Organizational Quality and Organizational Ethics

	Old Paradigm		New Paradigm	
	Damage Detection	*Focused Control*	*Coordinated Assurance*	*Strategic System*
Unit or units accountable for organizational ethics	Security department inspecting-in and detecting wrong-doing after the fact; moral norms maintained by fear of getting caught; high turnover	Legal, accounting, and human resource departments building-in moral norms by selectivity, audits, prosecutions, and/or targeted sanctions	All functional departments designing-in moral norms by companywide programs on compliance with legal, externally imposed standards	All functional departments educating-in moral norms as a collective commitment and strategic priority with benchmarked processes that improve the pace of achieving system integrity
Unit or units accountable for organizational quality	Inspection and shipping departments inspecting-in quality after the fact at the end of the mass production line just before shipping; high rework costs	Engineering, production, and operations departments building-in quality by statistical control of variation and focused fixes of deviations	All functional departments designing-in quality by: preventing costs of poor quality; adhering to companywide decision standards; and use of reliability engineering	All functional departments educating-in quality as a collective commitment and strategic priority with benchmarked processes that accelerate the pace of system improvement

tional ethics is the responsibility of security departments who detect wrong-doing at work and punish bad apples after the fact. The scope of the accountability structure for organizational ethics under this paradigm is extremely narrow (i.e., a single unit), and the reactive response is the moral norm (e.g., surveillance cameras to spot and plainclothes security personnel to apprehend and detain shoplifters). In a parallel manner, organizational quality is inspected-in by a single unit after the production process, but before the product/service goes out the door (e.g., final inspection in the shipping department at the end of an automobile assembly line to eliminate or rework substandard vehicles). The difficulty with the damage detection paradigm in organizational ethics and quality is that normally it is ineffective because it overwhelms the detection resources of a single unit, risks unfair scapegoating because variance ranges are not maintained during the production process, and creates resentment against system integrity.

In the second form of old paradigm, focused control, organizational ethics is builtin by multiple departments through the use of tools (e.g., more selective integrity screening instruments for recruiting, random ethics audits, targeted sanctions for unethical conduct, and prosecutions for severe offenses) to control ethics at work (Ones, Visyvesvaran, & Schmidt, 1993). In the absence of system knowledge of acceptable variation levels, however, managers risk undercontrolling destructive behavior or overcontrolling acceptable conduct (e.g., interpreting any behavioral deviation as statistically significant and overcontrolling acceptable moral variation). The predatory, righteous manager who is always trying to catch someone doing something wrong and who is quick to blame employees for any error, instead of improving the work process that allowed the error to occur, is particularly prone to this lack of integrity.

Similarly, under the focused control paradigm, organizational quality is builtin and customized by multiple departments through the use of statistical quality control tools that identify and maintain upper and lower limits on process variation (Deming, 1982, 1988; Evans & Lindsay, 1996). *Processes*, as sets of interconnected activities that often cut across functional units within a system, can vary from common, natural causes to special, assignable causes. Because variation increases the cost of doing business, statistical quality control tools are used to distinguish one cause from the other (Wheeler, 1993). Because special causes arise from external sources that are not inherent in a process (e.g., a bad batch of material purchased from a supplier, a poorly trained operator, excessive tool wear, or temporary personnel exhaustion), they need to be statistically identified and eliminated. A system governed only by common causes, however, is stable and does not require managerial intervention (Deming, 1982, 1988).

Well-intentioned managers can make two fundamental quality mistakes in attempting to fix a process: (a) treat as a special cause any fault or complaint when it actually came from common causes and (b) attribute to common causes any fault or complaint when it actually came from a special cause. In the former case, managerial tampering with a stable system will actually make matters worse and increase costs. In the latter case, managers can miss the opportunity to eliminate unwanted variation by assuming that it is not controllable (Deming, 1982, 1988; Lindsay & Petrick, 1997). Knowledge of system integrity, therefore, is crucial to ethicists if they are to avoid witch-hunts at work.

The difficulty with the focused control paradigm in organizational ethics and quality is that it limits accountability to a select few department managers and provides them with focused tools that fix certain processes (often scapegoating bad apples along with acceptable, creative, moral individuals) but damage the system as a whole.

In the first form of the new paradigm, coordinated assurance, organizational ethics compliance programs are designed in across all functions to assure conformity with legal and regulatory standards that are externally imposed (e.g., the U.S. Sentencing Guidelines that specify financial benefits for legal compliance and an operational (OEDS) Organizational Ethics Development System), or affirmative action employment regulations followed cross-functionally and measured statistically to preclude unintentional discrimination through disparate impact on protected populations (Fiorelli & Rooney, 1996). In a parallel way, organizational quality is designed in to prevent the costs of poor quality and partial fixes, and to accelerate the link between statistics and engineering, known as reliability engineering, that assures coordinated compliance with government mandated quality standards (Evans & Lindsay, 1996). Cross-functional, internally coordinated processes are the norm to assure the quality of goods/services going to customers.

The difficulty with the coordinated assurance paradigm in organizational ethics and quality is that it is driven by external standards without internalized commitment, is not accorded strategic priority by top leadership, and does not use benchmarked processes to promote organizational learning/global certification and system integrity improvement.

Finally, in the second form of new paradigm, strategic system, organizational ethics is cultivated when top leadership accords strategic importance to building and maintaining collective commitment to an OEDS. The OEDS includes leadership by moral example to guide and align all ethics initiatives, regular organizational ethics needs assessments, ethics training to improve judgment and conduct, ethics enforcement and commendation procedures, audits to monitor organizational moral progress, and benchmarked processes to measure and enhance moral reputation for system integrity (Cohen, 1993; Petrick & Quinn, 1997; Weber, 1993). In a parallel manner, organizational quality is educated in with top leadership, according strategic priority to quality in order to successfully adapt to external challenges, to companywide training to increase organizational learning and build collective commitment to ongoing quality performance improvement, and to benchmarked processes based on comparative data to accelerate the pace of system improvement (Lindsay & Petrick, 1997). This last paradigm is essential for educating in and internalizing the collective commitment to and shared pride in system integrity and quality.

The shift in ethics and quality paradigms from detection and control to coordination and strategic impact is a response to the inadequacies of the old paradigm. Organizations that try to inspect and control ethical conduct and quality performance typically create dysfunctional cultures characterized by predatory management behavior, low employee morale, and poor organizational performance (Cohen & Cohen, 1993; Jackall, 1988). It is only when the last paradigm is adopted that system integrity can become a reality.

PROCESSES IN ETHICS AND QUALITY (*THE THIRD P*)

After knowledge of organizational ethics and quality perspectives and paradigms enhances their judgment and system integrity, managers need to focus on the operational methods or processes they use to implement collective purposes. Unlike traditional managers who use bottom-line performance results as the exclusive indicator of success, building organizational integrity and quality requires managers to achieve a broader, balanced range of process competencies. In fact, *process integrity*, as the repeated alignment of ethical awareness, judgment, motivation, and performance, does not occur without taking more than performance into consideration (Petrick & Quinn, 1997). For organizational integrity and quality it is as important how one achieves goals as that one achieves them at all. Implementing paradigms by illegal and immoral methods or operationally suspect shortcuts jeopardizes both organizational integrity and quality.

Table 7.3 provides a graphic illustration of the parallel ways in which four key processes—awareness, judgment, motivation, and performance— are to be repeatedly aligned for process integrity to occur.

In Table 7.3, the first organizational ethics process is awareness, consisting of ethics perception and sensitivity. Managers increase their ethics awareness by perceiving (i.e., seeing and attending to) the moral issues in a business situation and by being sensitive to (i.e., valuing the significance of) unethical conduct at work. For example, managers with moral attention deficit disorder who are insensitive to the moral offensiveness of sexual harassment at work need ethics training to improve their moral awareness. Similarly, the first organizational quality process is awareness, subdivided into quality perception and sensitivity. Managers also increase their quality awareness by perceiving (i.e., identifying and recognizing) the quality issues in a business

TABLE 7.3
Processes of Organizational Ethics and Organizational Quality

	Awareness	Judgment	Motivation	Performance
Organizational ethics processes	Ethics perception and sensitivity	Ethics analysis and resolution	Readiness to enact ethics	Responsible and sustainable enactment of ethics
Organizational quality processes	Quality perception and sensitivity	Quality analysis and resolution	Readiness to enact quality	Responsible and sustainable enactment of quality

situation and by being sensitive (i.e., according importance) to substandard products, services, or processes. Quality training is a remedy for managerial misperception and insensitivity to organizational quality.

The second organizational ethics process is judgment, consisting of ethics analysis and resolution. Managers increase their ethical judgment by analyzing (i.e., understanding and ranking the multiple causes of a moral situation) and resolving (i.e., arriving at a sound justifiable and balanced solution) the moral issue at hand. Managers who exhibit sound ethical judgment use all the ethics perspectives, arguments, and cognate resources (e.g., legal, managerial, organizational, political, and communication resources) available to understand employee theft, for example, and then decide on a solution that comprehensively resolves the problem. Managers that remain stuck in the paralysis of moral analysis never arrive at moral resolutions, and, therefore, develop a reputation for weak, indecisive judgment and poor process integrity. Likewise, the second organizational quality process is judgment, subdivided into quality analysis and resolution. Managers improve their quality judgment by analyzing (i.e., collecting and interpreting data from all process measurement indicators to determine the root causes of quality problems) and by resolving (i.e., arriving at a timely, comprehensive solution) quality problems. Managers who exhibit sound quality judgment analyze the root causes of problems and decide on a sound course of action to solve quality problems (Lindsay & Petrick, 1997).

The third organizational ethics process is motivation, subdivided into the cognitive and volitional readiness to enact ethics. Managers strengthen the collective cognitive readiness to act ethically by using their intellectual virtues to vividly imagine a preferred organizational future and to compellingly communicate its value. Next, they cultivate collective, volitional readiness to act ethically by demonstrating and rewarding the display of moral virtue (e.g., justice, courage, moderation, self-discipline), emotional virtue (e.g., sincerity, resilience, emulation rather than resentment, trust), and social virtue (e.g., cooperativeness, sense of humor, civility, and organizational citizenship). They censure work vices that might erode organizational character (i.e., the collective readiness to act ethically) by, for example, refusing to condone resentment of coworker success and instead, advocating emulation of success or refraining from favoritism in appraisal and compensation decisions and instead, acting fairly and impartially (Greenberg, 1996; Hosmer, 1995; Sheaffer, 1988; Wilkins, 1989). Similarly, the third organizational quality process is motivation, subdivided into the cognitive and volitional readiness to enact quality. Managers improve the cognitive readiness of their organizations to enact quality by clarifying their visions of a preferred future and expanding their knowledge and use of statistical quality control tools. They improve their organization's volitional readiness to enact quality by rewarding cross-functional projects that measure and improve work processes to encourage teamwork (Scholtes, Joiner, & Streibel, 1996).

Finally, the fourth organizational ethics process is performance, subdivided into responsible and sustainable enactment of ethics. Organizations that engage in socially responsible conduct consider the interests of all key stakeholders to sustain their personal and organizational reputations as solid community citizens (Fombrun, 1996). In addition, organizational ethical conduct is demonstrated by sustainable development processes and practices that address the environmental impact of moral decisions (e.g., recycling processes; Shrivastava, 1996; Stead & Stead, 1996). In a parallel manner, the fourth organizational quality process is actual performance, subdivided into responsible and sustainable enactment of quality. Responsible enactment of quality entails considering the feedback of upstream suppliers, downstream distributors, and community stakeholders in the implementation of quality programs. Furthermore, ensuring responsible ecological management is part of quality performance in diverse environments (Wever, 1996; Willig, 1994).

In essence, process integrity requires regular managerial and organizational linking of ethics and quality awareness, judgment, motivation, and performance. Managers must walk the talk and organizations must exhibit organizational alignment between moral rhetoric and daily work reality or jeopardize their process integrity by developing hypocritical reputations that breed cynicism and resistance (Wanous, Reichers, & Austin, 1994).

PRINCIPLES IN ETHICS AND QUALITY
(THE FOURTH P)

Finally, once managers address their organizational perspectives, paradigms, and processes, ethics and quality are simultaneously impacted by the informal operating principles that prevail in the workplace. These informal principles reflect the development of moral reasoning maturity in workplace cultures (Kohlberg, 1984; Robin & Reidenbach, 1991). Managers and work cultures with low moral reasoning development are likely to be selfish and permit conniving practices to prevail; those with average moral reasoning development will foster practices that comply with external standards and adhere to the letter of the law; and those with high moral reasoning development will nurture just, inclusive practices that treat others respectfully out of internalized commitment to universal principles. *Developmental integrity*, as the improvement of moral reasoning at the individual and collective levels from self-interest through compliance and internalized commitment to universal ethical principles, is the final dimension of organizational integrity. Without developmental integrity, new perspectives, paradigms, and processes will be resisted at work as threats to short-term self-interest.

Table 7.4 provides a graphic illustration of the parallel ways in which prevailing informal operating principles are related to stages of organizational moral development, and, in turn, create three different work cultures, only the last of which supports organizational integrity and quality (French & Granrose, 1995; Gilligan, Ward, & Taylor, 1989; Kohlberg, 1984; Petrick & Quinn, 1997).

TABLE 7.4
Prevailing Organizational Operational Principles
and Organizational Integrity and Quality

Informal Operating Principles	Organizational Moral Development Stages	Work Cultures Created
1. Get it done now or else! (Coercive Power)	1. Social Darwinism stage	The House of Connivance
2. What's in it for me? (Reward Power)	2. Machiavellian stage	
3. Go along with group norms to get along (Referent Power)	3. Popular conformity stage	The House of Compliance
4. Obey laws and commands of authority (Legitimate Power)	4. Authority allegiance stage	
5. Involve all by voting but benefit the majority of people; the minority will absorb the cost (Political Expert Power)	5. Democratic participation stage	The House of Integrity and Quality
6. Act out of universal, prioritized moral principles and virtuous intentions to achieve system consensus (rather than only majority endorsement) or stand alone on principle (Moral Expert Power)	6. Principled integrity stage	

In Table 7.4, the first informal work operating principle is the threatening command to act or be fired. It is based on the coercive power of direct force and is typical of the first stage of organizational moral development, Social Darwinism. Social Darwinism is the lowest stage of collective moral reasoning; it advocates self-interest and survival of the fittest by force.

The second informal work operating principle is the manipulative bargaining ploy of demanding self-interest. It is based on reward power and indirect force (i.e., only those actions that are personally rewarding will be done). It is typical of the second stage of organizational moral development, Machiavellianism, which assumes that members will routinely engage in dishonest and treacherous behavior for personal career advancement or organizational gain. Organizations that operate at the first two stages create the house of connivance work culture and their predatory practices preclude the enactment of organizational integrity and quality initiatives (Dunlap, 1996).

The third informal operating principle is formed by conforming to work group norms and accepting the popular conformity stage of organizational moral development. It is based on the power one's reference group exerts on interpersonal, social, and work expectations, after people from the house of connivance are no longer tolerated (Treviño & Nelson, 1995).

The fourth informal operating principle is enacted by compliance with externally imposed laws/regulations and obedience to commands of legitimate authorities (Fiorelli & Rooney, 1996; Kelman & Hamilton, 1989). This is the stage of allegiance to authority; it is based on legitimate power that overrides group reference conformity. Nevertheless, organizations that operate at stages three and four create the house of compliance work culture that maintains conventional law and order but risks institutionalizing mediocrity and obsolescence.

Finally, the fifth informal operating principle advocates reliance on majority vote at work. It is typical of the fifth stage of organizational moral development, democratic participation, in which challenging authority with expert, democratic political power is the norm, rather than risking crimes of obedience due to unreflective compliance (Dew, 1997).

The sixth informal operating principle advocates commitment to the highest, prioritized universal moral principles (e.g., justice, fairness, caring, respect) to achieve system consensus rather than only majority endorsement. It is typical of the principled integrity stage of organizational moral development, and is based on expert moral power by all key stakeholders (Petrick & Furr, 1995). The moral commitment to speaking with facts in order to arrive at the truth overrides the political search for majority trends.

Organizations that operate at stages five and six are continually strengthening their organizational character and their readiness to act ethically, and are constantly improving system stability (Petrick & Quinn, 1997). Virtuous habits, internalized commitment to principles, and stable processes, therefore, constitute the work culture of the house of integrity and quality. Thus, ensuring that the organization's informal operating principles and moral reasoning capacities are at the highest stages leads simultaneously to increased organizational integrity and quality as well as the prevalence of developmental integrity.

SUMMARY

In summary, building organizational integrity and quality entails expanded competencies in handling the new four Ps (perspectives, paradigms, processes, and principles). Judgment, system, process, and developmental integrity constitute organizational integrity and sustain organizational quality. They will not emerge automatically, but if cultivated, they provide guidance for practicing managers and a conceptual focus for future scholarly research. Research agendas could include empirical studies in the following areas: perceived relationships between managerial ethics and quality perspectives and their managerial practices; relationships between perceptions of managerial integrity capacity and organizational performance; comparison of operational priority of organizational integrity among Baldrige Award winners with nonwinners in the same industry; and specific empirical studies of the performance impacts of perceived absence of different dimensions of organizational integrity.

In effect, the new integrity/quality mix of four Ps is one promising way to address the problem of simultaneously managing people and processes ethically.

REFERENCES

Allinson, R. E. (1993). *Global disasters.* New York: Prentice-Hall.
ANSI/ASQC A3. (1978). *Quality systems terminology.* Milwaukee, WI: American Society for Quality.
Axelrod, R. (1984). *The evolution of cooperation.* New York: Basic Books.
Bottorf, D. L. (1997). How ethics can improve business success. *Quality Progress, 30*(2), 57–60.
Bounds, G., Yorks, L., Adams, M., & Ranney, G. (1994). *Beyond total quality management.* New York: McGraw-Hill.
Bounds, G. M., Dobbins, G. H., & Fowler, O. S. (1995). *Management: A total quality perspective.* Cincinnati, OH: South-Western Publishing.
Brandt, R. B. (1992). *Morality, utilitarianism and rights.* New York: Cambridge University Press.
Carter, S. (1996). *Integrity.* New York: Harper Perennial.
Ciulla, J. B. (1995). Leadership ethics: Mapping the territory. *Business Ethics Quarterly, 5*(1), 5–28.
Cohen, D. V. (1993). Creating and maintaining ethical work climates. *Business Ethics Quarterly, 3*(4), 343–358.

Cohen, W., & Cohen, N. (1993). *The paranoid corporation and eight other ways your company can be crazy.* New York: AMACOM.

Collins, J. C., & Porras, J. I. (1994). *Built to last.* New York: Harper Collins.

Cooke, R. A., & Szumal, J. L. (1993). Measuring normative beliefs and shared behavioral expectations in organizations: The reliability and validity of the organizational culture inventory. *Psychological Reports, 72*(3), 1299–1330.

De George, R. T. (1993). *Competing with integrity in international business.* New York: Oxford University Press.

Denison, D., Hoojiberg, R., & Quinn, R. (1995). Paradox and performance: Toward a theory of behavioral complexity in managerial leadership. *Organization Science, 6*(5), 524–540.

Deming, W. E. (1982). *Quality, productivity and competitive position.* Boston: MIT Press.

Deming, W. E. (1988). *Out of the crisis.* Boston: MIT Press.

Dew, J. R. (1997). *Empowerment and democracy in the workplace.* Westport, CT: Quorum Books.

Donaldson, T., & Dunfee, T. W. (1994). Toward a unified conception of business ethics: Integrative social contracts theory. *The Academy of Management Review, 9*(2), 252–284.

Dunlap, A. (1996). *Mean business.* New York: McGraw-Hill.

Dworkin, R. (1978). *Taking rights seriously* (2nd ed.). Cambridge, MA: Harvard University Press.

Ethics Resource Center. (1994). *Ethics in American business: Policies, programs and perceptions.* Washington, DC: Ethics Resource Center.

Etzioni, A. (1988). *The moral dimension.* New York: The Free Press.

Evans J. R., & Lindsay, W. M. (1996). *The management and control of quality* (3rd ed.). New York: West Publishing.

Fiorelli, P., & Rooney, C. (1996). *The federal sentencing guidelines: Guidelines for internal auditors.* Sarasota, FL: Institute of Internal Auditors - Research Foundation.

Fombrun, C. J. (1996). *Reputation: Realizing value from the corporate image.* Boston: Harvard Business School Press.

French, W. A., & Granrose, J. (1995). *Practical business ethics.* Englewood Cliffs, NJ: Prentice Hall.

Garvin, D. (1988). *Managing quality: The strategic and competitive edge.* New York: The Free Press.

Gilligan, C., Ward, J. V., & Taylor, J. M. (Eds.). (1989). *Mapping the moral domain.* Cambridge, MA: Harvard University Press.

Glendon, M. A. (1991). *Rights talk: The impoverishment of political discourse.* New York: The Free Press.

Glendon, M. A. (1994). *A nation under lawyers.* New York: Farrar, Strauss & Giroux.

Greenberg, J. (1996). *The quest for justice on the job: Essays and experiments.* Thousand Oaks, CA: Sage.

Halfon, M. (1989). *Integrity: A philosophical inquiry.* Philadelphia: Temple University Press.

Hosmer, L. T. (1995). Trust: The connecting link between organizational theory and psychological ethics. *The Academy of Management Review, 20*(2), 379–403.

Jackall, R. (1988). *Moral mazes.* New York: Oxford University Press.

Kelman, H. C., & Hamilton, V. L. (1989). *Crimes of obedience.* New Haven, CT: Yale University Press.

Kohlberg, L. (1984). *The psychology of moral development: The nature and validity of moral stages.* New York: Harper & Row.

Kotter, J. P., & Heskett, J. L. (1992). *Corporate culture and performance.* New York: The Free Press.

Kramer, R. M., & Tyler, T. R. (Eds.). (1995). *Trust in organizations.* Newbury Park, CA: Sage.

Kupperman, J. (1989). Character and ethical theory. *Midwest Studies in Philosophy, 13,* 98–111.

LeClair, D., Ferrell, O., & Fraedrich, J. (1998). *Integrity management.* Tampa, FL: University of Tampa Press.

Lindsay, W. M., & Petrick, J. A. (1997). *Total quality and organization development.* Delray Beach, FL: St. Lucie Press.

Martin, M. W. (1995). *Everyday morality.* Belmont, CA: Wadsworth.

McFall, L. (1987). Integrity. *Ethics, 98*(4), 5–20.

Moberg, D. (1997). Virtuous peers in work organizations. *Business Ethics Quarterly, 7*(1), 67–85.

Murphy, K. R. (1993). *Honesty in the workplace.* Belmont, CA: Brooks/Cole.

Ones, D. S., Visyvesvaran, C., & Schmidt, F. (1993). Comprehensive meta-analysis of integrity test validities: Findings and implications for personnel selection and theories of job performance. *Journal of Applied Psychology, 78*(2), 270–292.

Paine, L. S. (1994). Managing for organizational integrity. *Harvard Business Review, 94*(2), 106–117.

Paine, L. S. (1996). Moral thinking in management: An essential capability. *Business Ethics Quarterly, 6*(4), 461–476.

Paine, L. S. (1997). *Cases in leadership, ethics and organizational integrity.* Chicago: Irwin.

Petrick, J. A., & Furr, D. S. (1995). *Total quality in managing human resources.* Delray Beach, FL: St. Lucie Press.

Petrick, J. A., & Manning, G. E. (1990). Developing an ethical climate for excellence. *Journal for Quality and Participation, 14*(2), 84–90.

Petrick, J. A., & Manning, G. E. (1993). Paradigm shifts in quality management and ethics development. *Business Forum, 18*(4), 15–18.

Petrick, J. A., & Quinn, J. F. (1997). *Management ethics: Integrity at work.* Thousand Oaks, CA: Sage.

Posner, B., & Schmidt, W. (1992). Values and the American manager: An update updated. *California Management Review, 34*(3), 80–94.

Rawls, J. (1971). *A theory of justice.* Cambridge, MA: Harvard University Press.

Rest, J. R. (1986). *Moral development: Advances in research and theory.* New York: Praeger.

Robin, D., & Reidenbach, E. (1991). A conceptual model of corporate moral development. *Journal of Business Ethics, 10*(4), 273–284.

Scholtes, P., Joiner, B., & Streibel, B. (1996). *The team handbook* (2nd ed.). Madison, WI: Joiner Associates.

Sen, A., & Williams, B. (Eds.). (1982). *Utilitarianism and beyond.* New York: Cambridge University Press.

Sheaffer, R. C. (1988). *Resentment against achievement.* Buffalo, NY: Prometheus Books.

Shrivastava, P. (1996). *Greening business: Profiting the corporation and the environment.* Cincinnati, OH: Thomson Executive Press.

Sims, R. (1992). The challenge of ethical behavior in organizations. *Journal of Business Ethics, 11*(7), 520–529.

Slote, M. (1992). *From morality to virtue.* New York: Oxford University Press.

Solomon, R. C. (1992a). Corporate roles, personal virtues: An Aristotelian approach to business ethics. *Business Ethics Quarterly, 2*(3), 317–340.

Solomon, R. C. (1992b). *Ethics and excellence: Cooperation and integrity in business.* New York: Oxford University Press.

Stahl, M. J. (1995). *Management: Total quality in a global environment.* Cambridge, MA: Blackwell.

Stead, W. E., & Stead, J. G. (1996). *Management for a small planet* (2nd ed.). Newbury Park, CA: Sage.

Taylor, G. (1985). *Integrity: Pride, shame and guilt.* Oxford, England: The Alexander Press.

Thompson, D. F. (1995). *Ethics in Congress: From individual to institutional corruption.* Washington, DC: Brookings Institute.

Trevino, L., & Nelson, K. (1995). *Managing business ethics.* New York: Wiley.

Victor, B., & Cullen, J. B. (1988). The organizational basis of ethical work climates. *Administrative Science Quarterly, 33*(4), 101–125.

Vroman, H. W., & Luchsinger, V. P. (1994). *Managing organization quality*. Burr Ridge, IL: Irwin.

Wanous, J., Reichers, A., & Austin, T. (1994). Organizational cynicism: An initial study. In B. Keys & L. Dosier (Eds.), *Academy of Management Best Papers Proceedings* (pp. 269–273). Atlanta: Georgia State University.

Waters, J. A. (1988). Integrity management: Learning and implementing ethical principles in the workplace. In S. Srivastva and Associates (Eds.), *Executive integrity* (pp. 172–196). San Francisco: Jossey-Bass.

Weber, J. (1993). Institutionalizing ethics into business organizations. *Business Ethics Quarterly, 3*(4), 419–436.

Werhane, P., & Freeman, R. (Eds.). (1997). *Encyclopedic dictionary of business ethics*. Cambridge, MA: Blackwell.

Wever, G. H. (1996). *Strategic environmental management: Using TQEM and ISO 4000 for competitive advantage*. New York: Wiley.

Wheeler, D. J. (1993). *Understanding variation: The key to managing chaos*. Knoxville, TN: SPC Press.

Wilkins, A. L. (1989). *Developing corporate character: How to successfully change an organization without destroying it*. San Francisco: Jossey-Bass.

Willig, J. T. (1994). *Environmental TQM*. New York: McGraw-Hill.

CHAPTER EIGHT

If Politics Is a Game, Then What Are the Rules?: Three Suggestions for Ethical Management

Russell Cropanzano
Alicia A. Grandey
Colorado State University

The word *politics* conjures up negative images of favoritism, lies, old boy networks, and exploitation. As is seen here, these images are not entirely wrong; politics is often extremely painful and destructive. On the other hand, politics can challenge the status quo, provoke new ideas, and allow business firms to prosper. Political behavior seems to have strong detractors and equally strong proponents. The only thing that all observers agree on is that there is no escaping it.

In noting this, our objective is not to provide another scholarly description, as some excellent ones already exist (see especially Bacharach & Lawler, 1980; Mintzberg, 1983; Pfeffer, 1981, 1992). Nor do we intend to lament or celebrate the existence of politics. Rather, the question that occupies us here is a practical one: How can a well-intentioned manager behave ethically in an environment that is virtually defined by self-serving social maneuvering? If politics is systemic to organizational life, can ethics also be? To answer this question more fully, we first investigate the concept of organizational politics. Having done that, we then offer three sets of guidelines to help managers navigate this problem. The first involves rules-oriented formalist ethical systems. The second involves outcome-oriented ethical systems. The third involves applying three sets of ethical standards simultaneously.

WHAT IS ORGANIZATIONAL POLITICS?

There is more agreement on the ubiquity of organizational politics than there is on its definition. Most generally, organizational politics is a means of influencing or compelling others within an organization (e.g., Martin & Sims, 1974; Mintzberg, 1983; Pfeffer, 1992). It is behavior directed toward obtaining or maintaining social control. For example, Pfeffer (1981) discussed how political tactics are used to acquire power, legitimate and rationalize a decision, or increase the power of an individual. Tactics employed might include choosing certain facts and not others as criteria, keeping troublesome issues from surfacing, forming coalitions, or attempting to force conformity through involvement on committees. In fact, any influence tactic would be considered political under this definition.

Mayes and Allen (1977) narrowed the scope of this definition by considering two new factors: organizational sanctioning and outcomes of influence behaviors. If either the means or the ends are not sanctioned by the organization, the behavior is political, whereas influence behaviors that are sanctioned by the organization and achieve organizational goals are not. This work is important because it underscores the fact that politics, as understood here, can have either positive or negative consequences. On the positive side, political behaviors could overthrow bad policies or leaders, lead to the rise of good leaders, or improve productivity if the political behaviors influence employees successfully toward organizational goals (Kumar & Ghadially, 1989). From this perspective, what is good for the organization as a whole is considered functional—even if it hurts some individuals.

Politics has a dark side as well. Ferris, Russ, and Fandt (1989); Ferris and Judge (1991); and Ferris and King (1991) emphasized the negative consequences that political machinations can have on the work environment. As one might imagine, people do not like being manipulated or mislead. No one wants to be a pawn in someone's self-promotion. For this reason, workers tend to see politics in a very negative light. When they perceive political decision making, employees tend to report lower levels of job satisfaction, organizational commitment, and helpful citizenship behavior, while also reporting higher levels of turnover intentions, psychological withdrawal behaviors, stress, and job anxiety (e.g., Cropanzano, Howes, Grandey, & Toth, in press; Drory, 1990; Drory & Romm, 1988; Ferris, Frink, Galang, Zhou, Kacmar, & Howard, 1996; Ferris & Kacmar, 1992; Kacmar & Ferris, 1991, 1993; Randall, Cropanzano, Bormann, & Birjulin, in press).

This research documents a crucial fact: Politics comes with costs. These costs are not necessarily paid by the person who engages in the behavior. Rather, they can be borne by someone who is entirely unrelated to the activity. We have also seen that politics can be profitable. By this we mean that a lot of people can benefit, perhaps enough to compensate victims for their losses. Because of this delicate balance between functional and dysfunctional politics, these types of influence behaviors necessarily involve the consideration of ethics. However, ethical considerations are seldom easy. To simplify this task, we now consider three sets of suggestions.

SUGGESTION 1—PLAYING BY THE RULES:
USING A FORMALIST ETHICAL SYSTEM

Formalism refers to certain rule-based ethical systems. The assumption underlying formalistic ethical systems is that certain universal standards or guidelines can be either understood or developed by human beings. Behavior is ethical when it is in accord with these guidelines, whereas unethical behavior violates them. Thus, when managers have to decide whether a social behavior is unethical, they must acquire or develop some maxim of ethical behavior, and then assess whether not that action is in accordance with the rule. In other words, we have a moral obligation to behave in accordance with these guidelines. Ethicists refer to this ethical orientation as deontological, because the word *deontology* is adapted from the Greek term for duty (Hosmer, 1996, p. 93). A common example of formalism can be found in the codes of many professional associations (Brady, 1985). These codes provide a detailed set of rules and guidelines that are applicable to certain individuals in certain situations.

At this level of abstraction, it is difficult to ascertain the implications of formalism for organizational politics. We need to be more specific as to the rules in question. To help us in this regard, business ethicists have considered the ethical thinking of Immanuel Kant (1724–1804). Kant proposed a universal law of ethics that he called the *categorical imperative*. It was categorical in the sense of being categorically true. Kant presented two formulations of the categorical imperative. He believed that they were equivalent, though later philosophers have sometimes disagreed.

The first formulation states that we should behave only in a manner in which we desire that everyone in the world would behave, if faced with the same circumstances and morally relevant conditions. If we cannot wish that our actions set up a universal law, then the act is probably not ethical. One criterion for deciding whether the first formulation has been met is the criterion of reversibility. Velasquez (1990) summarized the reversibility criterion as follows: "The person's reasons for acting must be reasons that he or she would be willing to have all others use, even as a basis of how they treat him or her" (p. 81). From this first statement of the categorical imperative, philosophers have derived justice-based approaches to ethics (Rawls, 1971).

The second formulation of the categorical imperative states that "an action is morally right if and only if . . . the person does not use others merely as a means for advancing his or her own interests, but also both respects and develops their capacity to choose freely for themselves" (Velasquez, 1992, p. 82). From this second statement of the categorical imperative, philosophers have derived rights-based approaches to business ethics. We now discuss both justice-based and rights-based approaches to ethics in greater detail.

Ethics Based on Justice

Philosophical theories of justice are concerned with how things are distributed in organizations. This includes both benefits, such as the opportunity to work lucrative overtime, and costs, such as layoffs. In a just organization, these things should be meted out in accordance with some standard. Of course, this rule-based focus is what qualifies justice as a formalist system. However, unlike rights, which emphasize qualities of the person, justice emphasizes qualities of the distribution. Scholars have identified a variety of rules for assigning outcomes, such as rewarding people based on their efforts, their contribution, their needs, or simply giving everyone an equal share (Margalit, 1996). In practice, managers use a slightly smaller subset of these rules, though this varies somewhat by culture (James, 1993). In the United States, businesses seem to prefer equity norms (i.e., to each according to his or her contribution) for economic benefits, although equality is preferred among closely knit groups and for certain positive social outcomes, such as being invited to a company party (Chen, 1995; Cropanzano & Schminke, in press; Kabanoff, 1991; Martin & Harder, 1994). Of course, managers need some mechanism for choosing among these alternative allocation rules.

An influential solution to this problem was proposed by Rawls (1971). Rawls instructed us to imagine that we are in an *original position*. In this position, a group of people are gathering together to devise the ground rules for a new society. What rules would they choose? Rawls stipulated that these planners are behind a veil of ignorance. To be sure, they have some rudimentary understanding of human nature and interpersonal relationships, but they lack any knowledge regarding the economy, technology, or the environmental challenges that their society will be destined to face. Most of all, none in the group have any idea as to the roles that they will play in that brave new world. They do not even know what their own abilities and interests will be. With this in mind, Rawls' (1971) original position reduces to the following question: What type of rules would we make if we could be without self-interest? Those rules are likely to be the fairest ones. In the original position, we probably would not decide on a rule that says "gays cannot join the military," since we might be destined to be gay and to want to enlist.

The original position, or at least Rawls' (1971) solution to the problem, suggests that people are somewhat averse to risk. Because we might be poor, or unattractive, or sickly, we want to guarantee that social institutions will contain some provision to provide for the weakest among us. For this reason, many resources should be divided equally or by need. However, Rawls noted that this is not always the case. It is ethical to give talented people certain advantages, such as high pay or social status, as an incentive for them to raise the quality of life for all. Thus, we could conclude that, for Rawls, a just behavior is one that tends to be egalitarian, but not necessarily so.

More generally, we can say simply that a social behavior is unethical if it results in an unfair allocation of some resource. Because people often engage in politics to achieve some end they desire, this would be often. Suppose that one exploited a personal romance with a supervisor to earn a promotion. Soon, the individual is rewarded with a high-profile assignment. In accordance with Rawls' (1971) original position, this allocation is unfair. People sitting down to construct a society probably would not choose a maxim that says "people in personal relationships with authority figures get promoted." This is because (a) while in the original position one would not know whether one would have this advantage in life, and (b) if this rule were obeyed, then poorer performers would soon rise to the top—eventually wounding everyone's chances for prosperity and social harmony.

Of course, the justice rule does become tricky to apply. If an individual fabricates credentials to earn a promotion, that would surely be seen as unethical political behavior. Conversely, if individuals simply call attention to a qualification that they actually have earned, that would seem justified. Unfortunately, there is a vast gray ocean between these well-delineated coastlines. Individuals often puff their credentials in an effort to put themselves in the most positive light possible. Ultimately, whether puffing is acceptable will depend on the amount and on the norms of a particular firm. Despite these caveats, justice standards seem to be an effective means of reducing organizational politics (Cropanzano, Kacmar, & Bozeman, 1995), though our conclusions must be seen as tentative.

Problems With Justice-Based Reasoning

It is difficult to evaluate the efficacy of justice standards for reducing hurtful politics because this approach to ethics has received less attention in the business literature. Justice theorists have emphasized the creation of a good society (e.g., Galbraith, 1996) and have attended less to using justice as a means of regulating interpersonal behavior. For this reason, some of the comments that follow will necessarily be borrowed from the empirical literature on social justice perceptions.

Justice standards function best when everyone agrees with them and when everyone believes that they are being applied consistently. Unfortunately, people often show a self-interested bias in interpreting their treatment. For example, high performing workers seem to prefer equity allocations that allow them to profit, whereas lower performing individuals prefer equality rules that give them a larger share of the total earning (Greenberg & Bies, 1992). This makes it harder for managers to use justice-based principles effectively. Likewise, people will sometimes claim injustice as means of rationalizing their own poor performance.

Another problem is that these standards can be applied with too much rigidity. In the course of efforts to undercut politics, organizations may build up such an elaborate network of procedural safeguards that they become counterproductive (Sitkin & Bies, 1993). As a result, the process stops serving its larger objectives. It's too much of a good thing.

Ethics Based on Individual Rights

Many ethicists believe that human beings have certain basic rights. These rights are inviolate. They cannot be taken away. Instead, they are an inherent part of our humanity and apply universally to all people. Kohlberg (1981) stated that this rights doctrine is the official morality of the United States. According to Velasquez (1990), rights can be either negative or positive (see Moberg & Meyer, 1990, p. 866, for a similar distinction). *Negative rights* refer to one's freedom from interference by other people or by the state. No one is required to do anything for you, the only duty of others is to stay out of your way. This emphasis on certain negative rights, especially property rights, is still found in the work of libertarian economic thinkers (e.g., Friedman, 1962; Hayek, 1944; Rand, 1969). Others have extended this thinking to include so-called *positive rights*. Positive rights imply that someone has a duty to do something for you. Thus, if you have a positive right for due process, then the state is obligated to supply it to you.

If one takes a rights-based perspective, then a political behavior is unethical to the extent that it violates the rights of some individual or individuals. Rights-based ethical criteria are extremely useful means of humanizing the work environment as they simply eliminate hurtful political behavior, while encouraging us to provide aid and assistance to others. The easiest way to demonstrate this is by considering Kant's admonishment that people should never be treated only as means, but also as ends in themselves. That is, the worth of human beings accrues by virtue of being human, not by what they can do for you. Clearly, many sorts of backhanded maneuvering or double-dealing are precluded by this standard (for more detail on the particulars, see Moberg & Meyer, 1990). It is wrong to manipulate other people, although it is not wrong to work with them for mutually beneficial ends (so long as this alliance does not violate the rights of some other group, of course). Likewise, we can also see that it is wrong to inflict unnecessary pain on our coworkers or even to use them as means of self-aggrandizement.

Problems With Applying Rights-Based Reasoning

Despite clear benefits, there are problems with applying rights-based standards to business ethics. We consider two. First, it is difficult to prioritize these sundry rights. Second, rights-based reasoning can take on an absolutist moral quality, making it difficult to seek compromise.

Prioritizing Different Rights. Rights are not always consonant. Sometimes, they create dilemmas. The more rights multiply, the more likely these dilemmas will occur. To resolve them, a person needs to know which rights are relatively more important and which rights are less so. Unfortunately, such guidelines are not necessarily apparent, though rough standards exist (Velasquez, 1992). For example, suppose a person has applied to head a certain department. A group of individuals in the personnel office has decided, with only very limited consultation from others, to select this individual. On the surface, this might seem political. Perhaps all of the workers in the affected department have the right to participate in the process. But we also need to consider the applicant's right to privacy. Whose rights should be given more weight?

The Absolute Quality of Rights. Some have argued that rights have an absolutist quality about them (Howard, 1994; Sykes, 1992). If someone has a right to something, there is little left to discuss. For this reason, the overapplication of rights-based reasoning can cut off ethical deliberation almost as easily as it can encourage it. An interesting illustration of this possibility is provided by Ury, Brett, and Goldberg (1989). These three authors examined labor–management relations in a number of American coal mines. Prior to an extensive conflict management intervention, this relationship was poor. Each side engaged in a variety of political games, designed to one-up the other. For example, workers would file numerous, frivolous complaints to obstruct the grievance system. Ury and his colleagues argued that the conflict was difficult to resolve because it was not focused on pragmatic interests, but on symbolic rights and power. Sides, therefore, adhered strictly to their positions rather than seeking constructive compromises. Ury et al. suggested that less focus on moral rights and more on personal interests can facilitate conflict resolution.

Conclusion: How Serious a Problem? Although all of these criticisms have frequently been leveled at rights-based ethics, they may not be entirely fair. Some critics may be confusing legal rights with philosophical rights. The two are not necessarily the same (cf. Hosmer, 1996). It is true that legal rights have experienced an almost exponential growth (Howard, 1994). However, this may have resulted more from legal opportunism and less from the application of philosophical principles. Although possibly less flexible than other philosophical frameworks, a rights-based philosophy may be more adaptable than its critics give it credit for being. Keep in mind that the categorical imperative does not preclude us from using people as means, but from using them only as means. Others can be treated as a personal means, so long as that is not their only purpose. This attribute makes formalism adaptable to a wide variety of social dilemmas (for details see Moberg & Meyer,

1990). For example, if forming a political coalition, the others in the group might be a means by which an individual can achieve a goal. If they are aware of this prospect, give their consent, and stand to benefit personally, then this coalition could well be ethical. Similarly, rights-based philosophy certainly can make exceptions to the general rules. For example, Brady (1987) provided detailed guidelines for when rules should or should not be observed.

SUGGESTION 2—FOCUSING ON OUTCOMES: USING A UTILITARIAN ETHICAL SYSTEM

In formalist ethics, we render decisions by comparing a possible action to a standard or set of standards. As we have seen, this method of thinking may risk the possibility of inflexibility. To deal with this concern, a manager may substitute a utilitarian ethical framework. Utilitarianism is teleological in that it emphasizes the outcome of a given behavioral alternative. An action is ethical, if—when compared to alternative actions—it provides the greatest good for the greatest number of people. Otherwise, the action is likely to be unethical (Hosmer, 1996). When considering a social behavior, managers should first consider a wide range of alternatives. They should subsequently ponder the positive and negative consequences that are likely to result from each. A behavior is ethical when it yields the greatest good for the greatest number. Utilitarianism cautions against engaging in politics haphazardly. Remember: You need to consider all of the available alternatives.

Certain influence attempts that might be precluded by justice and rights-based approaches could be allowable within this teleological framework. For example, recall a paper reviewed earlier. Mayes and Allen (1977) argued that there are two types of politics: functional politics that uses sanctioned means to achieve sanctioned ends, and dysfunctional politics that achieves unsanctioned ends regardless of means. Although not stated by the authors, this framework is implicitly utilitarian. In other words, it is fine to bend the rules so long as something good results. This ends-oriented, or teleological, thinking is extremely flexible (Brady, 1985). In this way, it counters the legalism that can result from the misapplication of formalist standards. However, utilitarianism is not without its problems, either. We address these in the next section.

Problems With Utilitarian Reasoning

Computational Demands

Utilitarian reasoning is very demanding computationally. How is a manager to calculate all of the possible outcomes for every alternative action? One way to address this problem is through the use of *rule utilitarianism*.

In rule utilitarianism, the individual utilizes a set of rules that are believed to lead to the greatest good if consistently applied. For example, theft is disallowable because it would lead to a deterioration in the well-being of all. When faced with a potentially unethical action, a rule utilitarian manager would simply examine whether that action violates the guideline. This is much less cognitively demanding. In this sense, rule utilitarianism is much like formalism, except that the rules are legitimized on outcome-based grounds and not on the basis of some rights or justice standard.

Potential for Exploitation

The flexibility of utilitarianism is also its weakness. Bending the rules sounds good, until they get bent at your expense or at the expense of someone you care about. The relaxed standard could violate someone's rights or result in a less fair distribution of wealth (Velasquez, 1992). This is because utilitarianism is based on the greatest good for the greatest number. It is acceptable, therefore, to have a few suffer if the masses benefit. Taken literally, this can be a recipe for inequality. Research has shown that political behavior is often very painful (e.g., Cropanzano et al., in press). How much pain to a few is acceptable for the greater good? The rigid rules and guidelines that may result from formalism can be frustrating, but they at least have the potential to protect the weak and powerless.

Addressing These Concerns:
The Case of Value Utilitarianism

As we saw with formalism, critics are not always entirely fair. Some of them may have utilized an overly narrow reading of the utilitarian position. In this section, we attempt to address these concerns by taking a broader point of view. We call this perspective *value utilitarianism,* in order that we might distinguish it from the more circumscribed position that has provoked controversy in the business ethics literature. However, it should be emphasized that what we refer to as value utilitarianism is more or less what many philosophers see as utilitarian. In other words, this section responds to the aforementioned concerns by more fully explicating the philosophy.

Under utilitarian reasoning, inequality is acceptable, so long as the overall utility is maximized. However, to understand what this means, we must distinguish between two distinct meanings of utility. We distinguish here between two attributes that an object can be said to have an objective worth and a subjective value. The two are not necessarily the same. For example, a hamburger might be worth $5. The price is objective in the weak sense that it is quantified in a way that everyone who reads the price can agree on the sum. In addition, the worth is likely to be the same for everyone. However, the subjective value of that hamburger is greater for a starving person than for someone who is well fed. In other words, the amount of happiness (i.e., utility, but only if utility is understood as value) the hamburger gives the starving man is greater than the amount of happiness the hamburger gives the sated individual. In this example, we have used no more than the principle of decreasing marginal returns—the more you have of some object, the less the value of an additional increment (see Heilbroner & Thurow, 1994). We can see the relationship between value and amount in Fig. 8.1.

This principle suggests something else. If utility were defined as value and not as worth, then how would one distribute the hamburger in a way that maximized utility? The optimal value distribution could be achieved by giving most or all of the hamburger to the starving man. Giving it to the well-fed individual might maintain the hamburger's worth but would reduce its value. These considerations provide the basic principle of what we are calling value utilitarianism: It is ethical to provide the greatest value for the greatest number. In other words, good things should be distributed in a way that optimizes their value, whereas bad things should be distributed in a way that minimizes their (negative) value. This principle, consistently applied, will have the potential to minimize inequity and protect human dignity.

It is perhaps easiest to explain this principle with the simple example of money. The objective worth of money stays roughly constant (at least in the short term) regardless of how much or little one has. Going from $0 to $25,000 (roughly, the U.S. lower class, see Peterson, 1994, p. 57) is the same

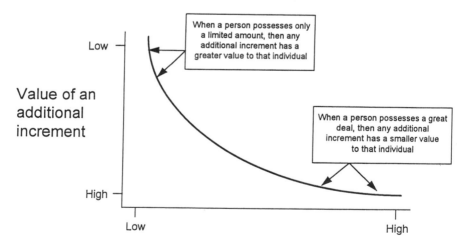

FIG. 8.1.   Diagram of a hypothetical value curve. Note the additional increment is of greater value for those who have less, and less value for those who have more.

as going from $200,000 to $225,000. However, the value of the money to each family is likely to be different. In the first case, the additional (or marginal) $25,000 is a vast improvement. This could make the difference between living on the government dole or being able to support one's family, albeit modestly. In the second case, it is an improvement of only 12.5%. This is likely to be the difference between a more or less luxurious automobile. As was the case with the hamburger, to maximize utility (if utility is understood as value, and all other things being equal), the $25,000 is best invested with the poorer family.

Notice the shape of the value curve in Fig. 8.1. At very low levels, a little bit of the outcome is extremely valuable. For example, consider a minimum-wage worker. A few hundred dollars, a new suit, or even a little bit of extra respect will mean a great deal. However, the curve decreases sharply and eventually flattens, suggesting two things. First, the value of an object decreases as more of it is obtained. This decrease proceeds at an accelerating rate. Second, at high levels, it takes large increases in worth to make a comparable change in value. A few hundred dollars are small change to a millionaire, but they are precious to the poor. Inequity is less ethical when it disadvantages the very needy or creates a class of very needy people.

The net result of this value utilitarianism, then, is that it places a sort of feedback loop into normal distribution rules. As a few people get more and more worthwhile things, the value of each new increment becomes less and less. The growth in their fortunes, whether this fortune be in money or in other benefits, does progressively less to optimize the total value for the collective as a whole. The best way to keep increasing the group's net value is to distribute some of these worthwhile benefits to the people who have the least—thereby maximizing the investment in value. Thus, gross inequalities are precluded by value utilitarianism.

Value utilitarianism gives us reasonably clear guidelines for engaging in politics. Politics is acceptable as long as it yields benefits and as long as it does not produce a great inequality in these benefits. Political tactics that demean or disempower other persons are likely to result in an unequal distribution of opportunity and dignity, thereby rendering them unethical. Suppose one group favors the development of a new product and another opposes it. The former cabal conspires to humiliate and demean the latter, thereby ensuring a favorable decision outcome. Is this unethical? A traditional formalist analysis would probably say "yes." Value utilitarianism might concur, but would have to consider the amount of value that results from the new product, ways to alleviate the hurt experienced by the losing side, and less contentious lost opportunities. If the damage to the losing side was fundamental (for instance, if people lost their jobs), then the gain from the new product would have to be considerably larger to compensate for this loss.

What of Justice and Rights?

In value utilitarianism, there are neither moral rights nor justice standards as such. The only exception to this rule is the right to have your value maximized in accordance with the theory. However, there is a feedback mechanism built into the theory—the more someone has, the less any new increment increases (relative) value. Consequently, to optimize value, worthwhile benefits must be shifted to the those who are relatively less well off. This system does not guarantee complete equality; this is not its objective. However, observing these rules does ensure a final distribution that is relatively more just in terms of value.

A similar analysis applies to rights. Let us consider the case of worker empowerment in managerial decision making. Allowing someone control is usually beneficial, in the sense that workers typically enjoy the opportunity to exert influence over their work lives. In addition, empowerment helps employees ensure worthwhile outcomes for themselves. For example, an empowered worker is in a better position to argue for higher pay, health benefits, and so forth. Under value utilitarianism, empowerment is a worthwhile commodity. People will seek it out, and it can be assigned in a way that maximizes its value for the group as a whole. From a utilitarian perspective, very autocratic organizations are ethically questionable because the power to control the environment is unequally allocated; senior management gets it and workers are denied it. All other things being equal, a more ethical system may be to take some of the worthwhile control away from top managers and give it to workers. Because empowerment is more valuable when given to those who have less, this maximizes the value for the group as a whole. However, note that empowerment is not a moral right, in the sense that it is intrinsic to a person. Rather, it is a nice thing to have, and people who want it are morally entitled to it, if conditions allow.

We should not close this analysis without mentioning the flexibility of the utilitarian standard. In all of the examples we have mentioned, there are clear exceptions. If an unequal distribution of benefits can optimize value, then such a distribution is ethically acceptable. In other words, equality is not an unyielding standard because equality is not seen as an intrinsic good. For example, if upper level managers were not compensated with extra status and pay, few would opt for the additional job duties. For this reason, it is ethical to reward individuals unequally, if doing so maximizes value to all.

Ease of Use

Value utilitarianism includes all of the computational demands inherent in utilitarianism. The solution for this problem would seem to be in integrating value utilitarianism with rule utilitarianism. That is, ethicists could develop a set of rules or guidelines that maximizes value in most situations. Ethical decisions could then be made with respect to these rules. This would greatly simplify decision making. We can speculate that these rules would be much like the justice standards mentioned by formalists. We return to this point presently.

Although there are no philosophical rights under value utilitarianism, many things are morally proscribed. Therefore, the political system can codify these judgments as legal rights or as justice standards. These legal rights would act as heuristics to help us avoid unethical behavior. Let us illustrate this with the extremely odious case of chattel slavery. To put it mildly, this pernicious practice deprived people of an enormous number of benefits, including the opportunity to stay with their families, to practice their own faith, to choose jobs, to earn their own wealth, to avoid inconsistent and harsh punishment, and so on. These may or may not be moral rights, but they are desirable benefits indeed. Slavery gave relatively low value benefits to the so-called masters (who were a tiny fraction of the population) and seized them from a mass of people for whom they would have had great value. In fact, their value is so great that it is impossible for us to imagine how slavery could be justified, regardless of how much economic worth is generated. Given this, it makes good sense to enshrine a legal right to freedom into a constitution. Within the legal system, we can term this a right. Although this is not a moral right in the Jeffersonian sense (i.e., it is neither universal nor based on a categorical imperative nor fundamental to being human), it does have the same practical implications. In any case, the legal right acts as a simple rule to minimize the need for cognitive effort.

SUGGESTION 3—USE A SEQUENTIAL APPROACH

The previous section demonstrated that both formalism and utilitarianism have advantages and disadvantages when applied to organizational politics. To some extent, each compensates for the other's weaknesses, but, in doing so, acquires some of its own. For example, utilitarianism is more flexible than formalism, but becomes more intricate in turn. Formalism does a good job of protecting basic human rights, but risks becoming pedantic. When making ethical decisions, we would like to maximize the strengths of the approaches and minimize their weaknesses. One logical path from this dilemma would suggest a framework that incorporates all three ethical systems. Cavanagh, Moberg, and Velasquez (1981) proposed such a framework.

The theoretical model provided by Cavanagh et al. (1981) combined these three ethical sets as components of a decision tree. The authors suggested systematically considering the costs and benefits of each system, in any order. In addition, the model includes overwhelming factors that allow for situations where such criteria should not be used. These factors include

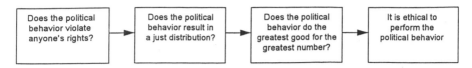

FIG. 8.2. A sequential representation of the model proposed by Cavanagh, Moberg, and Velasquez (1981).

conflicts between and within ethical criteria where a judgment must be made and when the decision maker lacks the capacity to use the ethical criteria for some reason (i.e., he does not have enough information). In theory, this would provide managers with a comprehensive method of making evaluations of behaviors occurring in their organizations. We first outline this model and then discuss some potential needs for further development.

The authors suggest that the order of the decision tree is arbitrary, although one might suggest otherwise. For example, Velasquez (1992, p. 105) argued that rights are generally given more weight than justice and justice is generally given more weight than utility. Velasquez's position seems reasonable, as it guarantees the protection of individual dignity before considering pragmatic costs and benefits. For this reason, Fig. 8.2 suggests that rights are a baseline of ethical behavior: If behavior is harming or withholding another person's rights, it is simply wrong. As a baseline, it would make sense for the rights-based system to be the first box of the decision tree. The manager would consider the political behavior and ask, "Does this respect the rights of others involved?" If the answer is no, this model demands that the manager consider any factors that would justify the annulment of such a right. If one person's or a group's rights are harmed by political behavior in order to acquire rights for another person or group, the manager must prioritize the value of the rights. As we have seen, there are no hard and fast prioritizing rules, but only a weighing of relative importance of interests, which enables the manager to make such decisions. If no one's rights were violated, then the manager would move on to the next set of criteria.

We suggest that this next stage be justice-based reasoning. As stated previously, justice in this context means that resources are allocated equitably. If political behavior redistributes outcomes unfairly, then the behavior is unethical. Here the manager asks, "Does this political behavior respect the basic principles of justice?" If the response is, "No, the behavior does affect distribution of resources in an inequitable way," then the model directs the manager to consider any special circumstances that would make this an acceptable violation.

If the political behavior passes both rights-based and justice-based reasoning, then the manager would move to the last stage: utilitarianism. This is the most computationally complex ethical system. As such, its placement at the end of the decision tree is justifiable: If the first two sets of criteria are not met, the manager would not have to cope with the time-consuming utilitarian system. By reaching this stage in the decision tree, the manager knows that the behavior has not harmed anyone's rights or led to an unfair distribution of rewards. Now the manager asks, "Does this behavior provide the most good for the most people, for the long run?" As discussed earlier, this can be very computationally demanding. The manager must consider all affected parties, both internal and external to the organization, and all possible alternative behaviors. If optimization of outcomes was not achieved, the model asks the manager if special factors justify this violation of the ethical criteria. If optimization is achieved, or the overwhelming factors allow for suboptimization, and the behavior had passed through the previous ethical systems, then the decision tree determines that the political behavior is ethically acceptable.

For instance, suppose two production teams are demanding more funding, and both previously had similar productivity levels. It would seem equitable to give them comparable amounts of funding. However, members of one of the teams begin to informally denigrate the output of the other department. Maybe they say the products are faulty, or the ideas are stolen from their own team. When the funding decision is made, this outspoken team acquires more of the allocation of resources. The manager of the department is called upon to decide if this decision was unethical.

The manager would begin by evaluating whether rights were violated on either side. If the outspoken team had been lying about the other team's output, this certainly would have been unethical. But, what if it were true? If the manager determined no rights were violated, the manager would then ask if justice had been done. The team that did not acquire the funding probably sees the political behavior by the other team as very unfair and the outcomes as a violation of justice. But, the team that received the extra funding would find the outcomes very equitable, if the members truly believed they produced higher quality products. The manager must determine whether an inequitable allocation occurred. If not, then the manager would determine if the outcome optimized the possible good. Although the political behavior led to more resources for one set of people over another, the manager could determine that, in the long run, this outcome would provide the most good for the organization as a whole. If the more highly funded department developed better products, this would yield more revenue for the company and would lead to better customer relations. If this is the case, the manager comes to the final conclusion that this particular political behavior of informal campaigning was not unethical.

Problems With the Sequential Model

Cavanagh et al.'s (1981) sequential model has much to recommend it. When determining the ethical nature of a political behavior, each ethical system's criteria are considered in turn. This allows each system an opportunity to respond to weaknesses in the others. In a manner of speaking, each theory of justice holds the other two accountable, thereby addressing some concerns raised earlier. In effect, Cavanagh and his colleagues (1981) summed the three ethical perspectives together. Although this is a useful corrective, it only addresses places where an ethical system has a deficit. For example, the utilitarian's relative inattention to exploitation is precluded by a consideration of rights and justice. However, the summative process implied in the sequential model does not address problems that are surfeit. That is, it does less to correct the situation in which a given ethical framework does too much of something.

In the case of surfeit, considering each rule in sequence risks multiplying some of the weaknesses in each model. We illustrate this by returning to the example of rights. If one uses rights as the starting point for the model, then justice and utilitarian concerns remain subordinate to a rights-based perspective. The absolutist quality of rights remains as unfinished business, in the sense that the needs of the community only come into play after the needs of the individual. Likewise, the complexity of utilitarian considerations may be added to sophisticated and legalistic thinking about justice, thereby making the process even more intricate. To make Cavanagh et al.'s model fully operational, we need to solve the problem of excess. What happens if one perspective tells us to do too much? We might be able to partially address these concerns, if we construe Cavanagh et al.'s model more holistically and less sequentially.

A Holistic Interpretation of the Cavanagh et al. Model

So far we have been discussing the Cavanagh et al. (1981) model serially, in which one ethical theory is considered after another. However, our interpretation may be unfairly narrow. What is perhaps most valuable about the sequential model is that it lends itself to an alternative, more holistic, interpretation. It should be emphasized that all of the ethical theories we have considered have value. The core point of Cavanagh et al.'s work is that we should take the best from these different perspectives, not that we should multiply out the worst. Thus, rather than considering each ethical framework one at a time, managers should evaluate them simultaneously, with each having the ability to check the other. We call this approach holistic, rather than sequential, because it does not provide a single starting or ending point. No perspective is subordinate to the others; each can be used to check another.

An example might be useful in illustrating this point. Suppose an academic department in a university is considering an overseas degree program. All of the principals agree that this program would be valuable, and would not harm any existing programs (i.e., current interests are unthreatened). However, this university renders decisions only through elaborate, formal procedures. These procedures protect both justice and rights, and as such, are valuable. Moreover, as employees of the institution, everyone agrees to abide by these regulations. Unfortunately, as there is no written process for granting permission to overseas degree programs, the decision soon begins to languish. In time, the funding deadlines will expire and the program will die for lack of action.

Under these conditions, is it ethical for a group of faculty members to form a political coalition and push through the new degree program? In the sequential model, the answer might well be "no." Violating formalistic, procedural safeguards would be highly questionable at best, and the program might not be implemented. In a holistic model, the answer would probably be "yes." The interests of the many outweigh the justice and rights concerns embodied in formal procedures. Therefore, it is acceptable to make an exception in this circumstance (cf. Brady, 1987).

Notice that in the holistic model, rights and justice remain very important considerations, but they do not exercise veto power over utility. The reverse is also true. The holistic model requires parallel thinking rather than sequential addition. If we accept this integrative point of view, then it adds a new ethical dimension. An ethical person is neither a formalist nor a utilitarian; rather an ethical person is both a formalist and a utilitarian. A balanced perspective among the three ethical frameworks is every bit as important as adhering to one or the other.

Perhaps the metaphor that best captures our thinking is that of a three-legged stool. One leg represents justice; one, rights; and one, utility. Ethical managerial behavior is supported by all three together. To lose any one of these legs is as bad as having none at all. If one breaks, then the stool becomes useless clutter. More subtly, but equally important, the legs must be properly balanced. If one is too long or too short, then the stool will prove uneven and precarious. In a like fashion, each ethical framework must be strongly represented, but must also be aligned with the others. A manager's challenge is to maintain the whole by striking a delicate balance between three sets of competing concerns. Before engaging in political behavior, managers should consider the needs of the community (justice), the individual (rights), and do so while maximizing value for all (utilitarianism). The order in which the different perspectives are considered is less important than is the fact that each is weighed against the other two.

CONCLUSION

Political behavior is a permanent, albeit sometimes unpleasant, fixture in organizations. In the course of this chapter, we attempted to provide the reader with the means to determine when these political behaviors are ethical or unethical. Depending on the ethical criteria, managers may draw different conclusions about the same behaviors. If a manager follows a more formalistic, rule-based strategy, the political acts themselves may be seen as unethical in that they use people as a means toward a self-serving end. A utilitarian mind-set would call for an analysis of the outcomes of those same behaviors. In this view, politics is unethical to the extent that it harms more people than it helps. Understanding how ethics plays a role in politics helps to explain the difficulties researchers have had in agreeing on whether politics is a healthy or harmful component of organizations. There is little of Pollyanna in our view. As we discussed, each ethical system has both strengths and shortcomings, and our attempt at reconciliation was a very rudimentary one. We are only partially apologetic for this. Thinking about ethical issues is certainly a worthwhile endeavor, as no ethical rule book can anticipate and answer all questions in advance. Ultimately, individuals need the tools to make their own decisions.

This observation not withstanding, guidelines—though lacking throughout much of the literature—would certainly be helpful. Perhaps the absence of a clear blueprint results from a more fundamental asymmetry. The term *business ethics* attempts to subsume two quite different human endeavors. Business, as it is conducted in a capitalist society, is largely predicated on the assumption that people will rationally act to maximize their own self-interest. Ethics, on the other hand, is predicated on the assumption that people will rationally consider the needs of others. When what is profitable is also helpful (or at least not harmful), then ethical thinking is largely moot. Ethical dilemmas arise when economic ends threaten to clash with human concerns (Hosmer, 1996). These clashes are inevitable when a person carries a moral code that emphasizes the needs of others into an environment that emphasizes profit. This dilemma will not be resolved soon. In the meantime, politics will remain a challenging game to play.

REFERENCES

Bacharach, S. B., & Lawler, E. J. (1980). *Power and politics in organizations.* San Francisco, CA: Jossey-Bass.

Brady, F. N. (1985). A Janus-headed model of ethical theory: Looking two ways at business/society issues. *Academy of Management Review, 10,* 568–576.

Brady, F. N. (1987). Rules for making exceptions to rules. *Academy of Management Review, 12,* 436–444.

Cavanagh, G. F., Moberg, D. J., & Velasquez, M. (1981). The ethics of organizational politics. *Academy of Management Review, 6,* 363–374.

Cropanzano, R., Howes, J. C., Grandey, A. A., & Toth, P. (in press). The relationship of organizational politics and support to work behaviors, attitudes, and stress. *Journal of Organizational Behavior.*

Cropanzano, R., Kacmar, M. K., & Bozeman, D. P. (1995). The social setting of work organizations: Politics, justice, and support. In R. Cropanzano & M. K. Kacmar (Eds.), *Organizational politics, justice, and support: Managing social climate at work* (pp. 1–18). Westport, CT: Greenwood.

Cropanzano, R., & Schminke, M. (in press). Justice as the mortar of social cohesion. In M. Turner (Ed.), *Groups at work: Advances in theory and research.* Mahwah, NJ: Lawrence Erlbaum Associates.

Drory, A. (1990). Perceived political climate and job attitudes. *Organization Studies, 14*(1), 59–71.

Drory, A., & Romm, T. (1988). What organizational politics is: Organization members' perceptions. *Organization Studies, 9*(2), 165–179.

Ferris, G. R., Frink, D. D., Galang, M. C., Zhou, J., Kacmar, K. M., & Howard, J. E. (1996). Perceptions of organizational politics: Predictions, stress-related implications, and outcomes. *Human Relations, 49,* 233–266.

Ferris, G. R., & Judge, T. A. (1991). Personnel/human resources management: A political influence perspective. *Journal of Management, 17,* 447–488.

Ferris, G. R., & Kacmar, K. M. (1992). Perceptions of organizational politics. *Journal of Management, 18,* 93–116.

Ferris, G. R., & King, T. R. (1991). Politics in human resource decisions: A walk on the dark side. *Organizational Dynamics, 20,* 59–71.

Ferris, G. R., Russ, G. S., & Fandt, P. M. (1989). Politics in organizations. In R. A. Giacalone & P. Rosenfeld (Eds.), *Impression management in organizations* (pp. 143–170). Newbury Park, CA: Sage.

Friedman, M. (1962). *Capitalism and freedom.* Chicago: University of Chicago Press.

Galbraith, J. K. (1996). *The good society: The humane agenda.* New York: Houghton Mifflin.

Greenberg, J., & Bies, R. J. (1992). Establishing the role of empirical studies of organizational justice in philsophical inquiries into business ethics. *Journal of Business Ethics, 11,* 433–444.

Hayek, F. A. (1944). *The road to serfdom.* Chicago: University of Chicago Press.

Heilbroner, R., & Thurow, L. (1994). *Economics explained* (Rev. ed.). New York: Touchstone.

Hosmer, L. T. (1996). *The ethics of management* (3rd ed.). Chicago: Irwin.

Howard, P. K. (1994). *The death of common sense: How law is suffocating America.* New York: Random House.

James, K. (1993). The social context of organizational justice: Cultural, intergroup, and structural effects on justice behaviors and perceptions. In R. Cropanzano (Ed.), *Justice in the workplace: Approaching fairness in human resource management* (pp. 21–50). Hillsdale, NJ: Lawrence Erlbaum Associates.

Kabanoff, B. (1991). Equity, equality, power, and conflict. *Academy of Management Review, 16,* 416–441.

Kacmar, K. M., & Ferris, G. R. (1991). Perceptions of organizational politics scale (POPS): Development and construct validation. *Educational and Psychological Measurement, 51,* 193–205.

Kacmar, K. M., & Ferris, G. R. (1993). Politics at work: Sharpening the focus of political behavior in organizations. *Business Horizons, 36,* 70–74.

Kohlberg, L. (1981). *The philosophy of moral development: Moral stages and the idea of justice.* San Francisco: Harper & Row.

Kumar, P., & Ghadially, R. (1989). Organizational politics and its effects on members of organizations. *Human Relations, 42,* 305–314.

Margalit, A. (1996). *The decent society.* Cambridge, MA: Harvard University Press.

Martin, J., & Harder, J. W. (1994). Bread and roses: Justice and the distribution of financial and socioemotional rewards in organizations. *Social Justice Research, 7,* 241–264.

Martin, N. H., & Sims, J. H. (1974). Power tactics. In D. A. Kolb, I. M. Rubin, & J. M. McIntyre (Eds.), *Organizational psychology: A book of readings* (pp. 177–183). Englewood Cliffs, NJ: Prentice-Hall.

Mayes, B. T., & Allen, R. W. (1977). Toward a definition of organizational politics. *Academy of Management Review, 2,* 672–678.

Mintzberg, H. (1983). *Power in and around organizations.* Englewood Cliffs, NJ: Prentice-Hall.

Moberg, D. J., & Myer, M. J. (1990). A deontological analysis of peer relations in organizations. *Journal of Business Ethics, 9,* 863–877.

Peterson, W. C. (1994). *Silent depression: Twenty-five years of wage squeeze and middle-class decline.* New York: Norton.

Pfeffer, J. (1981). *Power in organizations.* Boston: Pitman.

Pfeffer, J. (1992). *Managing with power: Politics and influence in organizations.* Boston: Harvard Business School Press.

Rand, A. (1969). *Introduction to objectivist epistemology.* New York: The Objectivist.

Randall, M. L., Cropanzano, R., Bormann, C. A., & Birjulin, A. (in press). Organizational politics and organizational support as predictors of work attitudes, job performance, and organizational citizenship behavior. *Journal of Organizational Behavior.*

Rawls, J. (1971). *A theory of justice.* Cambridge, MA: Harvard Univeristy Press.

Sitkin, S. B., & Bies, R. J. (1993). The legalistic organization: Definitions, dimensions, and dilemmas. *Organization Science, 4,* 345–351.

Sykes, C. J. (1992). *A nation of victims: The decay of the American character.* New York: St. Martin's Press.

Ury, W. L., Brett, J. M., & Goldberg, S. B. (1989). *Getting disputes resolved: Designing systems to cut the costs of conflict.* San Francisco: Jossey-Bass.

Velasquez, M. G. (1992). *Business ethics: Concepts and cases* (3rd ed.). Englewood Cliffs, NJ: Prentice-Hall.

CHAPTER NINE

Interpersonal Manipulation: Its Nature and Moral Limits

Mark A. Seabright
Western Oregon University

Dennis J. Moberg
Santa Clara University

There is a certain amount of fibbing in promotion; we tell people that a certain service is just about to sell out even though it's half sold; they rush to reserve space.
                                        —Waters, Bird, and Chant (1986, p. 377)

Shades of truth are required in negotiating with suppliers. One may offer me a product at $3.50/unit and I tell him I have a promotion and need it at $3.00. After he says okay, I tell him to hold on and then go out to look for a promotion.
                                        —Waters et al. (1986, p. 378)

In one plant we visited, an engineer confided to us (obviously because we, as researchers on human relations, were interested in psychological gimmicks!) that he was going to put across a proposed production layout change of his by inserting in it a rather obvious error, which others could then suggest should be corrected. We attended the meeting where this stunt was performed, and superficially it worked. Somebody caught the error, proposed that it be corrected, and our engineer immediately "bought" the suggestion as a very worth while one and made the change. The group then seemed to "buy" his entire layout proposal.
                                        —Lawrence (1954, p. 56)

Charlie, the executive vice president, . . . has reluctantly concluded that Lee must be taken out of his position as Director of Engineering. Charlie recognizes that it would demoralize the other managers if he were to

fire Lee outright. So, Charlie decides that he will begin to tell selected
individuals that he is dissatisfied with Lee's work. When there is open
support for Lee, Charlie quietly sides with Lee's opposition. He casually
lets Lee's peers know that he thinks Lee may have outlived his usefulness
to the firm. He even exaggerates Lee's deficiencies and failures when
speaking to Lee's coworkers. Discouraged by the waning support from
his colleagues, Lee decides to take an early retirement.
                          —Cavanagh, Moberg, and Velasquez (1981, pp. 369–370)

One of the many forms of influence in organizations is manipulation. Although the social science literature has devoted considerable attention to
power, authority, and other orthodox forms, the darker side of influence
has been relatively neglected (Conger, 1990). This oversight can be attributed
both to practical difficulties and to normative concerns. Manipulation is
mostly an underground phenomenon—by and large, successful manipulation goes unnoticed and unknown. This fact makes interpersonal manipulation inherently difficult to study. Normatively, the ethical ramifications of
manipulation give the topic a certain taboo quality. Knowledge about manipulation could enhance the legitimacy of its use or provide a road map
for would-be manipulators. Studying manipulation is incomplete, and possibly irresponsible, without addressing the ethics of manipulation.

There are two reasons for developing a better understanding of manipulation and its ethical implications. One is that manipulation is a relatively
common organizational influence tactic (Green & Pawlak, 1983; Porter, Allen,
& Angle, 1981). In a survey of managers' perceptions of the use of political
tactics, Allen, Madison, Porter, Renwick, and Mayes (1979) found that the
second and third most commonly mentioned categories of tactics were "use
of information" and "creating and maintaining a favorable image," both of
which included examples of manipulation. Especially illustrative were informational tactics involving the "distortion of information to create an impression by selective disclosure, innuendo, or 'objective' speculation about
individuals or events" and overwhelming the target with information "to
bury or obscure an important detail the political actor believes could harm
him, when the risk of withholding information is too great" (p. 79). In a
very different research context, Rosenberg and Pearlin (1962) found that
psychiatric nurses selected "benevolent manipulation" as the second most
likely tactic to use in influencing patient behavior in a hypothetical scenario,
with "persuasion" being the most frequently chosen category. Interestingly,
manipulation was ranked first in terms of probable effectiveness. Additional
evidence is provided by Mowday's (1978) study of upward influence among
elementary school principals. Across three hypothetical decision situations,
principals reported a moderate likelihood of relying on manipulation as an
influence tactic. Although they indicated that they were most likely to use
legitimate authority or persuasive arguments, they were more likely to use

manipulation than threats or rewards. Mowday also found that manipulation was the only influence tactic related to principal effectiveness, that is, high-effectiveness principals reported that they were more likely to use manipulation than low- or medium-effectiveness principals. Together, these studies place manipulation as a prevalent feature of organizational life.

The second reason for the importance of this topic is that manipulation is emotionally and ethically charged. Feelings of moral outrage (Bies, 1987) and revenge (Bies & Tripp, 1996; Bies, Tripp, & Kramer, 1997) can accompany a sense of being the object of a manipulation attempt. This experience may even be a defining event in an individual's organizational life. Furthermore, the collective practice of manipulation undermines trust in social relations (Green & Pawlak, 1983; Williams & Coughlin, 1993).

The purpose of this chapter is to explore interpersonal manipulation both descriptively (construct, determinants, and consequences) and prescriptively (its ethical implications). After identifying examples from the organizational literature, we define *manipulation* and distinguish it from related influence tactics. We then address the determinants, tactics, and consequences of manipulation attempts. Our prescriptive analysis considers the general moral case against manipulation as well as specific conditions that introduce ethical nuance. We conclude by discussing the implications of our analysis.

ORGANIZATIONAL EXAMPLES

The social science literature provides several examples of the use of manipulation in organizations. Most of the examples relate to impression management (e.g., Greenberg, 1990; Schlenker, 1980), organizational politics (e.g., Moberg, 1977; Riker, 1986), or leader behavior (e.g., Conger, 1990; Dyer & Condie, 1972), with considerable overlap among these categories. Some illustrative examples include:

- Hollow justice or engendering an impression of being fair without actually behaving in a fair manner (Greenberg, 1990, p. 139).
- Heresthetics or a type of political manipulation in which the situation is structured in such a way (e.g., agenda setting) that others will fall in line without any persuasion (Riker, 1986, p. ix).
- A managerial style based on facades, with tactics such as avoiding self-exposure, developing the appearance of integrity, seeming to pursue good causes, showing concern, and bluffing (Blake & Mouton, 1985, pp. 155–169).
- Illusory participation or appearing to adopt a participatory decision-making approach in order to co-opt participants rather than to use their

input (Dyer & Condie, 1972, pp. 104–108; Lawrence, 1954; Leavitt & Bahrami, 1988, pp. 145–146).

- Pseudo-Gemeinschaft or creating a false group feeling so that managers can use group influence processes to their advantage (Gouldner, 1950, pp. 653–654; Merton, 1946, p. 142–144).
- Benevolent autocrat or a leader who feigns a kindly, paternalistic style to hide, or hide behind, an autocratic stance (Bradford & Lippitt, 1945).
- Ingratiatory behaviors that are both instrumental and deceitful, such as using flattery or other-enhancement to curry the favor of a superior (Jones, 1964; Liden & Mitchell, 1988; Ralston, 1985).
- Altercasting or projecting role expectations in order to shape the target's self-definition to one's own advantage (Weinstein & Deutschberger, 1963).

DEFINING MANIPULATION

The sense of manipulation as used in the preceding organizational examples derives from a more basic definition, to "handle or treat skillfully" (Barnhart, 1988, p. 630; see also Rudinow, 1978; Simpson & Weiner, 1989, p. 319). The first use of the word as a type of interpersonal influence tactic is attributed to Carlyle (n.d.) in his 1864 biography of Frederick the Great (Barnhart, 1988, p. 630). He stated that, as part of Belleisle's overall plan, "he had got his Electors manipulated, tickled to his purpose" (p. 112). The transition in meaning from a manual or intellectual operation to an interpersonal ploy retains the sense that the manipulator exercises considerable skill in trying to alter the target's state.

Current definitions of interpersonal manipulation usually contain three elements: influence, deception, and intention or advantage. A sampling of definitions of manipulation shows these elements clearly:

- The substitution of judgment in such a way that those influenced are not aware that it is happening—at least, not while it is taking place. It is accomplished by a controlled distortion of the appearance of reality as seen by those affected (Gilman, 1962, p. 107).
- Conscious control of another's behavior, without his knowledge or consent, by the control of communications or activities that have meaning to the other person in order to achieve one's own objectives (Green & Pawlak, 1983, p. 36).
- Manipulative persuasion . . . involves the deliberate attempt of the agent to conceal or disguise his/her true objectives, *even though* the agent is *open* about the fact that an influence attempt is taking place—it is the

objective, not the influence attempt, that is concealed. . . . Manipulation . . . involves the concealment of *both* the intent of the political actor *and* the fact that an influence attempt is taking place (Porter et al., 1981, pp. 130–131).

- A method of getting someone to behave in the desired way without this person being aware that this is the power-wielder's intention (Rosenberg & Pearlin, 1962, p. 336).

- A attempts to manipulate S iff [if and only if] A attempts the complex motivation of S's behavior by means of deception or by playing on a supposed weakness of S (Rudinow, 1978, p. 346).

- To manage by dexterous contrivance or influence; especially to treat unfairly or insidiously for one's own advantage (Simpson & Weiner, 1989, p. 319).

- Any deliberate and successful effort to influence the response of another where the desired response has not been explicitly communicated to the other (Wrong, 1988, p. 28).

Most of these definitions suggest that manipulation is a type of interpersonal influence in which the manipulator intentionally deceives the target; some add that the objective is personal gain or advantage. We consider each of the elements in turn.

Influence

There are several typologies of interpersonal influence that include manipulation or potentially manipulative behaviors (Buss, 1992; Buss, Gomes, Higgins, & Lauterbach, 1987; Cody, McLaughlin, & Jordan, 1980; Dahl & Lindblom, 1953; Falbo, 1977; Falbo & Peplau, 1980; Gilman, 1962; Howard, Blumstein, & Schwartz, 1986; Kipnis, 1976; Kipnis & Schmidt, 1983; Kipnis, Schmidt, & Wilkinson, 1980; Porter et al., 1981; Tedeschi, Schlenker, & Bonoma, 1973; Tedeschi, Schlenker, & Lindskold, 1972; Wrong, 1988). Three inductive studies are especially relevant. Falbo (1977, p. 540) identified 16 influence strategies in undergraduate essays on the topic "How I Get My Way," including the manipulative, or potentially manipulative, strategies of deceit ("attempting to fool the target into agreeing by the use of flattery or lies"), emotion-target ("agent attempts to alter emotions of target"), and thought manipulation ("making the target think that the agent's way is the target's own idea"). Multidimensional scaling indicated that the 16 strategies reflected two underlying dimensions: rational/nonrational and direct/indirect. Manipulative strategies, such as deceit and thought manipulation, were designated as indirect and nonrational. Cody et al. (1980) analyzed subjects' responses to three compliance-gaining scenarios and found four general strategies: direct-rational, manipulative, exchange, and threat. Manipulative strategies included hinting, deceit, and flattery. Kipnis et al. (1980) coded lower level managers' descriptions of successfully influencing their bosses, coworkers, or subordinates, revealing 14 categories ranging from direct requests and rational discussions to clandestine activities and ingratiatory behavior. Some of the examples given for clandestine actives are clearly manipulative (e.g., "acted in a pseudo-democratic manner" and "manipulated information"); others are potentially manipulative (e.g., "lied to the target" and "showed understanding (pretended) of the target's problem"; p. 442). Factor analysis of these categories identified eight dimensions: assertiveness, ingratiation, rationality, sanctions, exchange, upward appeals, blocking, and coalitions. The dimensions of ingratiation and blocking include manipulative behaviors. In their review of inductive studies of interpersonal influence, Kipnis and Schmidt (1983) concluded that three tactics—assertive, rational, and nondirective or manipulative—summarize most of the findings.

Although this literature indicates that manipulation is one type of influence, it provides little conceptual guidance as to how it is similar to and different from other influence tactics. Sometimes, manipulation is viewed as a broad class of tactics to influence or change the environment (e.g., Buss et al., 1987). In other cases, it is restricted to specific behaviors, such as flattery or behaving seductively (e.g., Howard et al., 1986). Similarly, ingratiation has been treated as inherently manipulative (Ralston, 1985) or as an orthogonal construct (Liden & Mitchell, 1988).

Deception

Another area of confusion concerns the relationship between manipulation and deception. Counter to most definitions (and possibly common usage), manipulation does not always necessitate deception (Blum, 1973; Rudinow, 1978). Consider the following example provided by Rudinow (1978):

> Smith presents himself to the admitting officer at the psychiatric clinic. He wants to be admitted to spend the night in the hospital, saying that he has just had another terrible battle with his wife and claiming that if he is not admitted he will, as usual in such circumstances, wind up drunk, brawling, and finally either in the emergency ward or in jail. The admitting officer refuses his request, explaining that to admit Smith under these circumstances and for the reasons he gave would constitute inappropriate use of already overburdened facilities. Smith responds, "All right then, if you won't admit me now I will get you to admit me. I will climb to the top of the water tower and create such a scene that you'll have to admit me," and departs. Half an hour later Smith reappears at the admitting officer's desk, this time escorted by policemen, who report having "talked him down" from the water tower and suggest that he be admitted overnight for observation. Smith is admitted.

The admitting officer, in relating the episode, reported having felt manipulated. (p. 340)

Rudinow (1978) added that, although Smith employed deception in manipulating the policemen, he manipulated the admitting officer without lying. Manipulation, it appears, does not necessarily require deception.

Intention and Advantage

Another common element in definitions of manipulation is the notion that it is intentional and self-serving. Although it is difficult to conceive of manipulation occurring without any intent, there are degrees of awareness both of the means of influence (manipulative tactics) and of the ends themselves (alteration in the target's behavior). A manipulator may not be fully aware of employing manipulative tactics, or of the intended outcome, but manipulation is impossible if both means and ends are unconsciously enacted. In addition, we note that manipulation attempts are not always self-serving; they may be intended to aid others. It is important to add, however, that, even in such cases, the manipulator is interjecting his or her perception of what is best for the target. There is always that potential for a gap between the manipulator's sense of what is best for the target and the target's own assessment of self-interest. As Wilson (1978) concluded, "a person's judgments concerning his own interests have a primacy, therefore, which derives, not from the fact that they are more often correct than the judgments of others, but from the fact that it is his judgments—actual or hypothetical— which make correct the judgment of others" (pp. 314–315).

Types of Manipulation

Much of the problem with previous definitions of manipulation is that manipulation is not a unitary concept. Following Parsons (1963), we propose that it is composed of one type of influence that focuses on the target's situation and quite another that focuses on the psychological state of the target. Situationally based manipulation alters the objective or perceived features of the situation, such as the decision options, consequences, or rules, in a way that is likely to shape the targets' behavior or intentions (Cartwright, 1965). There is nothing inherently indirect about this form of manipulation. Like most coercion or exchange, the target may know the identity of the influencer, the nature of the desired response, and the salient features of the influence episode. In the Rudinow (1978) example quoted earlier, Smith manipulated the admitting officer's behavior by involving the police; the admitting officer could not easily ignore or challenge the policemen's request to admit Smith, irrespective of his knowledge that the water tower incident was a baseless ruse. Other examples of situational manipulation include agenda setting and Riker's (1986) heresthetics. Accordingly, we define *situational manipulation* as a form of influence in which targets' situations are managed such that targets perceive no apparent alternative but to revise or forego their preferences.

Psychological manipulation influences the target by affecting the target's underlying psychological properties or processes, such as attitudes, expectations, or values. Manipulation of this sort is necessarily indirect. During the influence episode, the target may be unaware of the perpetrator's identity, the intended outcome, or the nature of the episode itself. To return to the Rudinow (1978) example, Smith psychologically manipulated the policemen by developing the erroneous belief that he was suicidal and in need of the professional help they were obliged to provide. Other examples include illusory participation (Dyer & Condie, 1972, pp. 104–108; Lawrence, 1954; Leavitt & Bahrami, 1988, pp. 145–146) and hollow justice (Greenberg, 1990).

Befuddled sensemaking is a distinguishing feature of psychological manipulation. It involves an effort to confuse, complicate, or misdirect the target's understanding of the influence episode. It is this interpretive ruse or feint that distinguishes it from more direct influence tactics such as coercion, persuasion, and even many types of ingratiation. The psychological manipulator's dissembling may include causal attributions about the manipulator's and other actors' behavior. As noted by Porter et al. (1981), the element common to different types of manipulation is the "deliberate attempt of the agent to conceal or disguise his or her true objectives" (p. 130). We suggest that, more generally, the manipulator may attempt to mystify or misdirect the target's attributions about the intentions of various actors, including the manipulator (Moberg, 1977). For example, manipulators may displace or mask their own objectives by recasting others' intentions. The manipulator may also attempt to shape the target's self-perception (Bem, 1972) concerning the behavioral or attitudinal change. In some cases, the success of the manipulation attempt rests on the targets' perception of autonomy and self-efficacy—that is, the belief that they freely and willingly decided to change the marked behavior or attitude (cf. Dahl & Lindblom, 1953, p. 105). A sense of personal volition is likely to enhance the target's commitment to the behavioral or attitudinal change (Salancik, 1977). This effect is essential to a broad range of psychological manipulations, either as a feature of the marked change itself (e.g., co-optation involves commitment) or as a means to enhance the degree of influence (e.g., making your boss believe it was his or her idea). In summary, *psychological manipulation* is an indirect form of influence in which the target's sensemaking of the influence episode is complicated, confused, or misdirected.

We are not arguing that situational and psychological manipulation are entirely orthogonal. Indeed, a particular act of manipulation may contain both psychological and situational components. However, there are instances of situational manipulation that have minimal, if any, effect on a target's sensemaking. And even if they do, they are unlikely to implicate the target's self-perception. Agenda setting, for example, operates by framing the situation so as to exclude certain options from view and, by doing so, may implicitly mask the manipulator's intentions. It does not, however, involve a change in the target's self-perception. Psychological manipulation, on the other hand, requires some change in self-perception, and such a change is facilitated by alterations in situational sensemaking or causal attributions or both. Illusory participation, for example, co-opts targets by creating a sense of personal involvement and commitment, with such self-perceptions founded on a misunderstanding of the situation (actual vs. illusory input) and of the manipulator's intent (voice vs. co-optation).

This treatment helps explain why a sense of being used, and the associated moral outrage, is stronger for psychological manipulation than it is for situational manipulation. Although the latter impairs the target's freedom of choice or self-determination, the former diminishes the target's autonomy in self-definition. Psychological manipulation creates a misunderstanding about some aspect of the influence episode in order to engender a change in the target's beliefs, attitudes, values, and so on. If targets have a veridical understanding of the situation, the actor's intentions, and their choices, the decision to change may have been shunned or redirected. Psychological manipulation is thus intrusive both in its targeted domain, personal characteristics, and in its method, restricted or illusory autonomy. For this reason, we would expect feelings of being used to be stronger to the degree that the psychological change implicates the self (i.e., involves a highly personal characteristic, such as basic values) and to the degree that targets erroneously believe that they made the change autonomously.

USE OF MANIPULATION

We propose that three standards—principled, normative, and instrumental (Greenberg, 1990; Greenberg & Cohen, 1982; Tetlock, 1985)—affect the use of manipulative tactics in interpersonal relationships. Personal values and internalized codes of conduct comprise the principled standard (Tetlock, 1985), whereas the collective force of others' expectations determines the normative standard (Greenberg & Cohen, 1982). The instrumental standard concerns the relationship between the behavior itself and its consequences, such as one's own and others' gain. From the actor's perspective, the three standards reflect self-expectations (principled), other-expectations (normative), and outcome-expectations (instrumental).

The social science literature suggests several variables that are likely to influence the content and relative salience of the three standards. In the following sections, we first examine the variables that may directly shape each standard and then consider the moderator(s) that are likely to increase the standard's salience.

Principled Standard

Moral Development. Theories of moral development address how individuals think through ethical dilemmas. Kohlberg (1969) proposed three general levels of moral development, each containing two sequential stages. At the preconventional level, Stage 1 is marked by direct obedience and avoidance of punishment, and Stage 2 is guided by instrumental self-interest and basic reciprocity. At the conventional level, Stage 3 focuses on social approval and pleasing and helping others; Stage 4 broadens this orientation to include a concern for maintaining social accord for its own sake. At the postconventional level, Stage 5 values the social contract, albeit arbitrarily determined, because it affords general welfare, and Stage 6 is guided by self-chosen moral principles of conscience or universal appeal. Clearly, moral development informs an individual's principled standard.

Self-Awareness. Self-awareness, or an inward versus outward focus of attention (Duval & Wicklund, 1972), is likely to affect reliance on the principled standard. An important consequence of self-focused attention is to make personal ideals salient and to set in motion a self-regulation process in which the current situation is compared with the ideal standard and behavior is adjusted to match the standard (Carver & Scheier, 1981). As indicated by studies in several different domains, the result of this process is to enhance adherence to personal ideals (e.g., Greenberg, 1990; Fiske & Taylor, 1984, pp. 199–203). By extension, we would expect self-awareness to engender conformity to personal moral standards (concerning manipulation).

Normative Standard

Organizational and Professional Culture. The shared beliefs and expectations that characterize the culture of an organization or profession determine the acceptability of various influence tactics, including manipulation. As Porter et al. (1981) suggested, "there is ample reason to believe that informal 'political' norms abound in organizations" (p. 114). Specific norms may address the extent to which manipulation is condemned, or condoned, in a given situation. We suggest that the makeup of an individual's normative standard is strongly shaped by organizational and professional culture.

Situation Strength. The strength of the situation enhances the salience of normative expectations, relative to principled and instrumental standards. For example, Christie and Geis' (1970) interactive model of Machiavellian behavior indicates that situation structure moderates the effect of Machia-vellianism (see later section on Machiavellianism) on the use of specific tactics. According to the model, high and low Machs behave similarly in highly structured situations, that is, when roles, rewards, and responsibilities are clearly defined. In loosely structured situations, however, high Machs tend to test limits, initiate structure, and exploit resources, whereas low Machs tend to adopt implicit limits, accept others' structuring, and become interpersonally involved. More generally, as Davis-Blake and Pfeffer (1989) concluded, strong situations tend to swamp dispositional effects.

Instrumental Standard

Relative Power and Objectives. There is substantial evidence that relative power or status affects the choice of influence tactic (Falbo & Peplau, 1980; Howard et al., 1986; Instone, Major, & Bunker, 1983; Kipnis & Schmidt, 1983; Kipnis et al., 1980; Krone, 1991; Tedeschi et al., 1973; Tedeschi et al., 1972). Studies of influence in intimate relationships indicate that dependence increases reliance on unilateral, indirect, and manipulative tactics (Falbo & Peplau, 1980; Howard et al., 1986). Studies of organizational influence show that downward influence attempts utilize a greater variety of tactics and rely more on directive strategies, such as assertiveness, than upward influence attempts (Kipnis & Schmidt, 1983; Kipnis et al., 1980). In a study of upward influence, Mowday (1978) found that manipulation was the only influence tactic related to the effectiveness of elementary school principals, with high-effectiveness principals reporting that they were more likely to use manipulation than low- or medium-effectiveness principals. In addition, Krone (1991) found that out-group subordinates (i.e., subordinates who characterized their relationship with their supervisors as formal and restricted) were more likely than in-group subordinates to use manipulative tactics in their attempts at upward influence. Collectively, these studies suggest that relative status and dependence can affect the feasibility or perceived efficacy of various influence strategies, including manipulation.

Whether an objective is organizationally sanctioned is also likely to affect the choice of influence tactic. Personal objectives, such as favors, suggest the use of indirect tactics (Kipnis & Schmidt, 1983; Kipnis et al., 1980). Whereas legitimate means are available for achieving sanctioned ends, the pursuit of nonsanctioned objectives requires either disguising the actual goal while using accepted strategies or adopting nonsanctioned tactics. Generally, we would expect manipulation to occur more often in the pursuit of non-sanctioned objectives. In terms of our general framework for use of ma-nipulation, objectives affect an individual's instrumental calculations.

Machiavellianism. Christie and colleagues originally conceived of Machiavellianism as a manipulative orientation with four defining features: a lack of emotional involvement with others, a utilitarian rather than moral view of behavior, a lack of gross psychopathology, and a low degree of ideological commitment (Christie & Geis, 1970). Using statements from Machiavelli's writings, they developed a 20-item instrument, the Mach scale, to measure this construct (Christie & Geis, 1970). Research results indicate that individuals with high scores on the Mach scale exhibit manipulative behavior more often, and devise more innovative manipulations, than do individuals with low scores on the Mach scale (Bass, 1990; Christie & Geis, 1970; Geis & Christie, 1970). High Machs are also found to be more successful in bargaining and persuasion situations than low Machs (Christie & Geis, 1970). Summarizing this research, Christie and Geis (1970) characterized the Machiavellian type as detached and calculative:

> In pursuit of largely self-defined goals, he disregards both his own and others' affective states and therefore attacks the problem with all the logical ability that he possesses. He reads the situation in terms of perceived possibilities and then proceeds to act on the basis of what action will lead to what results. (p. 350)

This description suggests that Machiavellianism enhances reliance on an instrumental standard. Machiavellianism does not imply a lack of principles or awareness of normative expectations; rather, it indicates that instrumental considerations dominate these other standards.

TACTICS OF MANIPULATION

It is important to distinguish between the resources used to manipulate and the actual manipulation tactics, although they are often confused (Kipnis & Schmidt, 1983). The resources supporting influence attempts reflect basic sources of dependence—effect and information (Johns, 1996; Jones & Gerard, 1967). For example, Tedeschi et al. (1973, 1972) proposed that manipulative influence is effected either by reinforcement control (rewards and punishments) or by information control (cue control, filtering, warning, and deception).

There has been little work, inductively or deductively, on actual tactics of manipulation. However derived, most typologies address general influence or power, rather than manipulation per se (e.g., Buss et al., 1987; French & Raven, 1959). A notable exception is Michener and Suchner's (1972) extrapolation of their power typology to deceptive tactics. They proposed four tactics that could be used manipulatively: blocking outcomes (e.g., agenda setting), demand creation (e.g., ingratiation), utilizing alternatives (e.g., clubmanship or inflating the choice set), and feigned withdrawal (e.g., playing hard to get).

CONSEQUENCES OF MANIPULATION

A manipulation attempt potentially affects the manipulator, the target, and the organizational or social context in which it occurs. We consider each here.

Manipulator

A successful manipulation attempt obviously produces the benefits that follow from the target's compliance, whereas these benefits are forgone if failure occurs. If the manipulation attempt involves deception, however, another possible outcome accompanying failure is detection. If the subterfuge is discovered, the consequences could include sanctions, retaliatory actions, and loss of reputation.

Manipulation tactics are also likely to affect the perpetrator's self-image and perception of the target. If successful, manipulators' sense of control and self-efficacy may be enhanced, whereas their image of the target may be devalued (Kipnis, Castell, Gergen, & Mauch, 1976; Kipnis & Schmidt, 1983).

Target

Manipulation, if successful, creates behavioral or attitudinal changes that are not freely chosen. Situational manipulation impairs the target's freedom of choice, whereas psychological manipulation diminishes freedom of self-definition. Although both types of manipulation attenuate the target's actual autonomy, an ironic consequence of an undetected ruse is that it may inflate the target's perceptions of autonomy. As noted by Dahl and Lindblom (1953), successful manipulation may "stimulate feelings of 'free choice' and evoke enthusiasm and initiative" (p. 105).

Assuming deception is involved, its detection may depend on the target's relationship with the manipulator. In a study of deception detection, McCornack and Parks (1986) found that greater familiarity or relational development strengthened "subjects' confidence in their ability to spot their partner's lies, which in turn were linked to increases in the presumption that partners were telling the truth, which ultimately resulted in significant *decreases* in accuracy" (p. 388). In addition, interpersonal trust is likely to enhance the target's vulnerability (Mayer, Davis, & Schoorman, 1995), including susceptibility to deception.

If a manipulative ruse is uncovered, the potential consequences include moral outrage (Bies, 1987), revenge (Bies & Tripp, 1996; Bies, Tripp, & Kramer, 1997), and reactance (Brehm & Cole, 1966; Krebs, 1982; Schopler & Thompson, 1968). Common to all of these responses are feelings of anger, resentment, or hostility. These emotions define moral outrage and often accompany revenge and reactance. Revenge, however, also finds expression in cognitive forms, such as fantasies of vengeance, and in behavioral acts, such as violence (Bies & Tripp, 1996; Bies, Tripp, & Kramer, 1997), and reactance leads to efforts to restore lost freedom, either directly or indirectly (Brehm & Brehm, 1981). Other possible consequences of a foiled manipulation attempt are an erosion of trust and an attenuation of the frequency and nature of future interactions between the target and the perpetrator.

Organizational or Social Context

An interesting question is whether manipulation is contagious. The use of nondeceptive manipulation models a route to influence. In addition, reliance on manipulation tactics is likely to erode collective trust (Green & Pawlak, 1983; Williams & Coughlin, 1993), thereby constricting the bases for interpersonal exchange and attenuating manipulation's illegitimacy. In the absence of trust, manipulation may become an acceptable, or seemingly necessary, means for gaining compliance.

ETHICS OF MANIPULATION

For those unfamiliar with ethical theory, the term *prima facie* has a special meaning in ethics. Literally defined as "based on the first impression," prima facie refers to an ethical principle so fundamental that only special circumstances would exempt its conclusion. For example, one might contend that prima facie, democracy is an ethically superior mode of governance than autocracy.

When it comes to manipulation, the moral case against this practice is so great that it is unanimously considered prima facie unethical. Because the ends of the perpetrator are served with no concern for the victim in typical acts of manipulation, utilitarians question whether other acts might promise even better aggregate ends (cf. Davis, 1984). Similarly, serious justice issues arise when one manipulates another (Nozick, 1974). But, the indictment is strongest among deontologists who, after Kant, consider using others for one's ends only to be most fundamentally wrong (e.g., Rudinow, 1978).[1]

The categorical imperative was Kant's (1785/1964) attempt to capture what he considered were basic, commonly held intuitions about morality. When dealing with the topic of manipulation, the second formulation of the categorical imperative is most directly relevant. It holds that one should never treat a person as a means only, but always at the same time as an end. This formulation is useful in understanding one of the most significant

---

[1]It is clear that manipulating and using others for one's ends only are not equivalent. However, because manipulating is a special case of using others, the moral objection to it is at least as strong.

insights of Kant's ethics, that is, that our most basic moral intuitions require a respect for persons not as instruments but as rational, autonomous agents.

This understanding suggests why the practice of manipulation is prima facie wrong. Manipulation operates by robbing the victim of autonomy, either in choice (situational manipulation) or in self-definition (psychological manipulation) for the sole purpose of advancing the perpetrator's objective. Situational manipulation corrals the victim into behavioral change, and psychological manipulation befuddles the victim's sensemaking. In both cases, the victim's standing as an independent, rational agent is compromised through the act itself, through the corralling or befuddling. It is this way of treating the victim—merely as a means—that violates Kant's principle.

It should be noted, however, that the Kantian prohibition against using others as a means only is not suggesting that it is morally wrong to use someone to achieve one's ends. Such a reading would imply incorrectly that the categorical imperative suggests that it is immoral to engage in commercial transactions or to influence people to freely choose to recycle their aluminum cans because doing so is obviously using someone to achieve one's ends. The Kantian principle, however, simply enjoins against using others as a means *only*, which would not apply to most commercial transactions or environmental awareness campaigns. Once again, to use others as a means *only* is to disregard their nature as autonomous agents. It is to use persons as one might use a hammer or a trained seal without any respect for their standing as independent, rational agents.

Although compelling and useful, a prima facie indictment against the practice of manipulation based on Kant's principle is not the entire story. Clearly, there are conditions in which an act of manipulation is only mildly objectionable and others in which it is especially egregious. We can imagine no case where it is ethically neutral or indicative of virtue.[2] What remains of this chapter, then, is an attempt to articulate the shades of gray associated with manipulation. In so doing, it is not our project to provide encouragement or succor to manipulators. Rather, it is to find in our complex moral intuitions (Davis, 1984) common reactions to important differences.

Consideration 1: Intent of the Manipulator

Some acts of manipulation are not completely conscious. For example, individuals thought to have Machiavellian predispositions are not always aware of how they exploit their adversary's weaknesses or their own relative advantages. These persons may be genuinely baffled by their ability to get others to do their bidding. In ethics, a fundamental canon of justice holds

---

[2]It is interesting that one historical instance of (situational) manipulation cited by Riker (1986) is attributed to Abraham Lincoln, a statesman of celebrated virtue. It would appear that great men and women do not necessarily live lives free of manipulation.

that, generally, one should not be held responsible for acts one does not freely choose. A similar example is embedded in Grice's maxim of conversational implicature that holds that one person may mislead while speaking the truth if what is said violates expectations about common communicative purposes (Grice, 1989). Consequently, most would judge acts of manipulation that are partially unconscious or unintentional to be less serious than acts that are carefully planned.[3]

The fact that intent is a consideration in our moralizing about manipulation offers manipulators direction for their deception. When accused, a manipulator may attempt to escape moral responsibility by various forms of impression management (e.g., Giacalone & Rosenfeld, 1989) including accounts, excuses, and justifications. In this vein, one hears the term deniability in cases of governmental involvement in espionage. Regardless of the attempts to spin the attribution process, moral forgiveness is reserved for genuine cases of a lack of volition rather than unsubstantiated pleas of innocent motives.

Consideration 2: Rewards for the Manipulator

The personal rewards that accrue to the manipulator also weigh in as a consideration about the morality of a particular act of manipulation. Most reprehensible are acts in which the victim is manipulated in order to advance the ends of the manipulator with no consideration for the ends of the victim. Such acts are exploitative and in clear violation of the categorical imperative (cf. Moberg & Meyer, 1990). Most people are not as quick to judge in cases of mixed motive manipulation, that is, when the ends of the victim are also advanced. Indeed, much of the manipulation in the marketplace is of that nature (Blumberg, 1989).

The most selfless acts of manipulation occur when the manipulator acts only to further the interests of the victim. Some parents, for example, will employ variations of so-called reverse psychology to manipulate their children. Teachers may also set students up to experience an epiphany. Not all such acts are truly manipulative as we have defined it, but some are, and as Wilson (1978) noted, there is substantial moral concern:

> To impose upon another, even by the gentlest and most loving pressure, a conception of his good which does not command his rational assent suggests a kind of dangerous arrogance. Failure to convert someone to a view of what is best for him must always cast doubt on it and any such view must always be in doubt until exposed to this test. (p. 314)

Many of us are less uncomfortable being the subject of paternalistic manipulation if manipulators use their superior power over us responsibly

---

[3]People have a duty to maintain some level of awareness about their own actions and the results they produce. In law, one finds that incapacitation is not an acceptable defense.

(Moberg, 1994). Indeed, we expect the professionals we consult (e.g., therapists, physicians, and accountants) to uphold special duties of disinterestedness, disclosure, and diligence in any situation in which an opportunity to manipulate occurs (Bayles, 1981).

Consideration 3: Damage Done to the Victim

Clearly, some acts of manipulation have serious effects on the victims whereas others can be shrugged off as life's lessons. The problem is that there is no single metric that enables one to ascertain the degree of damage one has suffered. For example, a $10,000 loss is devastating to some but a mere setback to others. Let us focus on three important factors: target of manipulation, impact on needs, and impact on self.

• Because behavior is more fleeting and less enduring than attitudes or beliefs, manipulation targeting behavior (buying a stove) rather than beliefs (gas stoves are better than electric stoves) is less objectionable. Our cognitions (attitudes and beliefs) serve a number of instrumental and expressive functions and help us organize our lives and learn from our experiences. If a cognitive map has an element that is defective, one's entire life course could be altered. On the basis of this principle, psychological manipulation is less acceptable than situational manipulation because the former necessarily distorts one's sensemaking about the self—a distortion that may have long-run consequences. Accordingly, we observe a convergence between most people's moral outrage and an application of ethical principles.

• There are many, many ways of classifying the importance of human needs. One is the distinction between basic needs and adventitious needs (Braybrooke, 1987). To say someone has a basic need for x is to say that the loss of x (or the loss of a significant opportunity to gain x) would result in a considerable decrease in one's prospects for survival or basic well-being. Included here are physiological needs together with fundamental psychological needs (such as the need to have some minimal level of self-esteem necessary for one's participation in society). In contrast, adventitious needs are those which come and go with particular projects. For example, if one is to prepare a cup of coffee, one needs drinking water. Although this is not a basic need, it is certainly a need in the sense that it is not possible to prepare a cup of coffee without drinking water. Clearly, it is more egregious to be manipulated into threatening one's basic needs than one's adventitious needs.

• Among adventitious needs, there are certainly some that are much more attached to self than others. Thus, if one has been working on a manuscript for years, and a publisher manipulates one to give away one's rights to it with no consideration, then that is a much more consequential (and therefore reprehensible) act of manipulation than if one were manipulated out of a stick of gum (Marietta, 1972).

Consideration 4: Weakness Preyed Upon and Strengths Leveraged

In cases in which the victim's vulnerability is one which is inescapable, the injustice created by manipulation is particularly heinous. Thus, if one capitalizes on the frailties of age, infirmity, or disability, one's manipulative acts seem despicable. At the other extreme, if the manipulator takes advantage of the victim's flaws of character that we generally associate with vices, we are commonly less troubled. The most renown model of vice is probably the seven deadly sins, so called because each required special penitence in the medieval Church. For the record, these sins are pride, envy, anger, sloth, avarice, gluttony, and lust. Accordingly, if it is a victim's pride or lust that is the leverage in an act of manipulation, then some may conclude that the victim got his just deserts. The lack of guilt among manipulative confidence men who prey upon the greedy supports this conclusion.

In a parallel sense, it is difficult to condone manipulative acts that reward the vices of the manipulator. For example, if a generous victim is manipulated at the hands of an envious manipulator, then our sense of justice would strongly favor the victim.

Consideration 5: Extent of the Breach of Trust

As we have seen, manipulation sometimes requires deception. If an act of manipulation requires painstaking or time-consuming acts of feigning trust, then the victim is deceived not once but on a series of occasions. Such acts are especially objectionable because they involve so much deception (Bok, 1979). Manipulators who fake their way into a family's inner circle (as servants, trusted confidants, or family members) only to abscond with some family resources entrusted to them are examples. So elaborate is their deceit that no family member is untouched by a sense of betrayal.

Some organizational relationships require more trust than others. There is more necessary trust between superior and subordinate than between peers, and more between peers than market partners (Moberg, 1994). Accordingly, one generally is more forgiving of manipulation in the marketplace than in the community, and manipulating one's superior or subordinates is especially shameful.

IMPLICATIONS

We hope that our approach in this chapter might provide direction for studying other taboo topics in organizational behavior. We suggest that part of the reason for the taboo quality of topics, such as manipulation or antisocial behavior is an uncertainty about how to treat their obvious normative ramifications. Because ethical issues are central to such topics, a purely descriptive approach that neglects these issues seems insufficient, at best, and unethical in its own right, at worst. We argue that studying taboo topics requires both descriptive and normative approaches and, based on our experience in developing this chapter, that there may be beneficial crossovers from combining these approaches. We found that our descriptive analysis led to distinctions (situational vs. psychological manipulation) that had important ethical ramifications and, in turn, that commonsense ethical insights (illusory autonomy) pointed to important descriptive features of the manipulation process.

A more specific implication of our analysis is that not all acts of manipulation are equally unethical. It is easy to think of manipulation as a single type of act that is patently wrong, either due to the connotation carried by the word itself or due to reflection on a specific, usually personally meaningful, example. Our analysis, however, has shown. that manipulative acts vary along several dimensions—manipulator's intent, consequences for both the manipulator and the victim, amount and type of subterfuge, etc.—that affect the strength of the moral case against such acts. These distinctions could be useful in formulating managerial responses to cases of manipulation.

Lastly, our treatment of psychological manipulation and its ethical implications suggests that the application of psychological knowledge to organizational behavior bears a certain responsibility both for the practitioner and for the researcher. Theories such as behavioral commitment (Salancik, 1977), self-perception (Bem, 1972), and reactance (Brehm & Brehm, 1981), to name just a few, are especially prone to manipulative use. More specifically, we are concerned that the management literature on the benefits of employee participation has been widely misused to co-opt employees without providing an actual voice in the decision-making process. The potential for such misuse raises a number of questions about professional responsibility. To what extent should practitioners go out of their way to avoid or disclose the use of such knowledge? Should theoretical treatments that are vulnerable to misuse include prescriptive advice? Do management faculty have an obligation to address the ethical implications of certain practices and theories, and if so, which ones?

There are some hopeful developments that may lessen the use of manipulation in the years ahead. Education in the behavioral sciences is more widespread today than ever before, inoculating more against the techniques of manipulation. In addition, trust is a topic of continuing importance in organizational affairs, leading to a cultivation of trustworthiness as part of one's reputation. Greater access to information in organizations would seem to nullify many manipulation attempts based on deceptive or uninformed sensemaking. Yet, it would be naive to assume that unethical manipulation is likely to go away soon as a social or organizational phenomenon. The reason is plain—manipulation is a process and a practice that is virtually impossible to control. It is often sensed too late to result in sanctions, if at all. Moreover, there is commonly an element of plausible deniability that diffuses responsibility. But, by shedding light on the nature of manipulation and its ethical implications, work on this subject may help to diminish a practice that diminishes persons.

REFERENCES

Allen, R. W., Madison, D. L., Porter, L. W., Renwick, P. A., & Mayes, B. T. (1979). Organizational politics: Tactics and characteristics of its actors. *California Management Review, 22,* 77–83.

Barnhart, R. K. (Ed.). (1988). *The Barnhart dictionary of etymology.* New York: H. W. Wilson.

Bass, B. M. (1990). Authoritarianism, power orientation, Machiavellianism, and leadership. In B. M. Bass (Ed.), *Bass & Stogdill's handbook of leadership: Theory, research, and managerial applications* (3rd ed., pp. 124–139). New York: The Free Press.

Bayles, M. D. (1981). *Professional ethics.* Belmont, CA: Wadsworth.

Bem, D. J. (1972). Self-perception theory. In L. Berkowitz (Ed.), *Advances in experimental social psychology* (Vol. 6, pp. 1–62). New York: Academic Press.

Bies, R. J. (1987). The predicament of injustice: The management of moral outrage. In L. L. Cummings & B. M. Staw (Eds.), *Research in organizational behavior* (Vol. 9, pp. 289–319). Greenwich, CT: JAI.

Bies, R. J., & Tripp, T. M. (1996). Beyond distrust: "Getting even" and the need for revenge. In R. M. Kramer & T. R. Tyler (Eds.), *Trust in organizations* (pp. 246–260). Thousand Oaks, CA: Sage.

Bies, R. J., Tripp, T. M., & Kramer, R. M. (1997). At the breaking point: Cognitive and social dynamics of revenge in organizations. In R. A. Giacalone & J. Greenberg (Eds.), *Antisocial behavior in organizations* (pp. 18–36). Thousand Oaks, CA: Sage.

Blake, R. R., & Mouton, J. S. (1985). *The managerial grid III.* Houston, TX: Gulf Publishing.

Blum, L. (1973). Deceiving, hurting, and using. In A. Montefiore (Ed.), *Philosophy and personal relations* (pp. 34–61). Montreal: McGill-Queen's University Press.

Blumberg, P. (1989). *The predatory society.* New York: Oxford University Press.

Bok, S. (1979). *Lying: Moral choice in public and private life.* New York: Vintage Books.

Bradford, L. P., & Lippitt, R. (1945). Building a democatic work group. *Personnel, 22,* 143–144.

Braybrooke, D. (1987). *Meeting needs.* Princeton, NJ: Princeton University Press.

Brehm, J. W., & Cole, A. H. (1966). Effect of a favor which reduces freedom. *Journal of Personality and Social Psychology, 3,* 420–426.

Brehm, S. S., & Brehm, J. W. (1981). *Psychological reactance: A theory of freedom and control.* New York: Academic Press.

Buss, D. M. (1992). Manipulation in close relationships: Five personality factors in interactional context. *Journal of Personality, 60,* 477–499.

Buss, D. M., Gomes, M., Higgins, D. S., & Lauterbach, K. (1987). Tactics of manipulation. *Journal of Personality and Social Psychology, 52,* 1219–1229.

Carlyle, T. (n.d.). *History of Friedrich the Second, called Frederick the Great* (Vol. 4). New York: John W. Lovell.

Cartwright, D. (1965). Influence, leadership, and control. In J. G. March (Ed.), *Handbook of organizations* (pp. 1–47). Chicago: Rand McNally.

Carver, C. S., & Scheier, M. F. (1981). *Attention and self-regulation: A control-theory approach to human behavior.* New York: Springer-Verlag.

Cavanagh, G. F., Moberg, D. J., & Velasquez, M. (1981). The ethics of organizational politics. *Academy of Management Review, 6,* 363–374.

Christie, R., & Geis, F. L. (Eds.). (1970). *Studies in Machiavellianism.* New York: Academic Press.

Cody, M. J., McLaughlin, M. L., & Jordan, W. J. (1980). A multidimensional scaling of three sets of compliance-gaining strategies. *Communication Quarterly, 28*(3), 34–46.

Conger, J. A. (1990). The dark side of leadership. *Organizational Dynamics, 19*(2), 44–55.

Dahl, R. A., & Lindblom, C. E. (1953). *Politics, economics, and welfare.* New York: Harper & Brothers.

Davis, N. (1984). Using persons and common sense. *Ethics, 94,* 387–406.

Davis-Blake, A., & Pfeffer, J. (1989). Just a mirage: The search for dispositional effects in organizational research. *Academy of Management Review, 14,* 385–400.

Duval, S., & Wicklund, R. A. (1972). *A theory of objective self-awareness.* New York: Academic Press.

Dyer, W. G., & Condie, S. J. (1972). Manipulation. In W. G. Dyer (Ed.), *The sensitive manipulator* (pp. 103–110). Provo, UT: Brigham Young University Press.

Falbo, T. (1977). Multidimensional scaling of power strategies. *Journal of Personality and Social Psychology, 35,* 537–547.

Falbo, T., & Peplau, L. A. (1980). Power strategies in intimate relationships. *Journal of Personality and Social Psychology, 38,* 618–628.

Fiske, S. T., & Taylor, S. E. (1984). *Social cognition.* Reading, MA: Addison-Wesley.

French, J. R. P., Jr., & Raven, B. H. (1959). The bases of social power. In D. Cartwright (Ed.), *Studies in social power* (pp. 150–167). Ann Arbor, MI: University of Michigan Press.

Geis, F. L., & Christie, R. (1970). Machiavellianism and the manipulation of one's fellowman. In K. J. Gergen & D. Marlowe (Eds.), *Personality and social behavior* (pp. 167–186). Reading, MA: Addison-Wesley.

Giacalone, R. A., & Rosenfeld, P. (Eds.). (1989). *Impression management in the organization.* Hillsdale, NJ: Lawence Erlbaum Associates.

Gilman, G. (1962). An inquiry into the nature and use of authority. In M. Haire (Ed.), *Organization theory in industrial practice* (pp. 105–142). New York: Wiley.

Gouldner, A. W. (1950). The problem of succession and bureaucracy. In A. W. Gouldner (Ed.), *Studies in leadership: Leadership and democractic action* (pp. 644–659). New York: Harper & Brothers.

Green, R. K., & Pawlak, E. J. (1983). Ethics and manipulation in organizations. *Social Service Review, 57,* 35–43.

Greenberg, J. (1990). Looking fair vs. being fair: Managing impressions of organizational justice. In L. L. Cummings & B. M. Staw (Eds.), *Research in organizational behavior* (Vol. 12, pp. 111–157). Greenwich, CT: JAI.

Greenberg, J., & Cohen, R. L. (1982). Why justice? Normative and instrumental interpretations. In J. Greenberg & R. L. Cohen (Eds.), *Equity and justice in social behavior* (pp. 437–469). New York: Academic Press.

Grice, P. (1989). *Studies in the way of words.* Cambridge, MA: Harvard University Press.

Howard, J. A., Blumstein, P., & Schwartz, P. (1986). Sex, power, and influence tactics in intimate relationships. *Journal of Personality and Social Psychology, 51,* 102–109.

Instone, D., Major, B., & Bunker, B. B. (1983). Gender, self-confidence, and social influence strategies: An organizational simulation. *Journal of Personality and Social Psychology, 44,* 322–333.

Johns, G. (1996). *Organizational behavior: Understanding and managing life at work* (4th ed.). New York: HarperCollins.

Jones, E. E. (1964). *Ingratiation: A social psychological analysis.* New York: Appleton-Century-Crofts.

Jones, E. E., & Gerard, H. B. (1967). *Foundations of social psychology.* New York: Wiley.

Kant, I. (1964). *Groundwork for the metaphysics of morals* (H. J. Paton, Trans.). New York: Harper & Row. (Original work published 1785)

Kipnis, D. (1976). *The powerholders.* Chicago: University of Chicago Press.

Kipnis, D., Castell, P. J., Gergen, M., & Mauch, D. (1976). Metamorphic effects of power. *Journal of Applied Psychology, 61,* 127–135.

Kipnis, D., & Schmidt, S. M. (1983). An influence perspective on bargaining within organizations. In M. H. Bazerman & R. J. Lewicki (Eds.), *Negotiating in organizations* (pp. 303–319). Beverly Hills, CA: Sage.

Kipnis, D., Schmidt, S. M., & Wilkinson, I. (1980). Intraorganizational influence tactics: Explorations in getting one's way. *Journal of Applied Psychology, 65,* 440–452.

Kohlberg, L. (1969). Stage and sequence: The cognitive-developmental approach to socialization. In D. A. Goslin (Ed.), *Handbook of socialization theory and research* (pp. 347–480). Chicago: Rand McNally.

Krebs, D. L. (1982). Prosocial behavior, equity, and justice. In J. Greenberg & R. L. Cohen (Eds.), *Equity and justice in social behavior* (pp. 261–308). New York: Academic Press.

Krone, K. J. (1991). Effects of leader–member exchange on subordinates' upward influence attempts. *Communication Research Reports, 8,* 9–18.

Lawrence, P. R. (1954). How to deal with resistance to change. *Harvard Business Review,* May–June, 49–57.

Leavitt, H. J., & Bahrami, H. (1988). Manipulation: Slippery styles for influencing behavior. In H. J. Leavitt & H. Bahrami (Eds.), *Managerial psychology: Managing behavior in organizations* (5th ed., pp. 142–147). Chicago: University of Chicago Press.

Liden, R. C., & Mitchell, T. R. (1988). Ingratiatory behaviors in organizational settings. *Academy of Management Review, 13,* 572–587.

Marietta, D. E., Jr. (1972). On using people. *Ethics, 82,* 232–238.

Mayer, R. C., Davis, J. H., & Schoorman, F. D. (1995). An integrative model of organizational trust. *Academy of Management Review, 20,* 709–734.

McCornack, S. A., & Parks, M. R. (1986). Deception detection and relationship development: The other side of trust. In M. L. McLaughlin (Ed.), *Communication yearbook 9* (pp. 377–389). Beverly Hills, CA: Sage.

Merton, R. K. (1946). *Mass persuasion: The social psychology of a war bond drive.* New York: Harper & Brothers.

Michener, H. A., & Suchner, R. W. (1972). The tactical use of social power. In J. T. Tedeschi (Ed.), *The social influence processes* (pp. 239–286). Chicago: Aldine-Atherton

Moberg, D. J. (1977, April). *Organizational politics: Perspective from attribution theory.* Paper presented at the meeting of the American Institute for Decision Sciences, Chicago, IL.

Moberg, D. J. (1994). An ethical analysis of hierarchical relations in organizations. *Business Ethics Quarterly, 4,* 205–220.

Moberg, D. J., & Meyer, M. J. (1990). A deontological analysis of peer relations in organizations. *Journal of Business Ethics, 9,* 863–877.

Mowday, R. T. (1978). The exercise of upward influence in organizations. *Administrative Science Quarterly, 23,* 137–156.

Nozick, R. (1974). *Anarchy, state, and utopia.* New York: Basic Books.

Parsons, T. (1963). On the concept of influence. *Public Opinion Quarterly, 27,* 37–62.

Porter, L. W., Allen, R. W., & Angle, H. L. (1981). The politics of upward inlfuence in organizations. In L. L. Cummings & B. M. Staw (Eds.), *Research in organizational behavior* (Vol. 3, pp. 109–149). Greenwich, CT: JAI.

Ralston, D. A. (1985). Employee ingratiation: The role of management. *Academy of Management Review, 10,* 477–487.

Riker, W. H. (1986). *The art of political manipulation*. New Haven, CT: Yale University Press.

Rosenberg, M., & Pearlin, L. I. (1962). Power-orientations in the mental hospital. *Human Relations, 15,* 335–349.

Rudinow, J. (1978). Manipulation. *Ethics, 88,* 338–347.

Salancik, G. R. (1977). Commitment and the control of organizational behavior and belief. In B. M. Staw & G. R. Salancik (Eds.), *New directions in organizational behavior* (pp. 1–54). Chicago: St. Clair Press.

Schlenker, B. R. (1980). *Impression management: The self-concept, social identity, and interpersonal relations*. Belmont, CA: Brooks/Cole.

Schopler, J., & Thompson, V. D. (1968). Role of attribution processes in mediating amount of reciprocity for a favor. *Journal of Personality and Social Psychology, 10,* 243–250.

Simpson, J. A., & Weiner, E. S. C. (Eds.). (1989). *The Oxford English dictionary* (2nd ed.). Oxford, England: Clarendon.

Tedeschi, J. T., Schlenker, B. R., & Bonoma, T. V. (1973). *Conflict, power and games*. Chicago: Aldine.

Tedeschi, J. T., Schlenker, B. R., & Lindskold, S. (1972). The exercise of power and influence: The source of influence. In J. T. Tedeschi (Ed.), *The social influence processes* (pp. 287–345). Chicago: Aldine-Atherton.

Tetlock, P. E. (1985). Toward an intuitive politician model of attribution processes. In B. R. Schlenker (Ed.), *The self and social life* (pp. 203–234). New York: McGraw-Hill.

Waters, J. A., Bird, F., & Chant, P. D.(1986). Everyday moral issues experienced by managers. *Journal of Business Ethics, 5,* 373–384.

Weinstein, E. A., & Deutschberger, P. (1963). Some dimensions of altercasting. *Sociometry, 26,* 454–466.

Williams, A. R., & Coughlin, C. L. J. (1993). "In God we trust, all others pay cash": A prologue to trust, vulnerability, and deceit in business organizations. *Business & Professional Ethics Journal, 12* (2), 67–90.

Wilson, J. R. S. (1978). In one another's power. *Ethics, 88,* 299–315.

Wrong, D. H. (1988). *Power: Its forms, bases, and uses*. Chicago: University of Chicago Press.

CHAPTER TEN

Software and Hard Choices: Ethical Considerations in the Facilitation of a Sociotechnical System

Terri L. Griffith
Washington University

Gregory B. Northcraft
University of Illinois

Mark A. Fuller
Baylor University

The past decade has seen exponential growth in technological capabilities. Computer chip speed doubles approximately every 18 months, and subsequent organizational and personal computing opportunities are keeping pace. The growth of computing and network capabilities are bringing anytime/anyplace work into reality. Working in a single office is giving way to hoteling, in which employees schedule shared workspace only for the time they need it; telecommuting, in which computers are used to work away from the office, at the client's place of business, at home, or on a plane; teleconferencing; and electronic meetings.

The World Wide Web and other Internet resources behind many of these advances also make it easier for software piracy, hacking, the dissemination of software viruses, and other electronic ills to affect millions of individuals and corporations worldwide. However, the ethical issues raised by these blatantly sociopathic behaviors are simplistic when compared to the subtle dilemmas raised by the nexus of social and technological (sociotechnical) aspects of work.

Sociotechnical systems are attempts ". . . to find the social and technological arrangement that meets both the needs of the [group members] in terms of the quality of their working life and organizational goals" (Pasmore & Sherwood, 1978, p. 41). The objective is to combine features of the social components of the organization with features of the technical components in balanced and synergistic relationships.

This chapter looks at *facilitation*, a specific role that has developed from one form of sociotechnical systems—group support systems—and expands the purview of the facilitation role to include a variety of sociotechnical settings. Ethical dilemmas are found in the paradoxical relationships between the expectations placed on facilitators and their abilities to facilitate. The ethical dilemmas arise because group support system (GSS) facilitation represents a subtle, but powerful, influence opportunity that must be managed.

The first step is to describe the GSS environment and the role of GSS facilitators. Included in this description is a review of power and influence within the facilitator role. Next, we use ethics as a lens to view the role of facilitation—in the process illustrating the *paradox of facilitation*. We then provide options for facilitators striving for ethical behavior in such complex settings. Finally, the paradox is considered in terms of a broader range of facilitators than just those in GSS environments.

Group Support Systems

In a GSS, users interact with and through computer-mediated communication systems to do collaborative work, such as meetings, brainstorming, and strategy planning (DeSanctis & Gallupe, 1987). Organizations can use a GSS to enable effective communication in groups. Research suggests that a GSS can reduce some aspects of process loss (those in which the dynamics of the group start to reduce the effectiveness of the group) inherent in using groups and teams in organizations (Benbasat & Lim, 1993). Increased meeting speed and participation are two generally accepted results of GSSs.

The group support sociotechnical system includes a variety of components that interact within the context of the task (e.g., decision making, information gathering): facilitators (both of the technology or of the group process—discussed later), group members participating in the interaction, other organizational members (such as bosses or other people relevant to the interaction), and technology (the GSS computer hardware and software).

GSS have largely been used in the context of same-time/same-place meetings where participants sit at a networked computer in a conference- or auditorium-style room and contribute to the meeting by typing in comments, voting, or otherwise participating as requested. More recently, different-time/different-place meetings have become more common, in which participants may be in their own offices, at a client's office, or otherwise away from the physical and temporal meeting place (Burke & Chidambaram, 1995; Chidambaram, Shakun, & Vogel, 1995).

Specialized software allows the group and the facilitator to process the information contributed. Some facilities provide group screens at the front of the room, whereas others may use just a space on each individual computer screen. Generally, GSS use full keyboards, though some have simpler keypads to reduce user entries and cost. The overall environment is as flexible as the hardware, software, group members, and facilitators will allow. The facilitator role is considered next, and group members are discussed in context with the facilitator role.

The Basic Facilitator Paradigm

Facilitation in this context usually entails operating the technology or facilitating the group's discussion or both (Clawson, Bostrom, & Anson, 1993; Niederman, Beise, & Beranek, 1995). Facilitation helps the participants, in the pursuit of their task, exploit the capabilities of the technology and their group. Certainly, group facilitation existed well before the advent of GSS. (See Hirokawa & Gouran, 1989, for a review.) However, the increased use and complexity of the group support sociotechnical system may increase the importance of facilitation.

The *American Heritage Dictionary* (1981) defines *facilitate* as ". . . to free from difficulties or obstacles; make easier . . ." (p. 469). Most descriptions of the facilitation process establish the facilitator role as one of strict impartiality; the facilitator is meant to enhance the manner in which a group makes decisions—not make content decisions for the group (e.g., Anson, Bostrom & Wynne, 1995; Broome & Keever, 1989; Doyle & Straus, 1982). Bostrom, Anson, and Clawson (1993) reinforced this view, describing facilitation as a ". . . set of functions or activities carried out before, during, and after a meeting to help the group achieve its *own* outcomes [italics added]. The essential characteristic of facilitation is to help make an outcome easier to achieve" (p. 147). A general sense of facilitation drawn from these descriptions is that facilitators should be impartial, that is, make only indirect contributions to the final solution through impartial enhancement of the processes of communication and information processing by the group. This is the *basic facilitator paradigm.*

Facilitator Roles

In practice, GSS facilitation has two distinct components: technical facilitation and group process facilitation (Clawson et al., 1993). Both facilitation functions—technical and group process—may be assumed by a single individual (e.g., Clawson et al., 1993). The technical facilitation role is to enhance group members' use of the communication and information technology; the group process facilitation role is to enhance group members' interactions with each other.

Technical Facilitation. Someone has to operate the technology in order for a group to function smoothly and productively in a sociotechnical setting, such as a GSS. Even a group that appreciates the advantages of using a GSS may not have the expertise to use the system without technical assistance. Clawson et al. (1993) used self-report measures to identify the dimensions of facilitator behavior, including behaviors we see as specific to technical facilitation: (a) appropriately selects and prepares technology, (b) creates comfort with and promotes understanding of the technology and technology outputs, and (c) understands technology and its capabilities (p. 556). The basic role of the technical facilitator is to provide the technology's advantages to the group members—perhaps by running the technology so that group members who could run the technology can concentrate instead on the group's task content, and certainly by assisting those group members who could not themselves operate the technology.

Group Process Facilitation. Although groups can meet—even effectively—without a group process facilitator, the fundamental role of the group process facilitator is to enhance (i.e., improve efficiency and effectiveness) the communication and interaction of group members. The facilitator's goal is to help the group achieve outcomes that make the best use of the resources available within the group. Clawson et al.'s (1993) survey also identified a variety of dimensions related to facilitator behaviors, thirteen that can be used to describe group process facilitation, including these: "(1) promotes ownership and encourages group responsibility; . . . (4) listens to, clarifies, and integrates information; . . . (10) presents information to the group (instructions, written materials); . . . (12) plans and designs the meeting process; . . . (13) manages conflict and negative emotions constructively; . . . (14) directs and manages the meetings" (p. 556).

The two basic components of facilitation—technical and group process— again highlight the intended neutrality and impartiality of the facilitator role. A sociotechnical system such as a GSS is a communication tool that can be used by groups to enhance their processes and outcomes (e.g., Benbasat & Lim, 1993). The facilitator roles are intended to assist groups in using the tool to enhance their communication processes and outcomes. The facilitator roles are intended to help the group achieve, better or faster, what the group wants to achieve. According to these characterizations of facilitator roles, a facilitator's own views regarding the outcome of the group's task or the facilitator's own agenda (beyond that of good facilitation) should be irrelevant to the group's processes or its outcomes. These issues of neutrality and impartiality resurface in the discussion of ethics that follows.

FACILITATOR INFLUENCE

What enables a facilitator to facilitate? The process of facilitation requires that the facilitator—whether technical, group process, or both—influence (i.e., change) the communication behaviors of the group.[1] A facilitator's ability to facilitate largely arises because sociotechnical systems are interacting social systems, and thereby are susceptible to a variety of social influence effects (e.g., Asch, 1972). Two bases of these social influence effects are *facilitator* power and *group member* information processing.

Facilitator Power

Communication structure, channels, networks, and rules are avenues of power, and GSS facilitators have a great deal of control over the communication of the group (Frost, 1987). Facilitators also have access to other sources of power (both more basic and more complex). Many basic explanations of power in organizations focus on an individual's influence over others, resulting from the ability to reward or punish them. Thus, your boss has power over you (and probably can influence your behaviors) because your boss controls important rewards and punishments in your life—such as pay raises, performance appraisals, and job assignments. French and Raven's (1959) classic description of power in organizations describes additional types of power which are not so directly tied to an individual's control over rewards and punishments. Three such sources of power are legitimate power, expert power, and status.

Legitimate power is authority, the right to give orders. Individuals accept and respect the dictates of legitimate authority figures in formal organizational hierarchies because legitimate authority carries with it control over rewards and punishments. In a sociotechnical system such as a GSS, the facilitator has legitimate power (e.g., Keltner, 1989). The facilitator must have some legitimate authority to give orders and to determine how things happen in order to facilitate the group's interaction. A facilitator's legitimate authority exists to the extent that the facilitator is perceived by the group members as having the right to structure the group's work. The group process facilitator may decide when the group is ready to begin, switch tools, or quit. The technical facilitator may choose the GSS tools that the group uses or decide how the selected tools are used by the group or both.

Deference to an authority figure in a sociotechnical system (e.g., the facilitator) can be traced to control over rewards and punishments (e.g., French & Raven, 1959). Groups use the tools that a sociotechnical system offers because the use of those tools (and the facilitator's direction) offers enhancement of group processes and outcomes—a reward. A group's or group member's unwillingness to abide by the directions of the facilitator carries an implicit risk of not receiving the rewards offered by the proper use of the tools and process.

---

[1]This section draws heavily from our work on facilitator power and influence (Griffith, Fuller, & Northcraft, in press).

A parallel case can be made for expert power. Expert power arises when one individual holds knowledge that others do not. Expertise results in power when the group perceives that to not follow the direction of the expert would result in worse process and outcomes (a form of punishment). Experts often are given authority (legitimate power) in groups precisely because they are expected to know the best course of action. Again, a facilitator (technical or group process) is an expert—an expert in the use of the sociotechnical system. Because the facilitator has expertise, the group's or any group member's unwillingness to abide by the facilitator's dictates carries a risk that group processes and outcomes will suffer. Additionally, perceptions of legitimate and expert power may be affected by whether the facilitator is a member of the organization or has been brought in from outside the organization. It may be that outside facilitators are perceived as having less legitimate power (given that they have no formal role in the reporting structure of the organization), but more expert power.

The status is related to legitimate and expert power. Status is deference or esteem accorded to an individual because of that individual's standing in a group. Status may arise from an individual's level of responsibility and authority, or from that individual's standing as an expert. Status can lend extra credence or weight to an individual's opinions or actions. Thus, a facilitator's status as an authority figure or expert might lead group members to be influenced by the facilitator even in areas in which the facilitator is not a legitimate authority figure or expert.

Group Member Information Processing

Facilitator power represents an obvious source of influence over group members in a GSS context. However, facilitators have available to them much more subtle sources of influence that derive from the information processing foibles of human decision makers (e.g., Kahneman, Slovic, & Tversky, 1982). Three examples of these information-processing sources of influence for facilitators are framing, anchoring, and salience.

Framing occurs when the manner in which a facilitator introduces or poses (frames) a question or issue influences the way that group members respond to that question or issue (Tversky & Kahneman, 1981). For example, individuals respond differently when presented with problems in terms of gains versus losses (Kahneman & Tversky, 1979); all other things being equal, decision makers will be risk-averse to protect gains and risk-seeking to avoid losses. Significantly, whether an issue or question is about gains or losses is often a function of the reference point presented (Kahneman, 1992; White & Neale, 1991). ("Are we doing better than company X?" "Are we losing ground against our goals?" "Do we want to protect our market niche?") Facilitators will elicit different risk preferences in group members, thereby yielding quite different decisions (e.g., Northcraft & Neale, 1986) based on how they choose to highlight the prospect of gains to protect (rather than losses to avoid). Indeed, the overall context in which a facilitator outlines a conflict or problem will influence the kinds of solutions the group considers and agrees to (e.g., Pinkley & Northcraft, 1994).

Anchoring is one related mechanism in which the way a facilitator introduces or talks about a question or issue dramatically influences the decisions a group makes (Northcraft & Neale, 1987). For example, if a facilitator asks a group to set a profit goal for the coming fiscal year and then reminds the group of last year's goal, last year's achieved profit, or last year's average profit within the industry, anchoring is likely to occur; any of these figures would provide a strong anchor for the group's deliberations and would influence the group's outcomes (toward the anchor provided by the facilitator). Past research on individual judgment has shown that even random, irrelevant information can anchor deliberations and thereby dramatically influence final decisions (Tversky & Kahneman, 1974).

Salience is an additional judgmental bias facilitators must consider. Salience refers to the point that information that is more cognitively available has a greater opportunity to influence decision makers' deliberations (Tversky & Kahneman, 1973). (Salience refers to the extent to which information stands out—that is, is particularly prominent, visible, eye-catching, or attention grabbing.) For example, the more vivid and concrete information is, the more likely it is to be remembered and so influence decision makers' deliberations (Wilson, Northcraft, & Neale, 1985). In the case of sociotechnical systems such as a GSS, the facilitator typically is more salient than any group member, precisely because of the facilitator's physical centrality as the legitimate authority running the session. This is particularly true in those GSS designs in which the facilitator is required to run the technology (Dennis, George, Jessup, Nunamaker, & Vogel, 1988) versus designs in which facilitation is optional.

The facilitator's greater salience means that the facilitator's comments are more likely to be remembered and thus are more likely to be considered than any group member's comments. This also means that any comments made by the facilitator will have a greater opportunity to frame or anchor the group's deliberations. Additionally, because facilitators control the flow of communication in a GSS, they may be more likely to speak first. Such first advocacy behaviors have been shown to anchor groups' thoughts, choices, or actions (Weisband, 1992).

Ethics and the Basic Facilitator Paradigm

Despite these obvious sources of influence available to facilitators, there have been relatively few discussions of ethics in the use of influence by group facilitators, let alone of ethics in the use of influence by facilitators in group support system environments. Zorn and Rosenfeld's (1989) exploration of the ethical dilemmas faced by facilitators of problem-solving groups identified the key tension for facilitation: that facilitators (be they technical, group process, or both) not only have a responsibility to the group, but also to the organization, to the individual members of the group, and to themselves. They present the following conundrum: "In working for the 'good,' how do [facilitators] decide whose 'good' should be considered first? Three potential conflicts exist; (a) self versus organizational 'good,' (b) management versus group 'good,' and (c) group versus group member 'good' " (p. 97).

The ethical tension that Zorn and Rosenfeld (1989) have identified arises because of the power and influence inherent in the facilitation role. Facilitator influence is what allows GSS facilitators to help a group achieve better outcomes, by altering the behaviors and cognitions of group members. Facilitator influence also provides the foundation for the paradox of facilitation. The paradox of facilitation is that facilitators are supposed to influence without being influential. Facilitators are supposed to influence (specifically, enhance) the group's process (i.e., efficiency and effectiveness) without determining the content of the group's decision (Anson et al., 1995; Rockwood, 1993; Schein, 1969). Yet, by improving the process, facilitators are working with the GSS and the group to enhance the quality of the outcomes (Nunamaker, Dennis, Valacich, & Vogel, 1991), and thus, inevitably, the content of the decision.

This paradox of facilitation would be difficult enough to manage even if all facilitators were saints and carried into facilitation only the best interests of their groups. Social influence need not be intentional to occur. Wellmeaning facilitators may not realize the extent of their power and influence over the group and the salience of their comments. Groups may turn to sociotechnical tools, such as a GSS, when they are uncertain about what to do, and uncertainty makes groups particularly susceptible to influence (Latane & Darley, 1970). Group process facilitators may be unaware of their framing of questions and issues or their anchoring of the group's deliberations and decisions. Technical facilitators may not fully realize the emphasis given to their suggestions about which tools to use. Facilitators may also be under pressure to be pulled into the dynamics of the ongoing session, perhaps losing some perspective on the meeting (Keltner, 1989, p. 24). Finally, a conscientious facilitator may try to assist the group by providing examples or making suggestions. Support for such assistance is even found in the description of Dimension 15 of facilitation behaviors (Clawson et al., 1993): "Encourages/supports multiple perspectives . . . uses techniques, metaphors, stories, examples to get the group to consider different frames of reference" (p. 556). However, if facilitators do not provide examples on both sides of an issue (or do not consider the impact of the particular example), unintentional influence may occur.

Of course, unintentional facilitator influence is impartial—it does not intentionally drive the group process and outcome in one direction or another. Nevertheless, it fundamentally alters the group's outcome. In doing so, any unintentional facilitator influence could be an ethical problem to the extent that the group members are unaware of the facilitator influence taking place and are unaware of its effects on their deliberations. Thus, unintentional influence may present a moral dilemma for facilitators.

Perhaps a second level of ethical concern arises because most facilitators are in fact not saints but instead normal human beings. As noted earlier, it is fundamental to the basic facilitator paradigm that any facilitator influence be (at the very least) impartial—not intended to take the group's deliberations in a particular direction. Unfortunately, from an ethical standpoint, impartiality may be a lot to ask of any facilitator because of two kinds of role conflicts (e.g., Katz & Kahn, 1972): (a) facilitators may have agendas that support their positions as facilitators and (b) facilitators may also be group members with a personal agenda regarding the group outcome.

Facilitators Have Agenda(s) That Support Their Position as Facilitators. A troubling possibility is that a facilitator's power and influence can be used to serve some agenda external to the group. For example, it is not unreasonable to think that a facilitator may want to be respected—to look like a good, competent facilitator (perhaps in order to be hired again). Kingsbury (1972) noted that a facilitator may be "concerned about his [sic] own learning in the group, his own gratification, and his standing with other members" (p. 110). Although little research seems to have addressed the issue of how facilitators are evaluated (Anson et al., 1995, provided a beginning), the general performance appraisal and goal-setting literature suggests that whatever dimension is perceived as being measured and rewarded will be the focal dimension for the performer (e.g., Locke & Latham, 1990, p. 95).

This creates a substantial (though possibly subconscious) conflict for the facilitator. Facilitators are supposed to help the group find the best solution; on the other hand, facilitators have a schedule to keep and other, personal goals to meet. This conflict could lead a facilitator to (even unintentionally) make decisions (e.g., format of the agenda, tool and technique selection) or comments (e.g., framing, anchoring) that influence the group toward completion of the task without necessarily influencing the group toward effective completion of the task.

Facilitators May Be Group Members. The problem of facilitator role conflict becomes an even more compelling issue when the facilitator is also participating as a member of the group (Keltner, 1989, p. 22). Whereas the basic facilitator paradigm implies that the facilitator role is occupied by a dispassionate, impartial third party, in some groups the facilitator may be a group member, complete with a group member's personal views about the preferred outcome. Facilitators in a GSS have ample opportunity to drive the group's deliberations in the direction of their vested interests, just as a traditional group leader who has a vested interest in the group's final decision has many opportunities to influence the group's processes and outcomes (Keltner, 1989). (Although again, any influence exercised by a facilitator in such a situation need not be intentional to occur.)

TOWARD ETHICAL FACILITATION

The central premise of this discussion has been that the very sources of power and influence that allow facilitators to enhance a group's processes and outcomes—to facilitate the group—create two levels of ethical dilemmas for facilitators. First, unintentional influence (even if impartial and neutral) may violate the tenets of self-determination and informed consent. Second, the intrusion of facilitators' own agendas into their sphere of influence over the group may violate the tenets of impartiality and neutrality. It is inevitable that a facilitator must have the power to influence the way a group interacts. A facilitator can not facilitate without altering the group's native process. However, this begs a difficult question: How is the ethical line drawn between facilitator influence that facilitates the group and facilitator influence that either unintentionally or unduly sways the content of the group's decisions?

This discussion of facilitator roles in the group support sociotechnical system has identified several critical ethical tensions. Of the different sociotechnical system elements, the facilitator would seem to be the weak link. This suggests two possible paths to making facilitation more ethical: (a) putting some controls on the behaviors of facilitators or (b) taking the facilitator out of facilitation.

The Ethical Facilitator

The real answer to the paradox of facilitation may be to do more to manage or control the behaviors of facilitators. In considering this possibility, it is useful to compare the close parallel between the role of GSS facilitator and that of dispute mediator. A dispute mediator controls the way that disputants interact, but does not control the agreement (if any) that they reach (Sheppard, 1984; Thibaut & Walker, 1975). As with the GSS facilitator role, neutrality and impartiality are key expectations of the mediator role. Cooks and Hale (1994), in describing mediators, noted that, "emphasis is placed on a qualified, impartial, third party who guides consenting parties through the process of reaching a mutually satisfactory agreement," where mutually presumably refers to the disputants—not the mediator. They continued by describing four cornerstones of mediator standards of practice: disputant self-determination, informed consent, mediator impartiality, and mediator neutrality (p. 61).

The definitions of neutrality and impartiality in mediation are under fire from some experts (e.g., Cooks & Hale, 1994; Feer, 1992; Rifkin, Millen & Cobb, 1991). However, mediation professional associations agree that impartiality is defined as "freedom from favoritism and bias in either word or action" (Feer, 1992, p. 63) whereas neutrality involves the relationship of the mediator to the disputant and issues (p. 63). Interestingly, Feer (1992) noted that some organizations step away from neutrality by expecting mediators to be concerned with fairness, which may contradict impartiality (e.g., Rifkin et al., 1991). Clearly, mediation researchers have a similar set of concerns to the paradox of facilitation previously described.

Within mediation, self-determination and informed consent both focus attention on the autonomy of the disputants. Self-determination means that the disputants or group members should themselves determine the final outcome of the deliberations; informed consent means that the disputants or group members should explicitly be made aware of the extent to which this goal of self-determination is not possible, or compromised. In facilitated situations, these issues can be complex. Organizational hierarchies may provide additional structure that may put a facilitator in the position of having to follow orders. These orders may or may not pressure the facilitator to break out of the facilitator paradigm. For example, facilitators may be privy to information that is not to be fully disseminated to the group or facilitators may be given boundaries regarding the agenda and the group's authority to vary from the agenda. These pressures clearly would impact on the goals of self-determination and informed consent but may be necessary in the organizational setting.

The cornerstones of the slightly more mature field of mediation identify ethical considerations that should be critical to facilitation; however, facilitation is a broader case than mediation in at least two ways. First, the sociotechnical system itself is more complex, both in the case of technology-supported sessions and manual ones; facilitators face obligations toward the organization, the group members, and themselves—rather than a more clearly defined set of disputants. Second, the context that facilitators may work in is more complex; mediators are dealing with a dispute, but facilitators may be brainstorming, problem solving with few boundaries, and so forth—or dealing with a dispute.

A review of these concerns suggests three ways to achieve more control over facilitators. First, GSS facilitators need to understand and acknowledge the sources of influence they control. Some of the more subtle forms of facilitator influence (such as framing and anchoring) may be important revelations even to those facilitators who are aware of the ways that they can drive a group's processes and outcomes (e.g., Northcraft & Neale, 1986, 1987).

There are several ways to achieve this understanding. Training and information provided by GSS documentation, professional groups, user feedback, and current literature are starting points for a detailed discussion of facilitator effects and experiences. Zorn and Rosenfeld (1989) suggested a "reflective" approach in their presentation of ways to improve ethical facilitation. They cited Paradise and Siegelwaks' (1982) work, and recommended that facilitators expose themselves to higher levels of ethical reasoning. Significantly, this suggests that awareness must be improved on two levels: awareness of the possibility (and sources) of influence, and awareness and understanding of the ethical burden that ability to influence carries with it. Historical accounts of facilitation scenarios and role-playing exercises also may provide mechanisms for increasing facilitators' awareness and understanding on both levels.

A second way to achieve more control is for facilitators to be trained to facilitate in a way that minimizes unintentional influence. A group process facilitator who fully understands the dangers of framing and anchoring can, for instance, be trained to avoid presenting issues in ways that unduly influence a group's deliberations and conclusions. Decision-making research suggests that experience alone is not sufficient to insulate facilitators from these problems (Neale & Northcraft, 1986, 1987). Experiential exercises (such as role-playing exercises; e.g., Hoover, 1977) that give facilitators the opportunity to practice the construction of neutral questions and prompts and to observe the outcomes of framing and anchoring may be especially helpful. Training similar to that provided for interview and survey administrators (i.e., unbiased interaction techniques) may also prove helpful (e.g., Dunham & Smith, 1979).

Again, facilitator training (like awareness) can be usefully taken to two levels: training about the sources of influence and training about the (ethical) use and misuse of that influence potential. Training has proven to be a powerful factor in enhancing the development of moral judgment (e.g., Rest, 1994). Perhaps of more ethical importance, training about influence without accompanying training about the ethics of its use begs the opportunity for abuse, particularly given the previously mentioned role conflicts that many facilitators may experience.

Finally, standards that spell out the obligations of facilitators with respect to the use of their influence need to be created. In fact, the articulation of these standards is probably a prerequisite to the development of effective training programs in the ethical use of influence opportunities in facilitation. Facilitators will need to struggle with the same issues raised by mediators in articulating these standards. Rest (1994) identified four determinants of moral behavior—moral sensitivity, moral judgment, moral motivation, and moral character—which could provide a useful blueprint for the parameters of ethical facilitation standards.

An important element of these standards should be the necessity of insuring informed consent. Facilitators might provide information regarding their relationship to the group (whether a vested interest exists, what form of facilitator evaluation is in place, their own goals, etc.). A request for this information could be programmed into GSS software to appear at the beginning of the session and the facilitator's response made part of the public record. A public statement of neutrality may increase facilitators' awareness and commitment to impartial proceedings, given that public statements are one way to engender commitment (Salancik, 1977).

It is important to acknowledge the limitations of putting controls on the behaviors of facilitators. Putting control on facilitator behaviors—even in the form of standards or a code of facilitator ethics—may miss the point. The role of a facilitator is to facilitate. Research from other domains on the use of standards as a control mechanism suggests that if a facilitator becomes preoccupied with standards compliance, the freewheeling creativity of a facilitator is likely to be constrained (e.g., Schlenker, 1982; Staw & Boettger, 1990; Tetlock, 1985), and the group's outcome is likely to suffer. For better or for worse, a facilitator who is focused on compliance with ethical standards cannot also be totally focused on facilitation.

The resolution of this final conundrum may be via the distinction between rule-focused versus client-focused ethics. (Building from Beauchamp, 1982, Grebe, Irvin, and Lang, 1989, described the classic deontological [formalist] and utilitarian theories of ethics. Here, we simplify our consideration to client-focused vs. rule-focused.) Rule-focused ethics provides a formalist approach to resolving ethical dilemmas (e.g., Beauchamp & Bowie, 1979). In rule-focused ethics, decisions are based on central standards of behavior, and the rules for behaving (in this case, the method of facilitation) are the focus. Client-focused ethics, on the other hand, represents a more utilitarian (e.g., Scarre, 1996) approach to addressing the ethical choices faced by facilitators. In client-focused ethics, decisions are based on the principle of client utility, in which the client's outcome is the focus.

Joyce (1995) proposed, from a mediation perspective, that rule-focused systems typically are less effective in adapting to the needs of diverse clients, diverse settings, and the rapidly changing demands of an emerging field. Client-focused ethics instead maintains the focus on a single principle—in this case, the needs of the system users—from which appropriate behaviors can be derived to address the needs of any contingencies.

Although some (e.g., Cavanagh, Moberg, & Velasquez, 1981) have counseled a balanced complementarity in formalist (rule-focused) and utilitarian (client-focused) approaches to ethical decision making, Brady (1985) specifically suggested that "not all business/society issues reflect both formalist and utilitarian interests" (p. 572). In the case of facilitation, the argument for the balance of ethical standards toward formalism is compelling.

As noted earlier, the evolution of facilitation to date has created conflicts of interest that argue against a utilitarian approach—in particular when facilitators may be group members, but also when facilitators have agendas that support their role as facilitators. In these cases, any claims by facilitators that their choices or decisions were motivated by a concern for maximizing the utility of a session necessarily begs the question of whose utility is being maximized—the group's, the facilitators', the individual who hired the facilitator, or some combination? Even in the cases in which a facilitator genuinely intends to maximize the group's utility, the facilitator's accurate understanding of the group's interest also must be suspect.

This may explain why self-determination is considered such a cornerstone standard of practice in mediation (the disputants get to decide what utility to maximize); it certainly points to the primacy of formalist ethics in typical GSS facilitation. However, in order to maintain an appropriate level of facilitator flexibility, it may be enough that these formalist standards extend only so far as behavioral intent. Limiting the standards to behavioral intent may help maintain some of the flexibility that would be lost if the standards extended to facilitation behaviors themselves.

Through understanding, acknowledgment, training, and standards, facilitators can become sensitized to the scope of their potential influence over groups. Then, facilitators can begin an on-going discussion concerning the appropriate management of that influence. Professional publications, such as "Facilitator Central" (http://hsb.baylor.edu/fuller/fac/), are one arena in which this type of discussion can take place. The remaining question is how to broaden the perceived need for facilitator ethics. For professional facilitators, the need may be clear; however, the facilitation role may extend beyond that currently acknowledged. Broadening the perceived boundaries of facilitation may be a substantial step.

Taking the Facilitator Out of Facilitation

Perhaps some group process functions could be built into the GSS itself (e.g., by having the computer monitor participants' communication frequency and goad nonparticipants back into the discussion). Limayem, Lee-Partridge, Dickson, and DeSanctis (1993) experimented with an automated GSS in which the GSS itself facilitates groups. An automated GSS would not beg the facilitator's paradox of impartial influence because the GSS itself can be assumed to be impartial (or at least known—particular designs ostensibly could favor one decision alternative over another—see later discussion). Interestingly, although Limayem et al. (1993) found that facilitated groups (either human or automated) achieved better postdecision consensus and perceived decision quality than did nonfacilitated groups, human and electronic facilitation did not produce significant differences on these dimensions.

There are two reasons that depending upon the automation of GSS tools to resolve the facilitator's paradox seems unfortunate. First, automation may only displace undue influence rather than do away with it. The influential decision in. a fully automated system becomes which automated system (which form of automated facilitation) to use. Users might not have gained at all in terms of self-determination.

Furthermore, depending on the transparency of the automated GSS action, informed consent might even be reduced. If participants are truly technical novices, explaining to them the implications of different alternatives (e.g., using different tools) might seem to fulfill the letter of informed consent, but would it fulfill the intent? A novice user would be unlikely to appreciate the importance of differences, and a choice made on information about which the user has no experience would be informed in name only. Finally, the person providing the description also would have the opportunity to slant presentation of particular tools to make them look more or less attractive. Objectivity in presenting the choice would be difficult at best and would provide an extremely subtle—but still important—opportunity for influence.

Second, this resolution of the paradox throws out the baby with the bath water. Facilitator influence itself is not the problem—facilitator influence carries with it the prospect of benefit in terms of group processes and outcomes. Technical facilitation is provided to help the group get the most out of the technology; group process facilitation is provided to help the group access all the group's resources. The challenge is making sure that a facilitator's influence does not produce less benefit than justified—are the trade-offs in terms of neutrality, impartiality, self-determination, and informed consent worth the benefit?

It is interesting to note that one of the reasons for creating technologies (like GSSs) to support group communication processes was precisely to insulate beneficial group processes from inappropriate influence, for instance by providing an anonymous way to contribute comments (Connolly, Jessup, & Valacich, 1990). It would appear, in retrospect, that the imposition of an additional component (such as a GSS) in group communication cannot remove influence but only transfer it elsewhere in the sociotechnical system. In the case of group process, moving influence to a technology such as a GSS begs the question of who in turn manages the GSS and its potential influence over group process. At best, the use of a GSS transfers that influence to sources—the facilitators—who have less (if any) vested interest in the outcome and whose use of that influence perhaps can be controlled. At worst, the use of a GSS transforms that influence into a more subtle form (for instance, framing and anchoring by a group member facilitator) that other group members may find difficult to recognize or resist.

CONCLUSIONS: BEYOND GSSs

The GSS is not the only sociotechnical system in which facilitation is an important (if not critical) element of organizational functioning. Indeed, as organizations look to technology to enable new organizational forms, it seems important to consider the ethical implications of this discussion in the broader context beyond GSS. All sociotechnical systems by definition have a technical component—a component which will require (to some degree) the presence and participation of a technician—a technically knowledgeable individual who runs the technology for the system users. The necessity of having a technical facilitator to run the technology raises—for all sociotechnical systems—the specter of inappropriate influence by the technician, whether intentional or not.

The World Wide Web provides a case in point. From the perspective of Web users, their interactions seem to be entirely with computers, software, networks, and data. Where is the room for facilitator influence? If (as we have defined earlier) a facilitator is someone who frees the user from difficulties using the technical system and (thereby) makes interactions with and on the technical system easier, then the work of technical facilitators runs throughout the sociotechnical system of the Web. Technical decisions are continuously being made concerning what data to make available, how to present that data, how to allow users to interact with the data, and so on. Unfortunately, the facilitators making those decisions may be no more likely to appreciate the potential influence (and potential ethical implications) of their decisions than the Web users who do not even realize the facilitators exist.

Interestingly, sociotechnical systems often are designed (e.g., as is the World Wide Web) to provide users with greater self-determination through access to data on their own terms. The inevitability of influence even in these circumstances suggests that no arrangement of technology probably can ever fully insulate users from facilitator influence. Even in sociotechnical systems in which the more intrusive forms of facilitation can be recognized, acknowledged, and removed (e.g., group process facilitation in a GSS), human influence still can and will play an influential role. This influence may come through sources as subtle as the initial conceptualization and design of the technology, but it will come. Facilitators cannot help but influence because of their assumptions regarding the technology and its use (e.g., Adaptive-Structuration Theory; DeSanctis & Poole, 1994) and through the activities they engage in and decisions they make as obvious and active partners in the use of the technology. We would not want to have it any other way, but that influence needs to be managed appropriately if the use of technology in organizations is to remain within ethical boundaries.

REFERENCES

The American heritage dictionary of the English language. (1981). Boston: Houghton Mifflin.

Anson, R., Bostrom, R., & Wynne, V. (1995). An experiment assessing group support system and facilitator effects on meeting outcomes. *Management Science, 41*(2), 189–208.

Asch, S. E. (1972). Group forces in the modification and distortion of judgment. In E. Hollander & R. Hunt (Eds.), *Classic contributions to social psychology* (pp. 330–339). New York: Oxford University Press.

Beauchamp, T. L. (1982). *Philosophical ethics: An introduction to moral philosophy.* New York: McGraw-Hill.

Beauchamp, T., & Bowie, N. E. (1979). *Ethical theory and business.* Englewood Cliffs, NJ: Prentice-Hall.

Benbasat, I., & Lim, L. H. (1993). The effects of group, task, context, and technology variables on the usefulness of group support systems: A meta-analysis of experimental studies. *Small Group Research, 24,* 430–462.

Bostrom, R. P., Anson, R., & Clawson, V. (1993). Group facilitation and group support systems. In L. M. Jessup & J. S. Valacich (Eds.), *Group support systems: New perspectives* (pp. 146–168). New York: Macmillan.

Brady, F. N. (1985). A Janus-headed model of ethical theory: Looking two ways at business/society issues. *Academy of Management Review, 10,* 568–576.

Broome, B. J., & Keever, D. B. (1989). Next generation group facilitation. *Management Communication Quarterly, 3,* 107–127.

Burke, K., & Chidambaram, L. (1995). Developmental differences between distributed and face-to-face groups in electronically supported meeting environments: An exploratory investigation. *Group Decision and Negotiation, 4,* 213–233.

Cavanagh, G. F., Moberg, D. J., & Velasquez, M. (1981). The ethics of organizational politics. *Academy of Management Review, 6,* 363–374.

Chidambaram, L., Shakun, M., & Vogel, D. (1995). Introduction to the special issue on distributed communication systems. *Group Decision and Negotiation, 4,* 191–192.

Clawson, V. K., Bostrom, R. P., & Anson, R. (1993). The role of the facilitator in computer-supported meetings. *Small Group Research, 24,* 547–565.

Connolly, T., Jessup, L. M., & Valacich, J. S. (1990). Effects of anonymity and evaluative tone on idea generation in computer-mediated groups. *Management Science, 36,* 689–703.

Cooks, L. M., & Hale, C. L. (1994). The construction of ethics in mediation. *Mediation Quarterly, 12*(1), 55–76.

Dennis, A. R., George, J. F., Jessup, L. M., Nunamaker, J. F., & Vogel, D. R. (1988). Information technology to support group work. *Management Information Systems Quarterly, 4,* 591–624.

DeSanctis, G., & Gallupe, R. B. (1987). A foundation for the study of group decision support systems. *Management Science, 33,* 589–609.

DeSanctis, G., & Poole, M. S. (1994). Capturing the complexity in advanced technology use: Adaptive structuration theory. *Organization Science, 5*(2), 121–147.

Doyle, M., & Straus, D. (1982). *How to make meetings work.* New York: Berkeley.

Dunham, R. B., & Smith, F. J. (1979). *Organizational surveys: An internal assessment of organizational health.* Glenview, IL: Scott, Foresman.

Feer, M. (1992). On "Toward a new discourse for mediation: A critique of neutrality." *Mediation Quarterly, 10*(2), 173–177.

French, J. R. P., & Raven, B. (1959). The bases of social power. In D. Cartwright & A. Zander (Eds.), *Group dynamics* (pp. 150–167). New York: Harper & Row.

Frost, P. (1987). Power, politics, and influence. In F. Jablin (Ed.), *The handbook of organizational communication* (pp. 503–548). Newbury Park, CA: Sage.

Grebe, S. C., Irvin, K., & Lang, M. (1989). A model for ethical decision making in mediation. *Mediation Quarterly, 7*(2), 133–148.

Griffith, T. L., Fuller, M. A., & Northcraft, G. B. (in press). Facilitator power and influence in group support systems: Some intended and unintended consequences. *Information Systems Research.*

Hirokawa, R. Y., & Gouran, D. S. (1989). Facilitation of group communication: A critique of prior research and an agenda for future research. *Management Communication Quarterly, 3,* 71–92.

Hoover, D. J. (1977). Experiential Learning: Conceptualization and definition. In R. E. Horn (Ed.), *The Guide to Simulations/Games for Education and Training (Vol. 2. Business)* (3rd ed., pp. 115–116). Cranford, NJ: Didactic Systems.

Joyce, D. P. (1995). The roles of the intervenor: A client-centered approach. *Mediation Quarterly, 12*(4), 301–312.

Kahneman, D. (1992). Reference points, anchors, norms and mixed feelings. *Organizational Behavior and Human Decision Processes, 51,* 296–312.

Kahneman, D., Slovic, P., & Tversky, A. (1982). *Judgment under uncertainty: Heuristics and biases.* New York: Cambridge University Press.

Kahneman, D., & Tversky, A. (1979). Prospect theory: An analysis of decision under risk. *Econometrica, 47,* 263–291.

Katz, D., & Kahn, R. L. (1972). *The social psychology of organizations* (2nd ed.). New York: Wiley.

Keltner, J. (1989). Facilitation: Catalyst for group problem solving. *Management Communication Quarterly, 3,* 8–32.

Kingsbury, S. (1972). Dilemmas for the trainer. In W. G. Dyer (Ed.), *Modern theory and method in group training* (pp. 107–115). New York: Van Nostrand Reinhold.

Latane, B., & Darley, J. (1970). *The unresponsive bystander: Why doesn't he help?* New York: Appleton-Century-Crofts.

Limayem, M., Lee-Partridge, J. E., Dickson, G. W., & DeSanctis, G. (1993). Enhancing GDSS effectiveness: Automated versus human facilitation. *Proceedings of the 26th Hawaii International Conferences on System Sciences, 5,* 95–101.

Locke, E. A., & Latham, G. P. (1990). *A theory of goal setting & task performance.* Englewood Cliffs, NJ: Prentice-Hall.

Neale, M. A., & Northcraft, G. B. (1986). Experts, amateurs, and refrigerators: Comparing expert and amateur decision making on a novel task. *Organizational Behavior and Human Decision Processes, 38,* 305–317.

Niederman, F., Beise, C. M., & Beranek, P. M. (1995). Issues and concerns about computer-supported meetings: The facilitator's perspective. *MIS Quarterly, 20*(1), 1–22.

Northcraft, G. B., & Neale, M. A. (1987). Expert, amateurs, and real estate: An anchoring-and-adjustment perspective on property pricing decisions. *Organizational Behavior and Human Decision Processes, 39,* 228–241.

Northcraft, G. B., & Neale, M. A. (1986). Opportunity costs and the framing of resource allocation decisions. *Organizational Behavior and Human Decision Processes, 37,* 28–38.

Nunamaker, J. F., Dennis, A. R., Valacich, J. S., & Vogel, D. R. (1991). Information technology for negotiating groups: Generating options for mutual gain. *Management Science, 37*(10), 1325–1346.

Paradise, L. V., & Siegelwaks, B. J. (1982). Ethical training for group leaders. *Journal for Specialists in Group Work, 7,* 162–166.

Pasmore, W. A., & Sherwood, J. J. (1978). *Sociotechnical systems: A sourcebook.* La Jolla, CA: University Associates.

Pinkley, R., & Northcraft, G. B. (1994). Conflict frames: Effects on dispute processes and outcomes. *Academy of Management Journal, 37*(1), 193–205.

Rest, J. R. (1994). Theory and research. In J. Rest & D. Narvaez (Eds.), *Moral development in the professions: Psychology and applied ethics* (pp. 1–26). Hillsdale, NJ: Lawrence Erlbaum Associates.

Rifkin, J., Millen, J., & Cobb, S. (1991). Toward a new discourse for mediation: A critique of neutrality. *Mediation Quarterly, 9*(2), 151–164.

Rockwood, G. F. (1993). Edgar Schein's process versus content consultation models. *Journal of Counseling & Development, 71,* 636–638.

Salancik, G. R. (1977). Commitment and the control of organizational behavior and belief. In B. M. Staw & G. R. Salancik (Eds.), *New directions in organizational behavior.* Chicago: St. Clair Press.

Scarre, G. (1996). *Utilitarianism.* New York: Routlege.

Schein, E. H. (1969). *Process consultation: Its role in organization development.* Reading, MA: Addison-Wesley.

Schlenker, B. R. (1982). Translating actions into attitudes: An identity-analytic approach to the explanation of social conduct. In L. Berkowitz (Ed.), *Advances in experimental social psychology* (Vol. 5, pp. 186–224). New York: Academic Press.

Sheppard, B. H. (1984). Third party conflict intervention: A procedural framework. In B. M. Staw & L. Cummings (Eds.), *Research in organizational behavior* (Vol. 6, pp. 141–190). Greenwich, CT: JAI.

Staw, B. M., & Boettger, R. D. (1990). Task revision: A neglected form of work performance. *Academy of Management Journal, 33,* 534–559.

Tetlock, P. E. (1985). Accountability: The neglected social context of judgment and choice. In B. M. Staw & L. Cummings (Eds.), *Research in organizational behavior* (Vol. 7, pp. 297–332). Greenwich, CT: JAI.

Thibaut, J., & Walker, L. (1975). *Procedural justice: A psychological analysis.* Hillsdale, NJ: Lawrence Erlbaum Associates.

Tversky, A., & Kahneman, D. (1973). Availability: A heuristic for judging frequency and probability. *Cognitive Psychology, 5,* 207–232.

Tversky, A., & Kahneman, D. (1974). Judgment under uncertainty: Heuristics and biases. *Science, 185,* 1124–1131.

Tversky, A., & Kahneman, D. (1981). The framing of decisions and the psychology of choice. *Science, 211,* 453–458.

Weisband, S. P. (1992). Discussion, advocacy, and computer-mediated communication effects in group decision-making. *Organizational Behavior and Human Decision Processes, 53*(3), 352–380.

White, S. B., & Neale, M. A. (1991). Reservation prices, resistance points, and BATNAs: Determining the parameters of acceptable negotiation outcomes. *Negotiation Journal, 7,* 379–388.

Wilson, M. G., Northcraft, G. B., & Neale, M. A. (1985). The perceived value of fringe benefits. *Personnel Psychology, 38,* 309–320.

Zorn, T. E., & Rosenfeld, L. B. (1989). Between a rock and a hard place: Ethical dilemmas in problem-solving group facilitation. *Management Communication Quarterly, 3*(1), 93–106.

CHAPTER ELEVEN

The Magic Punchbowl: A Nonrational Model of Ethical Management

Marshall Schminke
Creighton University

Organizations are not rational places. They teem with egos, politics, and hidden agendas. Under these conditions, it is unreasonable to expect that managers should always behave like rational decision makers: impartially identifying problems, gathering full information, and making optimal decisions. In fact, we know that often they do not.

However, many traditional approaches to ethical decision making assume that managers engage in a rational, linear decision process when addressing ethical dilemmas. That is, managers first correctly identify ethical dilemmas, then evaluate alternative solutions to them, and finally, choose the best alternative. But if that process does not reflect how managers actually make other decisions, it may not accurately describe how they make ethical decisions either.

In this chapter, I propose an alternative nonrational approach. I begin by briefly reviewing several recent rational models of ethical decision making. These provide the backdrop against which several themes in our current thinking about ethical decision making become clearer. Next, I contrast these with several models of nonrational decision making. These provide some context in which to better understand how our thinking about nonrational decision processes has progressed. Finally, I integrate these two approaches, and propose a nonrational punchbowl model of ethical decision making.

CURRENT MODELS OF ETHICAL DECISION MAKING

Three approaches to modeling ethical decision making have emerged in the literature. The first focuses on the characteristics of the individual making the decision. The second considers the setting or context in which the decision is made. The third approach goes beyond the individual and the context and focuses on the characteristics of the ethical issue or event itself.

Models That Focus on Individuals

Several authors have explored individual-level attributes as the central force behind ethical decision making. I briefly summarize four of them: Hogan's (1973) dialectical approach, Forsyth's (1980) moral judgment model, Kohlberg's (1981) cognitive moral development approach, and Rest's (1986) four component model.

Hogan (1973) presented the strongest view of the potency of individual traits on moral behavior. He focused on individuals' moral maturity, and in defining its parameters, he began with an image of humans as rule-formulating and rule-following animals. He then characterized how individuals differ across five dimensions, which captured their reactions to rule-governed behavior: moral knowledge, socialization, empathy, autonomy, and moral judgment.

Moral knowledge is the extent to which one understands the rules of moral behavior. Socialization describes the extent to which one believes these rules apply to him or her. Empathy reflects individuals' capacity to perceive situations from others' perspectives. Autonomy reflects the degree to which one's moral decisions are driven by a personal sense of duty, rather than peer or societal pressures. Finally, moral judgment addresses whether one considers human-generated laws (an ethic of responsibility) or higher order natural law (an ethic of personal conscience) as providing the more appropriate guide. Hogan presents specific assessment devices for each dimension and is clear in his belief that these individual-level characteristics dictate moral behavior regardless of setting; he suggests that this model "should help to explain moral conduct in *any* socio-cultural context" (1973, p. 220, italics added).

Forsyth (1980) explored a different set of individual-level dimensions of ethical ideologies. His Ethics Position Questionnaire (EPQ) reflects a belief that variations in individuals' moral judgment may be described by two dimensions: relativism and idealism. Relativism reflects the extent to which one rejects the premise that universal rules or principles of ethical behavior exist. Idealism reflects the extent to which one believes that doing the right thing will always lead to desirable consequences. The resulting two-by-two matrix (high or low on each of the two dimensions) creates a taxonomy of four ethical ideologies: situationists (high relativism, high idealism), subjectivists (high relativism, low idealism), absolutists (low relativism, high idealism), and exceptionists (low relativism, low idealism).

Forsyth (1980) tied each of these ideologies to existing ethical perspectives. For example, he related both the situationist and subjectivist perspectives (the high relativist pair) to ethical skepticism. He identified subjectivists as pragmatic ethical egoists; moral standards are relevant only with respect to one's own behavior. He linked situationist thinking with Fletcher's (1966) situation ethics; morality is not so much a question of right and wrong as it is of a fit between one's actions and the context in which they occur. He likened absolutists to deontological thinking, one that rejects considering the consequences of actions in determining their morality. Finally, he suggested that exceptionists endorse teleological beliefs, in which the consequences of actions determine the morality of actions.

The best known individual-level approach to ethical decision making is the cognitive moral development (CMD) framework. Based on Piaget's (1932/1948) early work on moral development, Kohlberg (1981) suggested that CMD, or moral maturity, is reflected in six stages, across three levels of moral reasoning. The preconventional level contains Stage 1 (punishment and obedience orientation) and Stage 2 (instrumental relativist orientation). At this level, individuals define morality in terms of the consequences of actions (e.g., reward and punishment) or the moral positions of authority figures. The conventional level includes Stage 3 (good boy–nice girl orientation) and Stage 4 (law-and-order orientation). Here, peer influences as well as family and societal norms become more instrumental in determining what constitutes moral behavior. This conventional reasoning defines morality in terms of maintaining family or social structures. Finally, the postconventional level includes Stage 5 (social contracts, legalistic orientation) and Stage 6 (universal ethical principles orientation). At this level, individuals define moral principles independently from self-interest, authority figures, and societal pressures. The postconventional individual defines morality in terms of personal conscience and universal principles.

Rest (1986) presented a similar framework of CMD. His description mirrored Kohlberg's in its emphasis on justice as the central criteria of morality and in its six-stage structure. However, Rest's approach differed from Kohlberg's on two dimensions. First, although Rest's approach is a justice-based one, it reflects individuals' increasingly sophisticated thinking regarding how social cooperation can be organized. Kohlberg's stages reflect a sense of justice in formalist terms (reversibility, universality, and prescriptivity). Therefore, Rest's conceptualization emphasizes justice as social cooperation. Kohlberg's conceptualization reflects justice in more individual terms, including individual rights and responsibilities imposed by both society and self. Second, Kohlberg's approach emphasized a more rigid, hard stage structure.

One is either in or out of a particular stage. Rest's model presents a softer stage structure reflecting ranges of responses to ethical dilemmas. Individuals' ethical reasoning may be affected by more than one stage influence at a time.

However, Rest (1986, 1994) took the CMD approach a step further in creating what he called a four-component model. He suggested that moral development (moral judgment) is not enough to ensure moral behavior. Rather, moral judgment is only one of four individual-level factors that contribute to moral behavior. The others include moral sensitivity, moral motivation, and moral character. Moral sensitivity addresses the extent to which individuals are aware that their actions might impact others. In other words, are moral issues even on the individual's radar screen? Moral motivation reflects the extent to which moral values are accorded greater or lesser importance than one's other values (e.g., self-actualization, wealth, self-preservation, or organizational preservation). Finally, moral character captures the extent to which individuals show the fortitude or courage to actually carry out the actions they have defined as moral. In all, Rest's model significantly expands our thinking about individual characteristics that may affect moral behavior. However, like the others, it is limited to individual-level characteristics. The next section briefly reviews several models that also consider the role of situational context.

Models That Include Situational Effects

Treviño's (1986) person–situation interactionist approach paved the way for models that consider not only the person facing the ethical dilemma but also the setting in which that dilemma occurs (cf. Treviño & Youngblood, 1990; Treviño & Victor, 1992). She suggested that moral cognitions (such as those proposed by Kohlberg) drive ethical behavior, but that that relationship is moderated by two factors. The first set of moderators includes other individual characteristics such as ego strength, field dependence, and locus of control. The second set of moderators includes situational factors such as job context (reinforcement contingencies and other pressures), organizational culture (including norms, values, obedience), and work characteristics (role taking and moral conflict resolution). Most adults operate from Kohlberg's conventional level of moral development, in which peer and social influences play a large role in determining what constitutes moral behavior (Treviño, 1986; Weber, 1990). Therefore, these situational influences should be especially salient in work settings and, thus, impact the relationship between CMD and ethical behavior.

Others have considered both individual and organizational factors in models of ethical decision making. For example, in Ferrell and Gresham's (1985) approach, individual factors include the teleological (outcome-based) and deontological (rules-based) assumptions individuals use for making ethical decisions. These assumptions follow Velasquez's (1992) description of utilitarian, rights, and justice principles. These principles provide the ethical frameworks by which individuals decide what constitutes moral action. Other individual factors in the model include knowledge, values, and attitudes. Situational factors include the ethical beliefs and actions of significant others as well as the opportunity for action.

Bommer, Gratto, Gravander, and Tuttle (1987) proposed an even broader model of situational and individual influences on ethical decision making. The individual attributes in this model include level of moral development, personality traits (such as locus of control), demographics (age, gender, education), motivational orientation (safety vs. esteem), personal goals and values, and other factors, such as life experiences and intelligence. Situational factors cut across five different contextual environments. An individual's personal environment includes family and peer influences on the ethical decision process. The professional environment reflects codes of conduct, licensing requirements, and the influence of professional meetings. The work environment may influence ethical decision making through stated policies, corporate culture, and pressures of corporate goals. The governmental and legal environment includes laws and regulations resulting from legislation, administrative agencies, and the judicial system. Finally, the social environment addresses the influence resulting from religious, humanistic, cultural, and societal values.

Several recent attempts to model ethical decision making centered on the theory of reasoned action (TRA; Ajzen & Fishbein, 1980; Fishbein & Ajzen, 1975). The goal of the TRA is to predict and understand a person's behavior, focusing on behavioral intent as the best predictor of that behavior. Intent, in turn, is influenced by both individual and situational factors. Individual factors include behavioral beliefs (Will the action lead to certain outcomes?), outcome evaluations (Are those outcomes positive or negative?), and attitudes toward the behavior itself. Situational factors include subjective norms such as whether significant others think the behavior should or should not be performed.

Some TRA-based models of ethical behavior stick closely to the Fishbein and Ajzen framework (e.g., Dubinsky & Loken, 1989). Others include a number of other individual and situational factors. For example, Kurland (1995) proposed a model based on both TRA and the theory of planned behavior (Ajzen, 1991), which adds perceived behavioral control to the situational constraints on behavior. Similarly, Hunt and Vitell (1986) proposed a general theory of marketing ethics based on the TRA that included sociocultural, industry and organizational norms, and individual factors such as deontological and teleological reasoning. Jones (1991) provided a synthesis of several models (Dubinsky & Loken, 1989; Ferrell & Gresham, 1985; Hunt & Vitell, 1986; Rest, 1986; Treviño, 1986) that embedded Rest's four components and TRA-based approaches in a broader situational context. Finally, Ferrell, Gresham, and Fraedrich (1989) integrated three approaches into a single model of ethical decision making. They combined Hunt and Vitell's TRA-based model with Ferrell and Gresham's (1985) deontologal/teleological model and added Kohlberg's CMD framework to create what they termed a synthesis of ethical decision models.

Models That Focus on the Ethical Issue

Recently, some authors have begun to expand their view of the influences on ethical behavior. These views go beyond individual differences and the setting or situation in which the event occurs to consider the nature of the ethical event itself. One example of this movement is Brady's (1990) Janus-headed view of ethical decision making. Brady's approach focused on individuals and their underlying ethical predispositions, but its application required consideration of the particular ethical event.

Brady contended that individuals have not one but two ethical faces, one formalist and the other utilitarian (roughly synonymous with deontological and teleological approaches, respectively). Formalist reasoning reflects an inclination to follow rules or principles in determining what constitutes ethical behavior. Utilitarian reasoning evaluates the results of actions, rather than the actions themselves, as ethical or not. Critical to Brady's approach is that formalism and utilitarianism do not represent an either/or proposition. Rather, each individual has both formalist and utilitarian tendencies, which play a greater or a lesser role when confronting issues that reflect formalist or utilitarian concerns, respectively.

In fact, many issues contain both. Brady illustrated the duality of these issue pairs in areas such as whistleblowing, overseas corporate bribery, pollution, corporate trade secrets, and software piracy. In many cases, these issues contain both formalist and utilitarian concerns. For example, in each case, formalists might seek a set of rules to help best balance the rights of various stakeholders whose interests are mutually incompatible. On the other hand, utilitarians might seek to maximize the net social good (or minimize the net social harm) arising from such conflicts of interest.

Brady noted that not all issues reflect formalist and utilitarian concerns equally. He cited new genetic engineering technologies and suggested that most of the ethical discussion surrounding these technologies has tended to focus on utilitarian concerns: Do the potential benefits of manipulating genetic structures in laboratory settings outweigh the potential harm (known and unknown) that might come from such tinkering? Likewise, nuclear power and nuclear weapons seem to generate largely utilitarian discussion. On the other hand, debate on employment discrimination seems to center around formalist issues: Should employers have the right to hire anyone they please?

Must employment selection be job-task related? The Janus-headed model suggests that individuals have the capacity to deal with each type of issue from each perspective. However, it is the nature of the issue itself that determines the decision-making perspective from which an individual will address the dilemma.

Jones (1991) also looked beyond the individual and the organizational setting in addressing how ethical decisions are made. He proposed an issue-contingent model of ethical decision making. In it, he suggested that the moral intensity of a situation—the extent to which an issue-related moral imperative exists—is a multidimensional construct that "focuses on the moral issue, not on the moral agent or the organizational context" (p. 373). Six dimensions characterize the moral intensity of an event. First, the magnitude of the consequences of an event is the sum of the harms (benefits) done to its victims (beneficiaries). Greater harms or benefits translate to greater moral intensity. Second, social consensus reflects the degree of social agreement that an act is good or bad. Greater consensus results in greater moral intensity. Third, probability of effect includes both the uncertainty of whether the event will take place and the likelihood that the predicted harm or benefits will occur if it does take place. Greater probability of effect will result in greater moral intensity. Fourth, temporal immediacy indicates the length of time between the act and the onset of its expected outcomes. Increased immediacy yields greater moral intensity. Fifth, proximity reflects the feeling of closeness (social, cultural, psychological, or physical) the decision maker has for the beneficiaries or victims of the act. Increased closeness results in greater moral intensity. Finally, concentration of effect reflects the degree to which a small or large number of individuals will be affected by an act of a given magnitude. Greater concentration results in greater moral intensity. Building on Rest's (1986) four component model, Jones (1991) suggested that moral intensity may affect ethical decision making at any stage of the decision-making process: recognizing that a moral issue exists, making moral judgments, establishing moral intent, or actually engaging in moral behavior.

Each of these models of ethical decision making—individual, situational, or issue oriented—operates under an assumption of systematic, rational decision making on the part of the individual facing the ethical dilemma. At times that assumption is implicit, but other times it is quite explicit. For example, in describing the theory of reasoned action, Ajzen and Fishbein (1980) stated:

> . . . the theory is based on the assumption that human beings are usually quite rational and make systematic use of information available to them. We do not subscribe to the view that human social behavior is controlled by unconscious motives or overpowering desires, nor do we believe that it can be characterized as capricious or thoughtless. Rather, we argue that people con-

sider the implications of their actions before they decide to engage or not engage in a given behavior. (p. 5)

However, we know that strict rationality does not describe many decision processes in real organizational settings (March & Simon, 1958). The next section summarizes several nonrational approaches to managerial decision making.

NONRATIONAL MANAGERIAL DECISION MAKING

Before exploring models of nonrational managerial decision making, one point needs to be made. Nonrational decision making is not synonymous with irrational decision making. That is, nonrational models do not imply any sort of mental ineptitude or instability on the part of decision makers. What they address is that, in real organizational settings, managers seldom meet the criteria of the rational decision maker that underlie most traditional economic decision models: correctly identifying the problem, knowing all relevant alternatives, identifying all relevant criteria, accurately weighing the importance of the criteria, accurately assessing each criterion vis-à-vis relevant goals, and accurately calculating and choosing the optimal alternative (Friedman, 1957). Rather, four approaches to describing nonrational decision making have emerged in the literature: bounded rationality, incrementalism, biases and heuristics, and escalation.

The earliest models of nonrational decision making operate from a premise of bounded rationality (March & Simon, 1958; Simon, 1957), that is, that decision makers lack information concerning the problem, alternative solutions, and relevant criteria. Furthermore, time and cost constraints may limit their search process. Finally, limited perceptual and cognitive abilities constrain decision makers' abilities to calculate optimal solutions (Bazerman, 1986). Thus, managers may employ less than optimal or rational decision models. That is, they tend to satisfice (selecting the first acceptable solution to a decision that comes along) rather than optimize (exploring and evaluating all possible alternatives fully before selecting the best one).

In a second view of nonrational decision making, Mintzberg and his colleagues described incremental decision approaches (cf. Mintzberg, Raisinghani, & Theoret, 1976). An incremental approach recognizes that managers are often incapable of addressing very large scale, complicated issues in a single decision cycle. Rather, they may muddle through a series of subissues, with no clear endgame in mind. For example, we may observe an organization's actions as it moves from Position A to, say, Position E. As outsiders, it may appear to us that a well-reasoned decision-making process allowed the organization to take the large step from A to E. However, it is more likely that the company moved incrementally, from A to B, then from B to C, then from C to D, and finally, from D to E. What to an outsider may have appeared to be revolutionary change was, in reality, a series of smaller evolutionary changes, as managers sought to reduce major decisions to smaller, more manageable portions.

A third view of decision making considers the shortcuts—and possible resulting decision errors—inherent in many decision processes. Specifically, Tversky and Kahneman (1974) noted several biases and heuristics in decision making that include representativeness, availability, and anchoring and adjustment. Representativeness reflects managers' tendencies to be swayed by stereotypes. Availability denotes managers' inclination to give greater weight to more recent or more easily recalled events. Finally, anchoring and adjustment reflects an individual's tendency to be influenced by initial figures in, say, negotiation settings, even when those figures are objectively irrelevant. Each of these denotes strategies that individuals use to simplify the decision process. (However, each may also lead to biased decisions or even serious, systematic errors; Bazerman, 1986.)

In a fourth example of nonrational decision making, Staw and others described the escalation phenomenon in decision making (cf. Staw, 1981). Research shows that managers often display escalating commitment to even a failing course of action. Ignoring the financial adage that sunk costs are irrelevant, managers often throw good money after bad, and this commitment to the failed action may increase as the sunk costs increase.

Of course, all of these issues—bounded rationality, incrementalism, biases and heuristics, and escalation—are present in the sticky world of ethical decision making as well. To make matters more complicated, managers facing ethical dilemmas confront ambiguity not only about what constitutes a correct or moral course of action but also about how to decide what constitutes moral behavior. In this chapter, I argue that ethical decision making is no more or no less rational than any other type of managerial decision making and, thus, is guided by similar nonrational processes. One additional nonrational decision model may help organize our thinking about ethical decision making: the garbage can approach.

A GARBAGE CAN MODEL OF DECISION MAKING

The garbage can model of decision making examines how managers make decisions under conditions of high uncertainty. In developing the model, Cohen, March, and Olsen (1972) described a type of high uncertainty organization or decision situation they called organized anarchies. Organized anarchies reflect three traits: problematic preferences, unclear technologies, and fluid participation. *Problematic preferences* imply that individuals' preference sets are unclear; the organization operates under a set of inconsistent and ill-defined goals and desires on the part of its members or coalitions of members. The organization or decision situation can be better described as "a loose collection of ideas than as a coherent structure" (p. 1). *Unclear technologies* indicate that even organization members find the decision processes to be ambiguous. Decisions are made but the process is not well understood. *Fluid participation* suggests that participants vary in the amount of time and effort they devote to various issues. Variation may also exist in the makeup of the decision team itself.

The garbage can approach notes four forces flowing through these organized anarchies. *Problems* provide concerns for organization members. They are the issues that require attention. *Solutions* are answers, but they are not static answers. They are someone's product, and as such, organizations may contain answers looking for questions. *Participants* enter and exit the mix. A variety of demands on members' time and resources requires that they constantly reevaluate their involvement with different projects or issues. Finally, *choice opportunities* present themselves on occasion when a decision or action is called for.

Cohen et al. (1972) viewed organizations as large garbage cans into which these four streams of organizational elements flow. The four ingredients mix and swirl over time, but of course this blending does not follow a rational pattern in which participants with choice opportunities discover decision alternatives, anticipate the likely outcomes of those alternatives, evaluate those outcomes relative to set goals, and finally reach a decision. The model views the process as much more random; organizations become "collections of choices looking for problems, issues and feelings looking for decision situations in which they might be aired, solutions looking for issues to which they might be the answer, and decision makers looking for work" (p. 2).

Garbage can decision processes describe some famous outcomes. For example, 3M's ubiquitous Post-it sticky notes grew from a new adhesive polymer developed by chemist Spencer Silver in 1964. However, it wasn't until 10 years later that another chemist, Arthur Fry, came up with a problem for Spencer's solution: bookmarks that kept falling out of his Sunday hymnal. After six more years of testing and marketing, Post-its finally saw national distribution (Mingo, 1994).

Similarly, Kimberly-Clark, a paper manufacturer in Wisconsin since 1872, began developing paper-based (cellulose) substitutes for absorbent cotton materials in 1914. As World War I escalated, cotton shortages led Kimberly-Clark to develop a variety of uses for the new product (Cellucotton), including bandages and gas mask filters. After the war, they owned a solution for which few problems remained. Responding, they produced Cellucotton in thin sheets, which became known as Kleenex tissues. Kimberly-Clark marketed the new product narrowly as a sanitary way to remove cold cream.

Later, marketing research revealed that two thirds of their customers did not use the product to remove cold cream at all, but rather as disposable handkerchiefs. After developing a new marketing campaign (that also encouraged using Kleenex as coffee filters!), sales soared (Mingo, 1994).

The garbage can model has been used to explore and explain a variety of decision issues. For example, Masuch and LaPotin (1989) used it as the basis for exploring artificial intelligence choice systems for organizations, and Goitein (1989) examined its application to decisions regarding energy conservation efforts. Levitt and Nass (1989) explored decision making in textbook publishing and found it to be consistent with a garbage can approach. Strategic decision making in organizations has also been viewed from the garbage can perspective (Eisenhardt & Zbaracki, 1992; Hickson, 1987). Others used a garbage can approach in broader contexts to understand public policy (Albaek, 1995; Mandell, 1989; Teasley & Harrell, 1996) and industrial policy (Atkinson & Powers, 1987) decisions. The model has also helped researchers to understand education issues, such as school choice (Dougherty & Sostre, 1992) and participation in school decision making (Bartunek & Keys, 1979).

The garbage can model has also been paired with other theoretical approaches to enhance our understanding of organizational issues. For example, to understand better the way ambiguity might affect decision making in structured settings, Padgett (1980) integrated the garbage can model with more traditional notions of classical bureaucracy. Similarly, Mezias and Scarselletta (1994) integrated a garbage can approach with institutional theory to explain the decision process of a public policy task force examining financial reporting standards. In all, the garbage can approach has proven useful in a number of organizational and societal settings. The question that remains is whether it applies to ethical decision making in organizations.

A GARBAGE CAN MODEL OF ETHICAL DECISION MAKING: THE "MAGIC PUNCHBOWL"

During an early review of the proposal for this book, a reviewer expressed concern over the label *garbage can approach*, noting that garbage cans are places we put things we no longer want. Certainly, ethical decisions and ethical organizations are not something to be discarded! Thus, I agree that the garbage can metaphor may not provide the positive image we seek. Therefore, for the remainder of the chapter, I will refer to this vessel of swirling decision-making ingredients as a magic punchbowl, as it is from this container that chaotic organizational forces may produce ethical decisions. For this punchbowl model to provide a framework that will enhance our thinking about ethical decision making, it needs to be able to accommodate and synthesize the individual, contextual, and issue-related forces outlined earlier in the chapter.

Note that, in discussing the ethical decision models, I have not suggested that the content of these frameworks—the constructs themselves—was not accurate. Rather, I have suggested that the linear, rational way in which the constructs are arranged—the way the decision process is portrayed—does not describe the way decisions are really made in organizational settings. Therefore, it is not my intent to dispose of the constructs set forth in any of the models I reviewed. To the contrary, building better theory often consists of taking existing models and reorganizing them to more accurately reflect reality. That is the goal of this final section: to synthesize existing constructs and models that address ethical decision making into a framework that more accurately describes the real ethical decision process. However, to apply a punchbowl approach to organizational ethics, the first question is whether ethical situations resemble organized anarchies. In the next sections I consider how ethical situations reflect the three distinguishing characteristics of organized anarchies: problematic preferences, unclear technologies, and fluid participation.

Problematic Preferences

Ethical situations do reflect problematic preferences; individuals' preference sets may be unclear, ill-defined, or inconsistent. For example, consider the moral judgment component of Rest's (1986) four component model. Moral judgment includes individuals' cognitive moral development (and other developmental approaches to ethical decision making such as Gilligan's [1982] ethics of care) and moral evaluation tools like deontological and teleological frameworks (Jones, 1991). These moral judgment characteristics provide the basic building blocks for individuals' ethical reasoning. Because individuals differ in terms of moral cognitions and moral frameworks, we can expect repeated confusion as to whether, say, utilitarian or formalist reasoning should determine what constitutes moral behavior.

Unclear Technologies

Ethical situations also reflect unclear technologies (decision processes); individuals often find the decision process to be ambiguous. First, because many ethical dilemmas (and thus, decisions) are by nature secretive, little shared understanding exists in most organizations about how they are, or should be, addressed. Second, no single ethical decision model has emerged as the acknowledged best empirical or theoretical descriptor of the ethical decision-making process. (Consider the variety of decision models outlined in the earlier section, Current Models of Ethical Decision Making.) In fact, the frequency with which new models appear suggests that, as researchers, we are not confident that we have found the model that accurately describes the process.

Fluid Participation

We may view participation in ethical decisions as fluid on at least three dimensions: presence, individual characteristics, and opportunity. First, consider participants' presence at or near the ethical issue. Turnover, transfers, and promotions are a fact of life in most organizations. Members come and go; their ability to participate in ethical debates waxes and wanes with their wandering.

Second, not all participants who do remain in an organizational setting participate in all moral issues that might arise. Three components of Rest's (1986) four component model may affect participation: moral sensitivity, motivation, and character.

Moral Sensitivity. To participate, one must be sensitive to the existence of an ethical issue. We have seen that individuals' moral sensitivity may be affected by a host of social, economic, organizational, and individual effects (Ferrell et al., 1989; Hunt & Vitell, 1986; Jones, 1991), and individuals with increased awareness of ethical issues are more likely to notice ethical problems when they arise.

Moral Motivation. To participate, an individual must also be motivated to act on the ethical issue. Moral motivation largely reflects moral intent. The TRA-based models described above suggest that moral intent flows from moral evaluations, organizational culture and opportunity, the ethics of significant others, and other individual-level factors (Ferrell et al., 1989; Hunt & Vitell, 1986; Jones, 1991). Moral motivation reflects the extent to which an individual places relatively greater importance on ethical values. Therefore, moral issues will be accorded greater weight, and scarce resources of time and effort will more likely be channeled to ethical problems and solutions.

Moral Character. To participate, an individual must possess the moral character to follow up on that motivation. A number of individual-level factors affect moral character, including ego strength, perseverance, and strength of conviction (Rest, 1986), and these characteristics played a role in several of the ethical decision frameworks presented earlier (e.g., Bommer et al., 1987; Ferrell & Gresham, 1985; Treviño, 1986). In a sense, moral character provides the glue that holds together the necessary ingredients long enough for ethical decisions to be made and ethical actions to be taken.

Presence and personal inclination are not enough to guarantee participation. Additionally, an individual must be in an organizational position that provides the opportunity to participate in a moral issue. A clerk at the university bookstore might be opposed to some of the hiring policies of the university, but he may not be in a position to affect the debate on the issue, although he may possess a surfeit of moral sensitivity, motivation, and character.

Thus, ethical dilemmas in organizational settings seem quite consistent with the Cohen et al. (1972) description of organized anarchies. That is, they reflect problematic preferences, unclear technologies, and fluid participation. Therefore, a punchbowl approach may provide a sound basis for exploring how ethical decisions are made in organizations.

Punchbowl Ingredients

Recall that four ingredients swirl in the punchbowl—participants, problems, solutions, and choice opportunities—and that these ingredients sometimes exist in isolation and sometimes link with one or more other ingredients. However, for ethical organizational behavior to happen, all four must join together simultaneously. The question is what each of these represents in terms of ethical decision processes.

Participants. A participant in the ethical punchbowl is simply a moral agent, which Jones (1991) identified as individuals involved in a moral decision (regardless of whether they recognize the issue as an ethical one). As we saw in the individual-based ethical models, these participants are complex ethical creatures who vary across a number of dimensions (cf. Forsyth, 1980; Hogan, 1973) including moral judgment, sensitivity, motivation, and character (Rest, 1986). Their participation is fluid and is enhanced by moral sensitivity, motivation, and character. However, for ethical action to occur, one or more participants must connect with the other three ingredients.

Problems. A problem in the punchbowl is a moral issue, which is "present when a person's actions, when freely performed, may harm or benefit others" (Jones, 1991, p. 367). Recall from the issue-based ethical models described earlier that these issues or problems are endowed with some degree of moral intensity (Jones, 1991). In the punchbowl, greater levels of moral intensity increase the chances that these problems will be noticed and acted upon. The moral intensity of an issue is the red flag that attracts participants and solutions and may lead to choice opportunities.

Solutions. Solutions to moral problems may abound due to the many (potentially conflicting) ethical preferences of participants. However, they may also be created and poured into the punch without organizational awareness of any specific problem to be solved. For example, many organizations regularly provide ethics training for employees. In most cases these efforts are not aimed only at extant ethical violators. Rather, they are cast broadly at organizational participants, seeking to prevent ethical violations. They may be solutions without specific, identifiable problems.

Choice Opportunities.   Opportunities to address and even solve ethical issues may arise either by chance or by design. In either case, they evolve from the organizational setting and, thus, are reflected in the situation- or context-based models described earlier. That is, ethically thoughtful organizations may create more opportunities to solve ethical problems than may exist by chance alone. For example, ethics officers or ethics hotlines may create situations in which organizations face ethical issues and seek action. In a sense, these choice opportunities are the flypaper to which the other ingredients—participants, problems, and solutions—may stick long enough to assemble themselves into meaningful clusters that include a participant, facing an ethical problem, armed with potential solutions, and in a context that provides the opportunity to do something to address the ethical issue.

These four forces flow continually through organizations. Sometimes they exist independently, and sometimes, two or three of them may link together. In these cases the rational ethical decision chain is not completed. That is, we may have opportunities with no willing participants. We may have problems for which there are no solutions. We may have participants with solutions for which no problems currently exist or participants that do not have the opportunity to apply the solutions. However, once in a while, the four ingredients do connect and hang together long enough to solve meaningful ethical issues. Note that this condition does not necessarily happen in the rational, linear way many current ethical decision models suggest. Rather, the four may—and do—come together in odd, nonlinear ways. To an outside observer, it might appear as if a rational ethical decision process has happened. But in reality, the random magic of the punchbowl's swirling ingredients did its job in linking the four factors.

IMPLICATIONS

The implications of a model such as this are many. First, it integrates a number of diverse ethical models and frameworks. One criticism of the field of business ethics as it has recently evolved is that, as we continue to explore issues, often from multiple perspectives, we do not do a very good job of integrating past, current, and emerging theory. This framework will accommodate a variety of managerial ethical issues, such as those in the previous chapters and beyond.

Second, it may account for some of the instability we see in trying to map individuals' ethical behavior. If the ethical punch in the bowl is full of a variety of actors and ethical frameworks, the model suggests that the same actor does not necessarily always align himself or herself with one particular framework. In one situation, a gender-driven model might dominate; in another, gender may play a minor role, and an outcome-based utilitarian framework may emerge as most applicable.

Third, it allows us to explore a host of sticky ethical questions. For example, why do we feel uncomfortable when teaching that some moral dilemmas simply seem to have no good solutions? This approach allows ethical dilemmas to exist in the absence of acceptable solutions. (Sometimes, there are no good solutions, or even if there are, the correct actors have not been able to link up with them in the punch.) Another often-troubling topic concerns when good companies do bad things. Because a punchbowl approach allows us to divorce ethical intentions from ethical outcomes, we are able to explore issues like this more meaningfully by making clear that being involved in a situation that resulted in bad outcomes does not imply immoral actors or intentions. These and other complex permutations of the five forces of the ethical process may be more easily—and accurately—framed using a punchbowl approach.

A final closing note is in order. That the process is often not a rational one does not imply that organizational members should throw up their hands in surrender. To the contrary, magic punchbowl decision systems—though nonlinear and nonrational—may be, must be, managed like any other. As with any recipe for punch, we may manage the quality of the ingredients, the flow rates of the ingredients into the bowl, and the enthusiasm with which the ingredients are stirred. Much of what we know about ethical decision making may play an important role in encouraging participation, raising ethical sensitivities, creating better quality moral solutions, and enhancing the chance that choice opportunities will arise. The particular order in which the ingredients link may be random, but enhancing the quality and frequency of those links represents an important management issue.

REFERENCES

Ajzen, I. (1991). The theory of planned behavior. *Organizational Behavior and Human Decision Processes, 50,* 179–211.

Ajzen, I., & Fishbein, M. (1980). *Understanding attitudes and predicting social behavior.* Englewood Cliffs, NJ: Prentice-Hall.

Albaek, E. (1995). Between knowledge and power: Utilization of social science in public policy making. *Policy Sciences, 28,* 79–100.

Atkinson, M. M., & Powers, R. A. (1987). Inside the industrial policy garbage can: Selective subsidies to business in Canada. *Canadian Public Policy, 13,* 208–217.

Bartunek, J. M., & Keys, C. B. (1979). Participation in school decision making. *Urban Education, 14,* 52–75.

Bazerman, M. H. (1986). *Judgment in managerial decision making.* New York: Wiley.

Bommer, M., Gratto, C., Gravander, J., & Tuttle, M. (1987). A behavioral model of ethical and unethical decision making. *Journal of Business Ethics, 6,* 265–280.

Brady, F. N. (1990). *Ethical managing.* New York: Macmillan.

Cohen, M. D., March, J. G., & Olsen, J. P. (1972). A garbage can model of organizational choice. *Administrative Science Quarterly, 17,* 1–25.

Dougherty, K. J., & Sostre, L. (1992). Minerva and the market: The sources of the movement for school choice. *Educational Policy, 6,* 160–179.

Dubinsky, A. J., & Loken, B. (1989). Analyzing ethical decision making in marketing. *Journal of Business Research, 19,* 83–107.

Eisenhardt, K. M., & Zbaracki, M. J. (1992). Strategic decision making. *Strategic Management Journal, 13,* 17–37.

Ferrell, O. C., & Gresham, L. G. (1985). A contingency framework for understanding ethical decision making in marketing. *Journal of Marketing, 49,* 87–96.

Ferrell, O. C., Gresham, L. G., & Fraedrich, J. (1989). A synthesis of ethical decision models for marketing. *Journal of Macromarketing, 9,* 55–64.

Fishbein, J., & Ajzen, I. (1975). *Belief, attitude, intention, and behavior.* Reading, MA: Addison-Wesley.

Fletcher, J. (1966). *Situation ethics.* Philadelphia: Westminster Press.

Forsyth, D. R. (1980). A taxonomy of ethical ideologies. *Journal of Personality and Social Psychology, 39,* 175–184.

Friedman, M. (1957). *A theory of consumption function.* Princeton, NJ: Princeton University Press.

Gilligan, C. (1982). *In a different voice: Psychological theory and women's development.* Cambridge, MA: Harvard University Press.

Goitein, B. (1989). Organizational decision-making and energy conservation investments. *Evaluation and Program Planning, 12,* 143–151.

Hickson, D. J. (1987). Decision-making at the top of organizations. *Annual Review of Sociology, 13,* 165–192.

Hogan, R. (1973). Moral conduct and moral character: A psychological perspective. *Psychological Bulletin, 79,* 217–232.

Hunt, S. D., & Vitell, S. (1986). A general theory of marketing ethics. *Journal of Macromarketing, 6,* 5–16.

Jones, T. M. (1991). Ethical decision making by individuals in organizations: An issue-contingent model. *Academy of Management Review, 16,* 366–395.

Kohlberg, L. (1981). *The philosophy of moral development.* San Francisco: Harper & Row.

Kurland, N. B. (1995). Ethical intentions and the theories of reasoned action and planned behavior. *Journal of Applied Social Psychology, 25,* 297–313.

Levitt, B., & Nass, C. (1989). The lid on the garbage can: Institutional constraints on decision making in the technical core of college text publishers. *Administrative Science Quarterly, 34,* 190–207.

Mandell, M. B. (1989). A simulation-based assessment of the value of enhancing the credibility of policy analysis. *Knowledge in Society, 2,* 39–56.

March, J. G., & Simon, H. A. (1958). *Organizations.* New York: Wiley.

Masuch, M., & LaPotin, P. (1989). Beyond garbage cans: An AI model of organizational choice. *Administrative Science Quarterly, 34,* 38–67.

Mezias, S. J., & Scarselletta, M. (1994). Resolving financial reporting problems: An institutional analysis of the process. *Administrative Science Quarterly, 39,* 654–678.

Mingo, J. (1994). *How the Cadillac got its fins.* New York: Harper Business.

214

Mintzberg, H., Raisinghani, D., & Theoret, A. (1976). The structure of "unstructured" decision processes. *Administrative Science Quarterly, 21*, 246–275.

Padgett, J. F. (1980). Managing garbage can hierarchies. *Administrative Science Quarterly, 25*, 583–604.

Piaget, J. (1948). *The moral judgment of the child.* Glencoe, IL: The Free Press.

Rest, J. R. (1986). *Moral development: Advances in theory and research.* New York: Praeger.

Rest, J. R. (1994). Background: Theory and research. In J. R. Rest and D. Narvaez (Eds.), *Moral development in the professions: Psychology and applied ethics* (pp. 1–26). Hillsdale, NJ: Lawrence Erlbaum and Associates.

Simon, H. A. (1957). *Models of man.* New York: Wiley.

Staw, B. M. (1981). The escalation of commitment to a course of action. *Academy of Management Review, 6*, 577–587.

Teasley, C. E., III, & Harrell, S. W. (1996). A real garbage can decision model: Measuring the costs of politics with a computer assisted decision support software (DSS) program. *Public Administration Quarterly, 19*, 479–492.

Treviño, L. K. (1986). Ethical decision making in organizations: A person-situation interactionist model. *Academy of Management Review, 11*, 601–617.

Treviño, L. K., & Victor, B. (1992). Peer reporting of unethical behavior: A social context perspective. *Academy of Management Journal, 35*, 38–64.

Treviño, L. K., & Youngblood, S. A. (1990). Bad apples in bad barrels: A causal analysis of ethical decision-making behavior. *Journal of Applied Psychology, 75*, 378–385.

Tversky, A., & Kahneman, D. (1974). Judgment under uncertainty: Heuristics and biases. *Science, 185*, 1124–1131.

Velasquez, M. G. (1992). *Business ethics.* Englewood Cliffs, NJ: Prentice-Hall.

Weber, J. (1990). Managers' moral reasoning: Assessing their responses to three moral dilemmas. *Human Relations, 43*, 687–702.

Contributors

G. Stoney Alder is a doctoral candidate at the University of Colorado at Boulder. He is pursuing a degree in organizational behavior and human resource management. His research interests include employee performance monitoring, organizational justice, and performance feedback. He has published articles on these topics in *Management Communication Quarterly, Journal of Business Ethics,* and *Journal of Applied Communication Research*.

Maureen L. Ambrose is an associate professor of management at the University of Colorado at Boulder. She received her PhD in industrial/organizational psychology from the University of Illinois at Urbana–Champaign, and served on the faculty at the University of Iowa prior to her move to the University of Colorado. Her research interests include electronic monitoring, organizational justice, and ethics. She has served on the editorial boards of the *Academy of Management Journal, Journal of Management,* and *Journal of Applied Psychology*. Her work has been published in numerous journals, including *Academy of Management Journal, Academy of Management Review, Administrative Science Quarterly,* and the *Journal of Applied Psychology*.

Russell Cropanzano is an associate professor of industrial/organizational psychology at Colorado State University. He received his PhD in I/O psychology from Purdue University in 1988. Cropanzano serves on the editorial board for the *Journal of Applied Psychology*. He has published more than

35 scholarly articles and chapters, appearing in such places as the *Journal of Applied Psychology*, the *Journal of Organizational Behavior*, and *Social Justice Research*. In addition, he has edited two books: *Justice in the Workplace* and *Organizational Politics, Justice, and Support*. He is a co-author of the forthcoming *Organizational Justice and Human Resources Management* and co-editor of two forthcoming books: *Advances in Organizational Justice* and *Justice in the Workplace* (Vol. 2). Cropanzano has lectured widely, delivering more than 25 talks, including papers in Australia, New Zealand, and the Netherlands.

Robert Folger is Freeman professor of doctoral studies and research, and professor of organizational behavior at the A. B. Freeman School of Business, Tulane University. He received his PhD from the University of North Carolina, Chapel Hill. His research interests include work motivation, fairness, performance appraisal, compensation, layoffs, workplace aggression, and ethics.

Mark A. Fuller is an assistant professor of information systems at Baylor University, having received his PhD from the University of Arizona's Management Information Systems Department in 1993. Prior to Baylor, Fuller worked extensively as a professional meeting facilitator, consulting with organizations on the use of groupware to support traditional meeting activities. Current research interests include the impact of technology on learning, meeting facilitation, virtual teamwork, and electronic commerce. Fuller has published in a variety of journals, including *Group Decision and Negotiation, Decision Support Systems,* and the *Journal of Mathematical Psychology*. He is currently the editor of the journal *Group Facilitation*.

Alicia A. Grandey is a PhD candidate in industrial/organizational psychology at Colorado State University. In 1996, she received her master's degree in I/O psychology. Grandey is a member of both the Academy of Management and the Society for Industrial/Organizational Psychology. Currently, she serves as the editorial assistant for the *Journal of Applied Psychology*. Her research interests include organizational politics, work stress, and emotional labor.

Terri L. Griffith is an assistant professor of organizational behavior at the John M. Olin School of Business, Washington University, St. Louis. She received her MS and PhD from Carnegie Mellon University, and her BA from the University of California, Berkeley. Her research and consulting interests include the implementation and effective use of new technologies. Most recently, she has worked with virtual teams and "negotiated" implementation strategies. Griffith's work has been published in journals such as: *Organization Science, MIS Quarterly, Journal of Engineering and Technology Man-*

agement, and *Organizational Behavior and Human Decision Processes.* She is a member of the Academy of Management and INFORMS, serves on editorial boards for *Journal of Engineering and Technology Management, Group Decision and Negotiation, Journal of Managerial Issues,* and is a senior editor for *Organization Science.*

Beverly Kracher is an assistant professor of business ethics and society at Creighton University. She received her PhD in philosophy from the University of Nebraska at Lincoln. Her current research involves applying an ethic of care to the business context. Her work can be found in the *Journal of Business Ethics* and *Business Ethics Quarterly.*

Dennis J. Moberg is professor of management and scholar with the Markkula Center for Applied Ethics at Santa Clara University. His research focuses on organizational ethics.

Terry W. Noel is an assistant professor in management at Vanderbilt University. He received his PhD in organizational behavior from the University of Colorado at Boulder in 1997. His research interests include group goal setting, work team innovation, and the concept of rights in organizational justice.

Gregory B. Northcraft is professor of business administration, and labor and industrial relations, at the University of Illinois. His PhD is from Stanford University (1981) in social psychology. His major research interests include conflict management, managerial decision making, processes of collaboration, and employee motivation and job design, particularly in high-technology manufacturing settings. His research has appeared in such places as *Organizational Behavior and Human Decision Processes, Academy of Management Journal, Academy of Management Review, Journal of Applied Psychology, Decision Sciences,* and *Organization Science.* He has held visiting professorships at Dartmouth College and Northwestern University, and also has taught in Thailand, Bulgaria, Australia, and the People's Republic of China. He serves on the editorial board of the *Journal of Managerial Issues,* and is associate editor of *Group Decision and Negotiation,* and associate editor of the *Academy of Management Journal.*

Joseph A. Petrick is associate professor of management at Wright State University in Dayton, Ohio. He earned his PhD from The Pennsylvania State University, with advanced international graduate work at the University of Bonn in Germany and the University of Tokyo in Japan. His co-authored books include *Total Quality in Managing Human Resources, Total Quality and Organization Development,* and *Management Ethics: Integrity at Work.*

He has published scholarly articles in the following journals: *Academy of Management Executive, Journal of Managerial Psychology, Journal of General Management, SAM Advanced Management Journal, Journal of Management Development, International Executive, Quality Progress, Industrial Management, Journal of Health and Human Resource Management, Journal for Quality and Participation,* and *Journal of Asian Business.* He has provided professional advice to a variety of organizations through Organizational Ethics Associates and Performance Leadership Associates.

Marshall Schminke holds the Robert B. Daugherty Chair in managerial ethics at Creighton University. He received his PhD in industrial administration from Carnegie Mellon University in 1986 and has taught at the University of Iowa and in the Dominican Republic. He is the executive director of Creighton's Center for Family Business and has published more than two dozen articles and book chapters in publications that include the *Academy of Management Journal, Business Ethics Quarterly, Journal of Applied Social Psychology, Journal of Business Ethics, Journal of Business and Psychology, Journal of Business Strategies,* and *Research in Organizational Behavior.*

Mark A. Seabright is an associate professor of management in the Division of Business at Western Oregon University. He received his PhD in organizational psychology and theory from Carnegie Mellon University in 1988. He has published articles in *Organizational Behavior and Human Decision Processes, Academy of Management Journal, Journal of Management Inquiry,* and *Business Ethics Quarterly.* His research interests include business ethics, organizational justice, and nontraditional organizational forms.

Dianna L. Stone is professor of management at the University of Central Florida. She received her PhD from Purdue University. Her research focuses on a variety of issues, including privacy in organizations, individuals' reactions to personnel selection procedures, race and disabilities in the workplace, and quality management. Results of her research have been published in the *Journal of Applied Psychology, Personnel Psychology, Organizational Behavior and Human Decision Processes, Journal of Management, Academy of Management Review,* and the new *Journal of Quality Management.* She is a past chair of the Human Resources Division of the Academy of Management, and currently serves on the editorial boards of the *Journal of Quality Management* and *Human Resource Management Review.*

Eugene F. Stone-Romero received his PhD from the University of California-Irvine in 1974 and is now professor of psychology at the University of Central Florida. He is a fellow of both the Society for Industrial and Organizational Psychology and the American Psychological Society and is a member of the Society of Indian Psychologists. He currently serves on the editorial boards of the *Journal of Applied Psychology, Personnel Psychology, Organizational Research Methods,* and *Technology Studies.* His work has appeared in such journals as the *Journal of Applied Psychology, Organizational Behavior and Human Performance, Journal of Vocational Behavior, Academy of Management Journal, Journal of Management,* and *the Journal of Educational Psychology,* and in such edited volumes as the *International Review of Industrial and Organizational Psychology* and *Research in Personnel and Human Resources Management.*

Linda Klebe Treviño is professor of organizational behavior at The Pennsylvania State University where she has been on the faculty since 1987. She holds a PhD in management, which has contributed to her unique focus on business ethics as a management (in addition to a philosophical) issue. Her research and writing on the management of ethical conduct in organizations is widely published and known internationally. She has consulted with a number of for-profit and nonprofit organizations and has co-authored a textbook with Katherine Nelson entitled *Managing Business Ethics: Straight Talk About How to Do It Right* (Wiley, 1995). Currently, she is interested in understanding how ethics management systems can be designed to fit a particular organization's culture and circumstances, and in conducting research to evaluate what works and what doesn't in ethics management. Her research has also expanded recently to include work on organizational justice as it applies to discipline in organizations and workforce reduction initiatives.

Gary R. Weaver is assistant professor of management at the University of Delaware. He received a BA in economics and philosophy from Bucknell University, a PhD in philosophy from the University of Iowa, and a PhD in business administration from The Pennsylvania State University. Weaver's research interests range over a variety of issues related to business ethics, at both organizational and individual levels of analysis and with both empirical and normative orientations. His articles or reviews have appeared in *Organization Studies, Business Ethics Quarterly, Journal of Business Ethics, Business and Society, Academy of Management Best Papers Proceedings, International Association of Business and Society Proceedings, Competitive Intelligence Review, Bulletin of Science, Technology and Society, The Review of Metaphysics,* and other publications. His work has been cited in the *Wall Street Journal, Christian Science Monitor, Federal Ethics Report,* and elsewhere.

Deborah L. Wells is an associate professor of management at Creighton University's College of Business Administration. Her primary research interests include human resources management, labor relations and collective bargaining, and organizational behavior. Wells holds a bachelor of science in sociology, a master of science in industrial relations, and a doctor of philosophy in industrial/organizational psychology from Iowa State University. She is a member of the Society for Human Resource Management and Academy of Management. Her publications have appeared in the *Journal of Applied Psychology,* the *Journal of Vocational Behavior,* and the *Journal of Business Ethics.*

Author Index

A

Adams, J. S., 50, 57, 14, 31, 32
Adams, M., 119, 128
Aiello, J. R., 61, 69-71, 74, 75, 78
Ajzen, I., 201, 203, 212, 213
Albaek, E., 207, 212
Alder, G. S., 44, 57, 62, 64, 74, 78
Alderman, E., 38, 57
Alexander, S., 102, 112
Allen, R. W., 134, 140, 152, 154, 172, 174
Allinson, R. E., 115, 128
Ambrose, M., 44, 57
Angel, N. F., 62, 78
Angle, H. L., 154, 174
Anson, R., 179, 184, 185, 193
Argyris, D. E., 91, 95
Arrow, K. J., 25, 32
Arvey, R. D., 100, 112
Asch, S. E., 181, 193
Asher, J., 85, 95
Atkinson, M. M., 207, 212
Austin, T., 125, 131
Axelrod, R., 116, 128

B

Bacharach, S. B., 133, 150
Bahrami, H., 156, 160, 174
Ball, G. A., 100-103, 110, 112-114
Barksdale vs. IBM 72, 78
Barnhart, R. K., 156, 172
Baron, R. A., 26, 29, 32, 33, 101, 110, 112
Barrick, L. J., 91, 95
Bartunek, J. M., 207, 213

Bass, B. M., 164, 172
Bassi, L. J., 90, 95
Bayles, M. D., 169, 172
Bazerman, M. H., 204, 205, 213
Beauchamp, T. L., 189, 193
Behson, S., 48, 50, 59
Beise, C. M., 179, 194
Bem, D. J., 160, 171, 172
Benbasat, I., 178, 180, 193
Benson, G., 90, 95
Bentham, J., 107, 112
Beranek, P. M., 179, 194
Bergsman, S., 90, 95
Berscheid, E., 15, 34
Beyer, J. M., 38, 48, 49, 59
Bies, R. J., 6, 11, 26, 33, 73, 78, 110, 112, 137, 138, 151, 152, 155, 165, 166, 172
Bird, F., 153, 175
Birjulin, A., 134, 152
Blake, R. R., 155, 163, 172
Blau, P. M., 109, 112
Blum, L., 158, 172
Blumberg, P., 168, 172
Blumstein, P., 157, 173
Bockanic, W. N., 43, 44, 57
Boettger, R. D., 189, 195
Bok, S., 170, 172
Bommer, M., 201, 209, 213
Bonoma, T. V., 157, 175
Bontempo, R., 105, 112
Borman, D. E., 82, 83, 85, 95
Bormann, C. A., 134, 152
Bostrom, R. P., 179, 193
Bottorff, D.L., 115, 128
Bounds, G. M., 115, 119, 128
Bowen, D. E., 85, 95

Bower, G. H., 94, 95
Bower, S. A., 94, 95
Bowie, N. E., 6, 10, 189, 193
Bowman, E. D., 62, 79
Bozeman, D. P., 137, 151
Bradford, L. P., 156, 172
Brady, F. N., 135, 140, 149, 150, 189, 193, 202, 213
Braithwaite, J., 106, 113
Brandt, R. B., 118, 128
Braybrooke, D., 169, 172
Brehm, J. W., 48, 57, 165, 166, 171, 172
Brehm, S. S., 166, 171, 172
Brenner, S. N., 73, 78
Brett, J. M., 139, 152
Brewer, J. F., 82, 96
Brislin, R., 104, 114
Brockner, J., 24, 33, 77, 78, 102, 113
Broome, B. J., 179, 193
Brown, M.L., 91, 95
Buchanan, A., 26, 33, 49, 50, 57
Bunker, B. B., 163, 173
Burke, K., 178, 193
Burris, L. R., 43, 58, 86, 91, 97
Buss, D. M., 157, 158, 164, 172
Butterfield, K. D., 103, 110, 112, 113
Bylinsky, G., 62, 72, 73, 78

C

Caldwell, D. F., 84, 95
Callahan, C., 43, 58, 86, 91, 97
Camerer, C. F., 21, 33
Campbell, J. P., 5, 8, 10, 10
Cappelli, P., 29, 33
Carayon, P., 70, 74, 78
Carter, S., 116, 128
Cartwright, D., 159, 172
Carver, C. S., 162, 173
Cascio, W. F., 39, 40, 47, 57, 86, 91, 95
Castell, P. J., 165, 174
Cavanagh, G. F., 145, 147, 148, 150, 154, 173, 189, 193
Chaiken, A. L., 46, 57

Chant, P. D., 153, 175
Chatman, J. A., 83, 95
Cheney, S., 90, 95
Chidambaram, L., 178, 193
Christie, R., 162, 164, 173
Ciulla, J. B., 6, 11, 116, 128
Clark, J. P., 43, 58
Clawson, V. K., 179, 180, 184, 193
Cobb, S., 187, 195
Cody, M. J., 157, 173
Cohen, M. D., 205, 206, 210, 213
Cohen, D. V., 122, 128
Cohen, N., 123, 129
Cohen, R. L., 161, 173
Cohen, W., 123, 129
Cole, A. H., 165, 172
Collins, J. C., 115, 129
Condie, S. J., 155, 156, 160, 173
Conger, J. A., 154, 155, 173
Connerly, M., 49, 58
Connolly, T., 191, 193
Conoley, J. C., 93, 95
Cooke, R. A., 118, 129
Cooks, L. M., 186, 187, 193
Cosmides, L., 21, 30, 33
Coughlin, C. L. J., 155, 166, 175
Cropanzano, R., 1, 11, 18, 30, 33, 73, 77, 78, 79, 134, 136, 137, 141, 150, 151
Cullen, J. B., 118, 130
CWA calls monitoring "menance", 73, 78

D

Daft, R. L., 5, 8, 10, 10, 11
Dahl, R. A., 157, 160, 165, 173
Damasio, A. R., 21, 33
Darley, J., 184, 194
Davis, M. S., 5, 6, 11
Davis, N., 165, 167, 173
Davis-Blake, A., 163, 173
Dawes, R., 21, 33
Dawis, R. V., 37, 47, 58
De George, R. T., 115, 129
de Wall, F., 21, 33

de Wolff, C. J., 84, 96
Decker, W. H., 6, 11
DeGeorge, R. T., 66, 78
Degoey, P., 16, 34
Deming, W. E., 116, 121, 122, 129
Denison, D., 116, 129
Dennis, A. R., 183, 184, 193-194
Derlega, V. J., 46, 57
Derry, R., 85, 96
Des Jardins, J. R., 65, 66, 78
DeSanctis, G., 178, 190, 192, 193, 194
Desselles, M. L., 62, 79
DeTienne, K. B., 61, 62, 78
Deutschberger, P., 156, 173
Dew, J. R., 127, 129
DeWitt, R. L., 102, 113
Dickson, G. W., 190, 194
Diessner, R., 92, 97
Dipboye, R. L., 39, 59
Dobbins, G. H., 115, 128
Dobson, J., 90, 96
Doe vs. B.P.S., 70
Donaldson, T., 4, 6, 11, 37, 57, 117, 129
Dougherty, K. J., 207, 213
Doyle, M., 179, 193
Drory, A., 134, 151
Dubinsky, A. J., 201, 213
Duckett, L. J., 94, 96
Duff, R. A., 106, 109, 110, 113
Dunfee, T. W., 6, 11, 117, 129
Dunham, R. B., 188, 193
Dunlap, A., 127, 129
duRivage, V., 62, 70, 75, 79
Duval, S., 162, 173
Dworkin, R., 117, 129
Dyer, W. G., 155, 156, 160, 173

E

Eddy, E., 44, 48-50, 59
Eisenhardt, K. M., 207, 213
Ellis, A., 109, 113
Emler, N. P., 109, 113

Etzion, A., 21, 33, 43, 51, 53-55, 57, 117, 129
Evan, W. M., 37, 41, 57
Evans, J. R., 115, 117, 121, 122, 129
Extejt, M. M., 43, 44, 57

F

Falbo, T., 157, 163, 173
Fandt, P. M., 134, 151
Feer, M., 187, 193
Feinberg, J., 109, 113
Ferguson, K., 89, 96
Ferrell, O. C., 115, 129, 200-202, 209, 213
Ferris, G. R., 134, 151
Festervand, T. A., 73, 80
Fickel, L., 63, 78
Field, H. S., 84, 92, 96
Fiorelli, P., 122, 127, 129
Fishbein, M., 201, 203, 212
Fiske, S. T., 162, 173
Flanagan, J. A., 61
Fleming, J., 3, 5, 11
Fletcher, J., 199, 213
Folger, R., 15, 18, 24, 26, 30, 33-34
Fombrun, C. J., 119, 125, 129
Forsyth, D. R., 7, 11, 198, 199, 210, 213
Fortado, B., 103, 113
Fowler, O. S., 115, 129
Fox, J. G., 66, 79
Fraedrich, J., 202, 213, 115, 128
Frank, R. H., 21, 33
Freeman, R. E., 6, 10, 37, 41, 57, 90, 97
French, J. R. P., Jr., 164, 173, 181, 193
French, W. A., 126, 129
Fried, C., 46, 49, 57
Friedman, M., 87, 97, 138, 151, 204, 213
Frink, D. D., 134, 151
Frost, P., 181, 193
Fukuyama, F., 28, 33
Furr, D. S., 127, 130
Fusilier, M. R., 49, 57

G

Galang, M. C., 134, 151
Galbraith, J. K., 137, 151
Gallupe, R. B., 178, 193
Garland, D., 106, 109, 113
Garson, B., 62, 70, 79
Garvin, D., 117-119, 129
Gatewood, R. D., 84, 92, 96
Geis, F. L., 162, 164, 173
George, J. F., 183, 193
Gerard, H. B., 164, 174
Gergen, M., 165, 174
Ghadially, R., 134, 151
Giacalone, R. A., 6, 11, 39, 47, 57, 168, 173
Gilbert, D. R., Jr., 37, 41, 57, 90, 97
Gilligan, C., 85-87, 89, 91, 92, 94, 95, 96, 126, 129, 208, 213
Gilman, G., 156, 157, 173
Glendon, M. A., 118, 129
Goffman, E., 39, 46, 47, 57
Goitein, B., 207, 213
Goldberg, S. B., 139, 152
Gomes, M., 157, 172
Gouldner, A. W., 156, 173
Gouran, D. S., 179, 194
Grandey, A. A., 134, 150
Granrose, J., 126, 129
Grant, R., 74, 79
Gratto, C., 201, 213
Gravander, J., 201, 213
Grebe, S. C., 189, 194
Green, R. K., 154-156, 166, 173
Greenberg, J., 6, 11, 73, 77, 78-79, 125, 129, 137, 151, 155, 160-162, 173
Gresham, L. G., 200, 201, 202, 209, 213
Grey, C., 104, 113
Grice, P., 168, 173
Griffith, T. L., 71, 79
Gross, M. L., 35, 53, 56, 58
Grover, S., 77, 78, 102, 113
Gueutal, H. G., 45, 58
Guzzo, R. A., 1, 11

H

Hackman, J. R., 37, 39, 47, 58
Hale, C. L., 186, 187, 193
Halfon, M., 115, 129
Hall, B., 67, 79
Hall, E. T., 38, 58
Halperin, R. R., 90, 96
Hamilton, V. L., 127, 129
Hamptom, J., 110, 113
Harder, J. W., 136, 151
Harrell, S. W., 207, 214
Hart, H. L. A., 108, 113
Hartman, C. L., 90, 97
Harvey, R. J., 84, 96
Hawk, S. R., 64, 79
Hayek, F. A., 138, 151
Heilbroner, R., 142, 151
Heneman, H. G., 83, 92, 96
Heneman, R. L., 83, 92, 96
Henriques, V. E., 62, 79
Heroux, M. A., 64, 79
Herrnstein, R. J., 26, 34
Heskett, J. L., 115, 129
Hickson, D. J., 207, 213
Higgins, C., 74, 79
Higgins, D. S., 157, 172
Hirokawa, R. Y., 179, 194
Hofstede, G., 48, 58, 105, 113
Hogan, R., 109, 113, 198, 210, 213
Hollinger, R. C., 43, 58
Hoojiberg, R., 116, 129
Hoover, D. J., 188, 194
Hosmer, L. T., 125, 129, 135, 139, 140, 150, 151
Howard, J. A., 157, 158, 163, 173
Howard, J. E., 134, 151
Howard, P. K., 139, 151
Howes, J. C., 134, 150
Hoyer, W. D., 49, 57
Hui, C. H., 104, 114
Hulin, C. L. 5, 8, 10, 10
Hume, D., 86, 96
Hunt, S. D., 201, 202, 209, 213
Huo, Y. J., 16, 33
Hyatt, D., 48, 49, 59

I

Impara, J. C., 93, 95
Instone, D., 163, 173
Irvin, K., 189, 194
Ivancevich, J. M., 100, 112

J

Jackall, R., 123, 129
James, K., 136, 151
Jessup, L. M., 183, 191, 193
Johns, G., 164, 173
Joiner, B., 125, 130
Jones, A. P., 100, 112
Jones, E. E., 156, 164, 174
Jones, G., 49, 59
Jones, J. W., 86, 96
Jones, T. M., 201, 203, 208-210, 213
Jordan, W. J., 157, 173
Jourard, S. M., 46, 48, 58
Joyce, D. P., 189, 194
Judge, T. A., 134, 151

K

Kabanoff, B., 136, 151
Kacmar, M. K., 134, 137, 151
Kahn, H., 43, 58
Kahn, R. L., 42, 55, 58, 185, 194
Kahn, W. A., 3, 7, 10, 11
Kahneman, D., 19, 20, 33, 182, 183,
   194, 195, 205, 214
Kant, I., 135, 138, 166, 167, 174
Karst, K. L., 49, 58
Katz, D., 42, 55, 58, 185, 194
Kavanagh, M., 45, 58
Keeley, M. C., 25, 33
Keever, D. B., 179, 193
Kelley, H. H., 40, 59
Kelman, H. C., 127, 129
Keltner, J., 181, 184-186, 194
Kennedy, C., 38, 57
Keys, C. B., 207, 213
Keyser, D. J., 93, 96
King, T. R., 134, 151

Kingsbury, S., 185, 194
Kipnis, D., 157, 158, 163-165, 174
Kircheimer, O., 111, 114
Klopfer, P. H., 46, 47, 58
Knetsch, J. L., 19, 33
Koehn, D., 89, 96
Kohlberg, L., 5, 11, 22, 23, 24, 30, 33,
   126, 129, 138, 151, 162, 174, 198,
   199, 202, 213
Komaki, J. L., 62, 79
Konovsky, M., 77, 79
Kotter, J. P., 115, 129
Kracker, B. J., 94, 97
Kramer, R. M., 117, 129, 155, 165,
   166, 172
Krebs, D. L., 165, 174
Kreitner, R., 100, 113
Krone, K. J., 163, 174
Kumar, P., 134, 151
Kupperman, J., 117, 129
Kurland, N. B., 201, 213

L

Laabs, J. J., 76, 79
Lafquist, L. H., 37, 58
Lanciault, D., 90, 96
Lang, M., 189, 194
LaPotin, P., 207, 213
Larrabee, M. J., 85, 96
Latane, B., 184, 194
Latham, G .P., 185, 194
Laufer, R., 46, 58
Lauterbach, K., 157, 172
Lawler, E. E., 37, 39, 47, 58
Lawler, E. J., 133, 150
Lawrence, P., 106, 113
Lawrence, P. R., 153, 156, 160, 174
Leavitt, H. J., 156, 160, 174
LeClair, D., 115, 129
Ledford, G. E., 85, 95
Lee-Patridge, J. E., 190, 194
Legrande, D., 70, 80
Lerner, M. J., 21, 33, 109, 113
Leventhal, G. S., 50, 51, 58
Levitt, B., 207, 213

Lewin, A. Y., 8, 11
Liden, R. C., 156, 158, 174
Liedtka, J. M., 87, 96
Lim, L. H., 178, 180, 193
Limayem, M., 190, 194
Lin, S., 105, 114
Lind, E. A., 15-18, 22-23, 31, 32, 33, 34
Lindblom, C. E., 157, 160, 165, 173
Lindsay, W. M, 115-118, 121-124, 129
Lindskold, S., 157, 175
Linowes, D. F., 36, 58
Lippitt, R., 156, 172
Little, D., 54, 55, 58
Little, M. O., 87, 96
Lobel, S., 105, 112
Locke, E. A., 185, 194
Locke, J., 65, 67, 79
Loken, B., 201, 213
Luchsinger, V. P., 115, 130, 131
Luthans, F., 100, 113

M

Machan, T. R., 67, 79
MacIntyre, A. C., 22, 33
Madison, D. L., 154, 172
Mael, F. A., 49, 58
Major, B., 163, 173
Malone, T. W., 90, 96
Mandell, M. B., 207, 213
Manning, G. E., 118, 119, 130
March, J. G., 204, 205, 213
Marcia, J. E., 92, 97
Margalit, A., 136, 151
Marietta, D. E., 170, 174
Marrs vs. Marriot Corp., 69, 70, 79
Martin, J., 136, 151
Martin, M. W., 116, 130
Martin, N. H., 134, 152
Marx, G. T., 74, 79
Masuch, M., 207, 213
Matheisen, T., 111, 113
Mathieu, A., 49, 50, 57
Mauch, D., 165, 174

Mayer, R. C., 165, 174
Mayes, B. T., 134, 140, 152, 154, 172
McCornack, S. A., 165, 174
McFall, L., 116, 130
McLaughlin, M. L., 157, 173
Merton, R. K., 156, 174
Meyer, M. J., 138, 139, 152, 168, 174
Mezias, S. J., 207, 213
Michener, H. A., 164, 174
Mill, J. S., 107
Millen, J., 187, 195
Miller, B. A., 91, 95
Miner, J. B., 82, 96
Mingo, J., 206, 207, 213
Mintzberg, H., 133, 134, 152, 204, 214
Mitchell, T. R., 156, 158, 174
Moag, J. S., 110, 112
Moberg, D. J., 117, 130, 89, 96, 138, 139, 145, 150, 152, 154, 155, 160, 168-170, 174, 189, 193
Molander, E. A., 73, 78
Morath, R. A., 49, 58
Morrison, E., 29, 34
Morton, M. S. S., 90, 96
Motowidlo, S. J., 82, 83, 85, 95
Mount, M. K., 91, 95
Mouton, J. S., 155, 172
Mowday, R. T., 154, 155, 163, 174
Murphy, J. G., 109, 113
Murphy, K. R., 117, 130
Murphy, L. L., 93, 96

N

Nash, L. L., 85, 87, 90, 96
Nass, C., 207, 213
Nathan, B. R., 85, 95
Neale, M. A., 182, 183, 188, 194
Nebeker, D. M., 62, 70, 71, 76, 79
Nelson, K. R., 127, 130
Newman, J., 29, 32
Newman, G., 100, 113
Niederman, F., 179, 194
Nine to Five, Working Women Education Fund, 70, 79

Noddings, N., 87, 89, 96
Noe, T. H., 6, 11
Northcraft, G. B., 183, 188, 194
Nozick, R., 166, 174
Nunamaker, J. F., 183, 184, 193
Nussbaum, K., 62, 70, 75, 79
Nuttig, K., 67, 79

O

Office of Technology Assesment,
   61, 62, 69, 72, 79
O'Leary, B., 24, 33
Olsen, J. P., 205, 213
O'Malley, M., 102, 113
Ones, D. S., 86, 96, 121, 130
O'Reilly, C. A., 84, 95, 102, 113
Organ, D. W., 83, 89, 97
Ostling, P. J, 66, 79
Ottensmeyer, E. J., 64, 79

P

Padgett, J. F., 207, 214
Paine, L. S., 115, 116, 130
Paradise, I. V., 188, 194
Parks, M. R., 165, 174
Parsons, T., 159, 174
Pasmore, W. A., 177, 194
Pawlak, E. J., 154-156, 166, 173
Payne, S. L., 6, 11
Pearlin, L. I., 154, 157, 175
Peplau, L. A., 157, 163, 173
Peterson, W. C., 142, 152
Petrick, J. A., 115, 116, 118, 119, 122-
   124, 126, 127, 130
Pettit, P., 106, 113
Pfeffer, J., 111, 113, 133, 134, 152,
   163, 173
Piaget, J., 199, 214
Picard, M., 76, 79
Piller, C., 51, 58, 76, 80
Pinch, W., 91
Pinkley, R., 183, 194
Pitts, L., Jr., 28, 34
Piturro, M. C., 62, 68, 70, 80

Poole, M. S., 192, 193
Popper, K. R., 1, 11
Porras, J. I., 115, 129
Porter, L. W., 37, 39, 47, 58, 154, 157,
   160, 162, 174
Posner, B. Z., 73, 80, 115, 130
Powers, R. A., 207, 212
Prelec, D., 26, 34
Preston, L. E., 37, 57
Primoratz, I., 109, 113
Puffer, S. M., 102, 113
Puka, B., 87, 97

Q

Quinn, J. F., 115, 116, 119, 122, 123,
   126, 127, 130
Quinn, R., 116, 129

R

Raisinghani, D., 204, 214
Ralston, D. A., 156, 158, 174
Rand, A., 138, 152
Randall, M. L., 134, 152
Ranney, G., 119, 128
Raven, B. H., 164, 173, 181, 193
Rawls, J., 13, 23, 30, 34, 117, 130,
135-137, 152
Rebello, M. J., 6, 11
Reed, T., 77, 78
Reed, T., 102, 113
Reich, W. T., 86, 87, 97
Reichers, A., 125, 131
Reidenbach, E., 126, 130
Reitan, E., 110, 114
Renwick , P. A., 154, 172
Rest, J. R., 5, 11, 22, 34, 93, 97, 116,
   130, 188, 195, 198-201, 203, 208-
   210, 214
Rifkin, J., 187, 195
Riker, W. H., 155, 160, 175
Roberson, C., 86, 97
Robertson, D. C., 7, 11
Robin, D., 126, 130
Robinson, S. L., 29, 34

Rockwood, G. F., 184, 195
Romm, T., 134, 151
Rooney, C., 122, 127, 129
Rosenberg, M., 154, 157, 175
Rosenfeld, L. B., 184, 188, 195
Rosenfeld, P., 39, 47, 58, 168, 173
Ross, S., 44, 58, 62, 70, 71, 76, 80
Rousseau, D. M., 29, 34
Rubenstein, D. I., 46, 47, 58
Ruderman, M., 102, 112
Rudinow, J., 156-160, 166, 175
Rusche, G., 111, 114
Russ, G. S., 134, 151
Ryden, M. B., 94, 96

S

Sackett, P. R., 43, 58, 86, 91, 97
Salancik, G. R., 160, 171, 175, 189, 195
Sanders, A. L., 62, 80
Sanders, K. J., 70, 80
Scarre, G., 189, 195
Scarselletta, M., 207, 213
Scheier, M. F., 162, 173
Schein, E. H., 184, 195
Schein, V. E., 35, 53, 58
Schelling, T. C., 26, 34
Schlenker, B. R., 155, 157, 175, 189, 195
Schmidt, F. L., 86, 96, 121, 130
Schmidt, S. M., 157, 158, 163-165, 174
Schmidt, W., 115, 130
Schmidt, W. H., 73, 80
Schminke, M., 1, 11, 197, 136, 151
Schnake, M. E., 102, 114
Schneider, B., 83, 97
Scholtes, P., 125, 130
Schoorman, F. D., 165, 174
Schopler, J., 165, 175
Schwartz, P., 157, 173
Sciarrino, J., 85, 95
Selznick, P., 28, 34
Sen, A., 118, 130
Shakun, M., 178, 193
Shea, G. P., 1, 11

Sheaffer, R. C., 125, 130
Sheppard, B. H., 186, 195
Sherwood, J. J., 177, 194
Shils, E. B., 35, 36, 42, 43, 58
Shrivastava, P., 125, 130
Siegelwaks, B. J., 188, 194
Simmons, D. D., 50, 58
Simon, H. A., 21, 26-29, 34, 204, 213, 214
Simpson, J. A., 156, 157, 175
Sims, H. P., Jr., 100, 101, 112
Sims, J. H., 134, 152
Sims, R., 116, 130
Sitkin, S. B., 138, 152
Skinner, B. F., 99, 100, 114
Skoe, E. E., 92, 94, 97
Slote, M., 117, 130
Slovic, P., 182, 194
Smith, F. J., 188, 193
Smith, H. J., 16, 33, 34, 54, 58
Smith, M. J., 70, 71, 75, 80
Smith, R. L., 54, 58
Solomon, R. C., 115, 117, 130
Solomon, R. L., 100, 114
Sostre, L., 207, 213
Spiegelberg, H., 29, 31, 34
Stafford, E. R., 90, 97
Stahl, M. J., 115, 119, 130
Stark, A., 7, 11
Staub, E., 93, 97
Staw, B. M., 189, 195, 198, 214
Stead, J. G., 125, 130
Stead, W. E., 125, 130
Stein, M. J., 10, 11
Steiner, G. A., 53, 56, 59
Steiner, J. F., 53, 56, 59
Stephens, C. U., 2, 11
Stone, D. L., 35-37, 39, 40, 42, 44-51, 53, 56, 59, 65, 80
Stone, E. F., 35-37, 39, 40, 42, 45-51, 53, 56, 59, 65, 80
Stone-Romero, E. F., 44, 48-50, 59
Straus, D., 179, 193
Streibel, B., 125, 130
Suchner, R. W., 164, 175
Susser, P. A., 74, 76, 80

Sweetland, R. C., 93, 96
Sykes, C. J., 139, 152
Szumal, J. L., 118, 129

T

Tannenbaum, S., 45, 58
Tapan, M. B., 91, 95
Tatum, C. B., 62, 70, 71, 76, 79
Taylor, G., 115, 130
Taylor, J. M., 126, 129
Taylor, S. E., 162, 173
Teasley, C. E., III, 207, 214
Tedeschi, J. T., 157, 163, 164, 175
Terris, W., 86, 96
Tetlock, P. E., 161, 175, 189, 195
Thaler, R., 19, 21, 33
Theoret, A., 204, 214
Thibaut, J. W., 15-17, 22, 23, 31, 34,
  40, 59, 186, 195
Thompson, D. F., 116, 130
Thompson, V. D., 165, 175
Thurow, L., 142, 151
Ting-Toomey, S., 105, 114
Toth, P., 134, 150
Treviño, L. K., 3, 4, 7, 11, 99, 101-
  103, 106, 109, 112, 112, 114, 127,
  130, 200, 201, 209, 214
Triandis, H. C., 104, 105, 112, 114
Trice, H. M., 38, 48, 49, 59
Tripp, T. M., 155, 165, 166, 172
Trubinsky, P., 105, 114
Tucker, T., 73, 80
Tunick, M., 109, 114
Tuttle, M., 201, 213
Tversky, A., 182, 183, 194, 195, 205,
  214
Twiss, S. B., 54, 55, 58
Twohey, D., 91, 97
Tyler, T. R., 15-18, 22, 23, 31, 32, 33,
  34, 73, 78, 117, 129

U

Uniform Guidelines 84, 97
Ury, W. L., 139, 152

V

Valacich, J. S., 184, 191, 193, 194
Velasquez, M., 135, 138, 139, 141,
  145, 150, 154, 173, 189, 193, 201,
  214
Victor, B., 2, 11, 118, 130, 200, 214
Viswesvaran, C., 86, 96, 121, 130
Vitell, S. J., 73, 80, 201-202, 209, 213
Vogel, D. R., 178, 183-184, 193-194
Volker, J., 91, 97
von Hirsch, A., 109, 114
Vroman, H. W., 115, 131

W

Waldron, J., 65, 80
Walker, L., 15, 16, 22, 23, 31, 34, 186,
  195
Walsh, V., 26, 34
Walster, E., 15, 34
Walster, G. W., 15, 34
Wanous, J., 125, 131
Ward, J. V., 126, 131
Wasserstrom, R. A., 36, 46, 49, 50,
  59
Waters, J. A., 116, 131, 153, 175
Watkins v. L. M. Berry & Co., 73
Weaver, G. R., 3, 4, 7, 11, 106, 114
Weber, J., 122, 131, 200, 214
Weick, K., 110, 114
Weinberg, S. L., 93, 97
Weiner, E. S. C., 156, 157, 175
Weinstein, E. A., 156, 175
Weisband, S. P., 183, 195
Weitz, B. A., 102, 113
Wells, D. L., 94, 97
Werhane, P., 66, 80
Westin, A. F., 36, 59
Wever, G. H., 125, 131
White, J., 90, 96
White, S. B., 182, 195
Whyte, W. H., Jr., 42, 53, 56, 59
Wicklund, R. A., 162, 173
Wicks, A. C., 90, 95, 97
Wilbur, J., 13, 34

Wilkins, A. L., 125, 131
Wilkinson, I., 157, 174
Williams, A. R., 155, 156, 175
Williams, B., 118, 130
Willig, J. T., 125, 131
Wilson, J. Q., 21, 34
Wilson, J. R. S., 159, 168, 175
Wilson, M. G., 183, 195
Wintersteller, E., 90, 96
Wisenfeld, B., 24, 33
Wolfe, M., 46, 58
Wrong, D. H., 157, 175
Wynne, V., 179, 193

Y

Yacker, N., 93, 97
Yorks, L., 119, 131
Youngblood, S. A., 200, 214

Z

Zbaracki, M. J., 207, 213
Zhou, J., 134, 151
Zorn, T. E., 184, 188, 195

Subject Index

A

Action guides
  legal, 54
  moral, 53-57
Adaptive-structuration theory, 192
Adult Personality Inventory, 93
Anchoring, 182, 183, 188, 191

B

Basic facilitator paradigm, 179, 183,
  185
Behaviorism, 99-100
Bounded autonomy, 25-29

C

California Psychological Inventory,
  93
Caring
  people, 86-90
  perspective, 91, 93-95
Categorical imperative, 135, 145,
  166-168
Client-focused ethics, 189
Computer monitoring of employee
  performance, 63, 70-72
Concretization, 87, 89-90
Conflict, 35-37, 40-41, 47, 52-57
Contextual activities, 82-86, 91
Control model, 23
Culture, 162

D

Deception, 156-159, 164-165, 168,
  170
Deontology/deontological, 5, 8,
  135, 189, 200-201, 208
Descriptive perspective, 99, 105,
  111

E

Eavesdropping on employees, 63,
  72-73
Egoism, 5-6, 23-24
Electronic monitoring
  and performance standards, 75-76
  categories/types, 63
Equity theory, 14-15, 31-32
Ethic of Care Interview (ECI), 92-93
Ethics and quality
  paradigms in, 119-123
  perspectives on, 116-119
  principles in, 125-128
  processes in, 123-125
Ethics of care, 82-83, 86-87, 89, 95
Expert power, 181, 182

F

Fairness-as-morality, 13-14, 17
Fairness-as-virtue, 14, 17, 21, 23-25,
  30, 32

Formalist/formalism, 7, 135, 139-
141, 144-145, 149, 189, 190, 202, 208
Four-component model, 198, 200-
201, 203, 208-209
Framing, 182, 188, 191

G

Group process facilitation, 179, 180,
184
Group value model/relational
model, 15-17, 22-23, 31

H

Human covenant, 25, 28-29
Human dignity, 28-30, 32

I

Impartiality, 179, 180, 185, 186, 187,
191
Influence tactics, 154-156, 158, 160,
162-163
Information control, 35-38, 47, 52-
55, 57
Information processing, 181, 182
Informed consent, 186, 187, 189, 191
Integrity
defined, 116
developmental, 126
judgment, 119
process, 123
system, 119
Interview, voice-centered , 91-92
Issue-contingent model, 203

J

Job analyses, 84
Job descriptions, 82-85
Just World hypothesis, 21
Justice, 50, 101-103, 105, 108-110,
136-137, 143-149
distributive, 14, 32
procedural, 14-16, 31

K-L

Kant, Immanuel, 166-167
Legitimate power, 181, 182

M

Machiavellianism, 162-164, 167
Managerial selection, 83, 89, 91
Mediation, 186, 187, 188, 190
Meta ethics, 5
Monitoring systems, characteristics
of, 63-64
Monitoring, ethical rules, 73-74
disclosure, 76-77
moderation, 74-76
Moral development, 21-22, 162
cognitive, 198-201, 208
conventional, 199-200
postconventional, 199
preconventional, 199
Moral intensity, 203, 210
Moral Orientation Scale, 93
Moral outrage, 155, 161, 165, 169

N

Naturalistic fallacy, 2
Neutrality, 180, 186, 187, 189, 191
Nonrational decision processes
biases and heuristics, 204-205
bounded rationality, 204-205
escalation, 204-205
garbage can, 205-207
incrementalism, 204-205
punchbowl, 197, 207-208, 211-
212
Normative perspective, 99, 105-
107, 109, 111, 112
consequentialist, 107-111
expressive, 107, 109, 112
reintegrative, 107, 110
retributive, 107-109, 112
Norms, 38, 41, 46-51, 53-54

O

Occupational Personality Questionnaire, 93
Organizational citizens/citizenship, 82-86, 89, 91-92, 95
Organizational citizenship behavior (OCB), 83, 93
Organizational integrity, 115
Organizational quality, 115
Organized anarchies, 205-206, 208, 210
Original position, 136-137

P

Paradox of facilitation, 178, 184, 186
Politics, political behavior, 133-134, 137-138, 141, 146-147, 149-150, 155
Power, 154, 157, 163-164, 168
Prima facie, 166-167
Privacy, 35-38, 40-41, 46-57
Processes, defined, 121
Psychological manipulation, 159-161, 165, 167, 169, 171
Punishment
affective reactions to, 100, 105, 111-112
and culture, 104-105
and social context, 103, 105, 111

Q-R

Quality, defined, 117
Reactance, 165-166, 171
Receptive listening, 87-88, 89
Referent cognitions theory (RCT), 18
Research approaches
descriptive, 2-3
empirical, 4-5
normative, 2-5
positivist, 2
prescriptive, 2
Revenge, 155, 165-166
Rights, 138-140, 143-149
conflict between employee and employer, 67, 68

health, 66, 70, 72
privacy, 65, 69-72
property, 67
Rule-focused ethics, 189

S

Salience, 182, 183
Self-awareness, 162
Self-determination, 186, 187, 190, 191, 192
Self-interest model, 15-17, 22
Selfishness, 15-16
Situation strength, 162
Situational manipulation, 159-161, 165, 167, 169, 171
Social influence, 184
Stakeholder, 35-42, 45-46, 51-57
Status, 181, 182
Surveillance of employees, 63, 69-70

T

Technical facilitation, 179, 180, 184
Teleology/teleological, 7, 140, 200-201, 208
Testing
integrity, 86
personality, 86
Theory of reasoned action, 201-203, 209
Title VII of the Civil Rights Act of 1964, 84
Training, 187, 190

U-V

Utilitarian/utilitarianism, 5-7, 140, 144-146, 148-149, 155, 165-166, 170-171, 189-190, 201-202, 208, 212
Utilitarianism
rule, 140-141, 144
value, 141-144
Values, 38-43, 45-48, 52-53, 55, 57
Voice(s), 87, 90